W9-BWF-109

*FROM
CRIME
TO
CHOICE*

Recent Titles in
Contributions in Women's Studies

Representations of Women: Nineteenth-Century British Women's Poetry
Kathleen Hickok

Women, Nazis, and Universities: Female University Students in the Third
Reich, 1933–1945
Jacques R. Pauwels

Cassandra's Daughters: The Women in Hemingway
Roger Whitlow

The World of Women's Trade Unionism: Comparative Historical Essays
Norbert C. Soldon, editor

Traditionalism, Nationalism, and Feminism: Women Writers of Quebec
Paula Gilbert Lewis, editor

Only Mothers Know: Patterns of Infant Feeding
Dana Raphael and Flora Davis

"Give to the Winds Thy Fears": The Women's Temperance Crusade, 1873–1874
Jack S. Blocker Jr.

Film Feminisms: Theory and Practice
Mary C. Gentile

At the Very Least She Pays the Rent: Women and German Industrialization,
1871–1914
Barbara Franzoi

With Ears Opening Like Morning Glories: Eudora Welty and the Love of
Storytelling
Carol S. Manning

Growing Up Female: Adolescent Girlhood in American Fiction
Barbara A. White

FROM
CRIME
TO
CHOICE

The Transformation of Abortion in America

NANETTE J. DAVIS

Contributions in Women's Studies, Number 60

GP

Greenwood Press
Westport, Connecticut • London, England

Library of Congress Cataloging-in-Publication Data

Davis, Nanette J.
  From crime to choice.

  (Contributions in women's studies, ISSN 0147-104X ;
no. 60)
  Bibliography: p.
  Includes index.
  1. Abortion—United States.   2. Social change.
I. Title.   II. Series.
HQ767.5.U5D38   1985   363.4'6'0973   85-8018
ISBN 0-313-24929-6 (lib. bdg. : alk. paper)

Library of Congress Catalog Card Number: 85-8018
ISBN: 0-313-24929-6
ISSN: 0147-104X

First published in 1985

Greenwood Press
A division of Congressional Information Service, Inc.
88 Post Road West
Westport, Connecticut 06881

Printed in the United States of America

∞™

The paper used in this book complies with the
Permanent Paper Standard issued by the National
Information Standards Organization (Z39.48-1984).

10 9 8 7 6 5 4 3 2 1

To my daughters,
Katherine, Susan, Elizabeth, and Patricia—
and granddaughters,
Carrie Rose and Meghann

Contents

Figures

Tables

Preface

Transformation refers to the action of changing in form, shape, or appearance, and it can be personal or social. In either case, it involves a crisis in meanings and often a shift in world view. Social transformations are not initially benign. They begin in periods of cultural disruption and grave personal stress when we lose faith in the legitimacy of our norms, the viability of our institutions, and the authority of our leaders. Invariably, a transformation calls attention to deep-seated cultural assumptions, challenging and undermining them.[1]

This has been true of abortion. For many of us socialized under the old "ground rules," it was natural to define abortion as a crime and to identify both providers and users as moral untouchables. The association of abortion with vice, the criminal underworld, corrupt physicians, sexual improprieties, sickness, and death was deeply embedded in our consciousness. In a word, these were facts of life, and they all added up to one thing: If one chooses respectability, abortion was negative and was to be avoided.

At the same time, we all knew that people were "doing it." Doctors were available for a price; desperate women sought it to cover up a sexual indiscretion, burdensome pregnancy, or intolerable responsibility; and kin groups, friends, and associates connived to create a support network that made abortion a manageable act. Abortion was rarely considered a *choice*. Rather, it was more likely a "necessary evil," "lesser evil," "act of desperation," or a "risky solution" to an otherwise unresolvable dilemma. Which is less hazardous to life—to carry an untimely pregnancy to term and probably raise an unwanted child (although, as many women discovered, an unwanted pregnancy did not equal unwanted child) or to involve oneself in a morally despicable act?

Abortion, then, was associated with warring priorities, stress, pain, p~~ adoxes, and conflicts. And there were few winners. Although a few p~ sicians managed to develop a highly lucrative abortion practice, the tr~

off was costly: professional isolation, loss of collegial respect, denial of hospital privileges, and surveillance by police. As for the non-physicians who made their living giving abortions, they were either short-term practitioners—they worked until consumer displeasure, police, or fatigue caught up with them—or merely local neighborhood women helping out a friend. In all the annals of abortion, we have little documentation of the friends-and-neighbors network of abortionists, although Pauline Bart's (1977) research on the pre-legal Jane operation, a feminist underground abortion network described later in the book, gives us a picture of how a group of dissidents carried it off. But Jane occurred in an already changing moral environment, which is to say, it was different from the stony silence that greeted most women's search for abortion before, say, 1965.

How did abortion make the transition from one form to another—from crime to a personal choice? And what are the implications? These are the central questions I try to answer in this book.

First, I begin with an evolutionary model of social transformation. I premise that the legal, medical, social, and psychological changes in abortion depend on other cultural upheavals. Abortion is not an isolated situation nor did it occur in a vacuum. The "consciousness-raising" strategies of an entire wave of social movements in the 1960s and early 1970s provided the original stimulus to abortion change by their rejection of the old order and their agenda, however inchoate, for the renewal of society.

Second, the book details four types of changes in abortion related to the way in which the social order responded to new and conflicting information. One was *change by exception*. The old ideas about abortion as bad remained intact but allowed for a handful of anomalies. Women who came into hospital emergency rooms with problems related to septic abortion were viewed as "the exceptions that prove the rule." Good girls don't get into trouble that necessitates an illegal abortion. In this system, in which such exceptions were taken into account and which endured for almost a century, there were no real challenges to the crime-control model of abortion.

Incremental change of abortion occurred bit by bit, but most physicians and hospitals remained unaware of having changed. Throughout the 1960s many physicians were treated to medical seminars on abortion techniques, even though there was little indication that they would ever use such skills. At one point, hospital abortion committees were enlarging the number of women who could legitimately come under the umbrella of therapeutic abortions: a medically supervised procedure in a standard surgical or obstetric ward. And once some states liberalized abortion laws, doctors in areas that denied abortion were sending expanding numbers of women to abortion clinics out-of-state. Yet there was almost no sharing among these medical professionals, hence no impact on the larger medical delivery system.

Then there was a *pendulum change*, the abandonment of the crime-control model and the adoption of the new freedom ethic: the right of a woman to abortion. The pendulum change failed to integrate what was right with the old and to discriminate the value of the new from its overstatements. Pendulum change rejected its own prior experience, women seeking support from kin and the involved man, going from one kind of partial system—abortion as a necessary evil—to another—abortion as a kind of passport or *rite of passage* to an adult woman's status at the height of the abortion movement. This pendulum shift shut out both moral considerations and personal doubts. It failed to harmonize abiding concerns of women with the integrity of their bodies—after all, abortion is an externally induced medical procedure—and the context and consequences of the abortion choice. This left the field open for moral entrepreneurs—clergymen, social workers, and physicians—who developed counseling formats that would make *them* comfortable with the abortion choice, often to the exclusion of the woman's needs or preferences. In this moral milieu, new forms of certainty emerged about women's autonomy that effectively rejected women's traditional kinship ties. Although this system preached a type of total freedom, its one-sidedness ignored the alienation and pain experienced not only by women who had the new legal abortions, but also by the doctors, nurses, family members, and man involved.

Paradigm change is the most radical mode of change, and we are still a long way from it, as the book clarifies. This involves integrating the old and new ideas to eliminate the delusion of either-or, of this-or-that. Paradigm change involves a new perspective because it relinquishes certainty and allows for different interpretations from different perspectives at different times. Where does that leave the current abortion situation? The old certainty—abortion is a criminal act—has been replaced by a new certainty—abortion is a personal choice, similar to having elective surgery or teeth extracted. And neither of these realities begins to approximate how most people cope with the decision to have (or to provide) an abortion. It also opens the door to vigorous societal reaction by opponents of this technological solution to unwanted pregnancy.

Because a paradigm change involves a shift of pattern, a spiral, and sometimes a cataclysm, it may be the most disturbing form of change. Until pro-choice and pro-life groups find a common vocabulary, we may continue to recycle outworn slogans, mutual recriminations, and violence. For example, twenty-four abortion clinics were bombed in 1984, and the property damage for just one clinic ran as high as a half million dollars. While opponents probably resent gender changes in any form, choosing abortion as their dominant symbol of what many believe is the degradation of moral and family life, pro-choice groups continue to regard pro-life groups (whether violent or nonviolent) as merely irrational and unprogressive.

Social transformation is not linear, however—a point that needs stressing. The entire culture is undergoing trauma and tensions that beg for new order, new solutions to the problems engendered by concentrations of power and wealth. Abortion is only one bitterly contested area out of which these more fundamental battles of power, wealth, status, and bureaucratic and professional models of control are being waged. Nuclear energy, worker participation in the economy, international distribution of jobs, social welfare entitlements, equal treatment of minorities, and protection of children and other vulnerable populations are among additional battlegrounds on which conflicting ideologies and social practices converge. We appear caught between two contradictory poles: technological efficiency and a social order that supports it (including capitalism, fascism, and communism as political mechanisms), and the right (and necessity) of individuals to make informed, responsible choices. In the latter case, political "isms" would have to make way for more human-centered, participatory strategies of political order.

What I'm saying here is that abortion is a world-shattering event in the sense that it arouses the best and the worst in human responses. It simultaneously offers a collective trigger for generating a new, more positive place for women in society, as well as allowing for absolute political control over entire populations. It is frightening in its paradox; hence we can begin to glimpse (even if we cannot accept) why it has become an object of terrorist attack. It is my belief, expressed throughout the book, that unless women are allowed to become fully human in the sense of controlling their own reproduction, all of us will be diminished and reduced.

How can I count the ways in which others have helped in bringing this book to completion? Mentors first: Bo Anderson, Bernard Meltzer, Nancy Hammond, and Ray Lerner. Informants next: Dr. Jack Stack and the countless individual clergymen, physicians, and women support group members who pointed out the track when it threatened to disappear in the historical dust. For all those who submitted so willingly to being questioned about their role in abortion change, or provided access to records and documents—and many of these people must remain anonymous because they are no longer involved or have even repudiated their role in the abortion movement—I am deeply grateful.

Friends, colleagues, and students from Portland State University contributed in invaluable ways to this book. I am especially indebted to Charles Bolton for reading earlier versions and offering useful suggestions; to Grant Farr for supplying methodological assistance; and to Nona Glazer for raising some fundamental questions that sent me back to the drawing board. Victoria Doerper's fine editing untangled many convoluted passages. Simon Fraser University generously provided financial assistance in preparation of the graphics during my stay as a visiting professor in the Department of Criminology (1985).

When you operate "on the fringes," as it were, your research often makes little sense to your family and friends. I owe the deepest debt of gratitude to my husband and six children, who tolerated my long absences, usually with good humor, and offered sustained support during my intense research and writing commitment, which appears to have gone on forever but in actuality spans a mere sixteen years. I can't say that I've grown "old" on abortion, although there were periods when the paradigm shift refused to develop a clear pattern and I wondered whether the project would ever be completed. My fervent hope is that I, and the family members, friends, students, and colleagues that I may have touched in my own search for the meanings of this often troubling reality, have grown considerably wiser about the human costs of repressive social control.

NOTE

1. An extraordinarily useful book for understanding the nature of contemporary change, and which I draw upon for insight in this section, is Ferguson (1980).

FROM
CRIME
TO
CHOICE

1

Introduction: Anatomy of Abortion

This book takes as its starting point that the Supreme Court failed to settle the abortion issue because it ignored the more fundamental problem: What are the social and economic conditions of human reproduction and who will control it? The juggling act of balancing the states' interest in reproduction with the virtual medical monopoly over contraception, pregnancy, abortion, and childbirth left women as reproductive dependents. Women continue to need state and professional permission in order to make the most personal decisions about their bodies. Still, the legal, social, and economic conditions of women's dependency have changed dramatically. And legal abortion has made the significant difference.

ABORTION AND REPRODUCTIVE CHOICE

★Abortion is intimately connected with other reproductive events, but it also has a structure, or anatomy, of its own. And it is worth dissecting the evolution and development of modern abortion because, I believe, abortion has made a demonstrative difference on how women view their own sexuality. The argument of this book will be that before the current abortion movement, reproductive choice did not exist. The official rhetoric stressed that having babies was natural; the willful rejection of motherhood was deviant. Women's bodies were presumed to be made for pregnancy and childbirth, and few people challenged the medical hegemony or spoke out against death at an early age for untold numbers of women over the centuries for whom pregnancy and illegal abortion were lethal (Shorter, 1982). Until the 1930s, "voluntary motherhood," a Victorian ideology, meant abstinence. Birth control and abortion were dangerous because "free" sexuality would undermine women's position within the family.[1] And until the abortion movement challenged the criminal law, abortion was almost universally identified with sin and crime, prostitution, illicit sexuality, illegitimacy, and a bad moral character.

Then, beginning with Alfred Kinsey's exposé of American adult sexual habits in the late forties and fifties, a new discourse emerged. The almost taboo subject of female sexuality could now be aired, along with discussions of pregnancy, induced abortion, techniques of illegal abortion, abortion-related deaths, and the need to expand medical responsibility for women's health. Kinsey's abortion data, based on a sample of 8,000 women, indicated that with each succeeding decade of a woman's fertility, the likelihood of abortion increases. The empirical reality of abortion as a *common* alternative to unwanted pregnancy was difficult to deny. In Kinsey's words, "Of almost all women in our sample ever married, ten percent of them had induced abortions by 25 years of age. By 45 years of age, approximately 22 percent of them had at least one induced abortion" (quoted in Calderone, 1958, 55). Kinsey observed that changes in norms affected the abortion rate, citing such shifts as family size; differential contraceptive use by race, age, and status groups; and variations in enforcement. Drawing on abortion statistics over a sixty-year period (1890–1950), Kinsey produced some surprising findings: There was widespread use of abortion among the unmarried—88 percent to 95 percent of the sample who were unmarried and who had been pregnant at least once had resolved their premarital pregnancy by induced abortion; and physicians had performed 87 percent of all these reported abortions.

In 1958 Dr. Mary Calderone, medical director of Planned Parenthood Federation, wrote *Abortion in the United States*, launching the abortion movement and breaking nearly a century of silence. Abortion, once a sacrosanct, morally untouchable, and medically aloof issue, had become a respectable medical concern. What did this family-planning expert reveal in her book?

First, the mere publication of an abortion book that seriously treated the issue in medical and scientific terms generated a profound interest. Ironically, it was doctors who attacked nineteenth-century abortion; and it was doctors who restored it to medical practice in the next century (Luker, 1984).

Second, the book indicted illegal abortion as the leading cause of maternal death, destroying the myth that only women of "bad" moral character had abortions. The *normality* of abortion was underscored, partly by citing Kinsey and other empirical studies and partly by having physicians with abortion practices report their experiences.

Third, people were astonished to read how even good-faith doctors operated to circumvent the law. "Therapeutic abortion"—a code name for the hospital screening committees with their psychiatric validation for abortion based on the woman's alleged insanity—had legally protected physicians and hospitals. But it also limited abortion practice to high-cost, highly selective patient care and maintained a two-tiered system: a legitimate hospital system for the few and a medically referred illegal system for the lucky. The rest, the majority of abortion seekers, went to "back alley" abortionists, so named because of the delapidated neighborhoods and grim operating settings associated with criminal abortion (Bates and Zawadski, 1964).

Fourth, we learned that throughout the thirties, forties, and fifties, abortion flourished, and while numbers appear to be indeterminate, there were estimated to be at least 200,000 abortions a year over those decades; some later insisted that the figure was closer to a million a year (Jaffe, et al., 1981; Sarvis and Rodman, 1974).

The ubiquity of abortion—its wide distribution among all races and classes of women—and the complicity of the medical profession in upholding what reformers emphasized was an unscientific, death-dealing, and unenforceable law helped to trigger a mass resistance to the states' abortion laws. It was a natural outcome of the sexually permissive doctrine and advanced medical technology, but abortion was still a crime. The social radicalism of the sixties opened up, perhaps for the first time, the possibility that, for millions of women around the world, human autonomy begins with bodily self-determination.[2] Having an abortion became a woman's "right" because abortion made it possible to make informed sexual and procreative decisions. Abortion changed from a negative, life-denying, and criminal act to a positive, live-giving force.

ABORTION AND CHANGING SOCIAL CONDITIONS

I may go a step further. If we ask why women before 1960 weren't openly demanding safe, medical abortion as their inherent right, one of the answers is their generally subordinated status and their almost exclusive identification with the family. Lacking an autonomous resource base, most women chose illegally what they could not acquire in a more licit way. Because they were confined to lower-level jobs and treated as temporary workers, economic independence was impossible. Having children provided a satisfying, if dutiful, life calling.

As conditions for women changed—the labor market opened up, the educational system expanded, and family ideology lost some of its feminine mystique—women eagerly embraced opportunities and expanded social roles (Banner, 1984). It became possible to think about reproductive freedom as part of a larger set of questions about human autonomy. "Children by choice," long the slogan of Planned Parenthood groups, could become a reality. As Linda Gordon (1976) points out, reproductive freedom requires not merely information about birth control, important as that is, but also freedom from the pressures of *having* to have children and, equally, the freedom to *have* children under healthy and socially liberating conditions. When the abortion movement entered the already turbulent decade of the sixties, many women lacked reproductive freedom in both senses.

We may thus think of the subordination of women, their inherent lack of reproductive knowledge and control, and their inability to secure medical abortions as the result of three kinds of victimization: gender, class, and ideology.

1. Women were victimized by professionals—doctors, law enforcement personnel, psychiatrists, social workers, and other gatekeepers—who controlled access to birth control and abortion. I spend several chapters on the pre-legal conditions of medical abortion and the selection process that excluded most abortion seekers and that created physical and mental hazards for many women.

2. Women were victimized by social class distinctions whereby well-to-do and well-connected women with medical advocates had access to medical abortions, while poor, minority women and those lacking medical advocates attempted to deal with unwanted pregnancies with hazardous, illegal procedures. Poor women's failure to secure good abortions will appear in their higher maternal mortality (Jaffe, et al., 1981).

3. Women were victimized by a patriarchal ideology in the form of various institutional pressures: tolerating male deviance, accepting unwanted pregnancies, and assuming self-blame was part of women's historic role (Schur, 1984; Davis, 1984). Thus rape, incest, woman battering, and pornography are not "modern" deviations invented by feminists. Instead, these male deviancies stand in the same relation to women in the eighties as coercive pregnancy did in the past: controlling women through their bodies and subjecting their wills to male-ordained interests. The struggle for reproductive rights is complicated by the fact that it takes place in a political context in which state and society have revoked their protective cloak over women (Davis, 1984).

Now, I am not arguing that women of today stand in the same relation to men and professional gatekeepers as they did during the nineteenth century, when the "cult of domesticity" raged throughout North America and England, and in the United States, promoted the "social (i.e., sexual) purity" movement, (Ryan, 1983; Bernard, 1981). In this country, Anthony Comstock (1844–1915) and other moralists capitalized on the anti-sexual ideology and passed laws against "vice" that were essentially laws against women: jailing prostitutes, outlawing contraception, and denying medical abortion. Modern feminists have altered the social contract considerably since that time.

The historical forces behind feminism are complicated and have to do with new demands for women workers, a new understanding of individual rights, a new consciousness about social equity (as well as recognizing that there is less social protection for women), and more equal relations between men and women. I am arguing, however, that abortion is an essential precondition for the emancipation of women, just as modern feminism is the precursor of a woman-centered abortion. Neither can survive without the other. Perhaps this is one reason that the New Right moves so zealously against *both* abortion and the Equal Rights Amendment.

THE PARADOX OF ABORTION

To propose that abortion is linked with major social, ethical, and symbolic changes in modern life does not imply that modernism represents a continuous, effortless move toward a future state of equality for women. On the contrary, the paradox of legal abortion is that the more society accepts it as merely a standard medical procedure, rather than as an emotionally charged social object, the more determined will be traditional forces—New Right groups, fundamentalist Christians, Roman Catholics, full-time housewives—to eradicate or effectively nullify the 1973 Supreme Court decision. Battle lines have already been drawn, as Noonan (1979, 1) observes:

Once or twice in a century an issue arises so divisive in its nature, so far-reaching in its consequences, and so deep in its foundations that it calls every person to take a stand. Abortion, it once appeared, was an unlikely candidate to be such an issue. . . . Politically, the subject was untouchable before the 1960s. No one in a public forum sought to challenge the accepted limits. Later when challengers did come forward, few politicians wanted to take sides: The issue cut across party lines, the parties had no pat partisan formulas for containing it, and each side was good at remembering its enemies. The politicians wished that the subject had never come up. Then they wished it would go away. In this respect abortion became what slavery had been: a plague for the parties and the party professionals.

Since this writing the 1984 Republican platform clarified that party's anti-abortion stance, apparently in a bid for conservative voters. The Democratic party's pro-abortion position may have been a miscalculated attempt to reach out to women voters. What the Republicans correctly banked on was that a significant percentage of voters (a) vote with their pocketbooks; (b) reject the liberation ethic associated with abortion; and (c) continue to feel ambivalent about abortion (even though supporting it in the opinion polls and practice) (see Luker, 1984, 216).

That abortion has galvanized the level of political and personal passion that it has should not be surprising. The stakes are momentous: the fundamental right of privacy for a woman to have control over her body and her life versus protection of the life of society's weakest member—the fetus. An enormous, unbridgeable gulf currently divides the two sides over the issue of what constitutes a "person" (Berger and Berger, 1983, 65). Is the fetus a person? If so, then any interference at any point of the pregnancy constitutes murder. Is the fetus simply part of a woman's body? If this is the case, then the woman has a prior claim to treat an unwarranted intrusion into her life space as an "invasion" and forcibly reject it.

The language used by each side further obscures the issues. Pro-abortionists (pro-choice) typically use language that avoids any suggestion of a human status for the fetus; anti-abortionists (pro-life) will regularly use the term "child," instead of "fetus," and rely on statistics which show that in view of the 1.5 million "murders" of "children" annually, abortion represents a legal permission for "genocide." This opinion is shared by conservative Protestants, Orthodox Jews, Eastern Orthodox Christians, as well as the more publicized anti-abortion views of the Roman Catholic Church. What opponents call a "casual" attitude toward abortion disturbs other groups as well: physicians, who find the permissive sexual codes surrounding reproductive choice morally repugnant; blacks, who reject what some leaders argue is the systematic reduction of their people through abortion and sterilization (Sarvis and Rodman, 1974); and traditional homemakers, for whom modernism spells loss of social status and whose life investment in bearing and rearing children appears to result in little social recognition. The concept of "life" used by anti-abortion groups is a final appeal—what is more essential than "life?"

Pro-abortion terminology has equally powerful emotional appeals. "Choice" signifies modernity, a positive attribute. To be modern involves a vast expansion in options and thus in human beings having more control over their lives. "Anti-choice," a label attached to opponents by abortion partisans, links anti-abortion with a deeply reactionary and mystifying stance. Conversely, "reproductive freedom" is said to demystify health questions for women and places abortion at the center of a new moral and political agenda. This agenda is still being created, largely by a new wave of feminist thinkers and activists (see, for example, Gilligan, 1979, 431–446).

Although abortion at the political level is stalemated in volatile one-issue oppositions—and more recently violence against abortion clinics—at the practical level it continues to be the most frequently performed surgical procedure in the United States (Goldstein, 1984). In 1980 there were 1.5 million abortions performed legally, and one-fourth of all pregnancies were terminated by abortion (Henshaw, et al., 1982). Although the Supreme Court ruling (*Roe v. Wade*, 1973) invalidated all state laws restricting first-trimester abortion, it gave the states a wide latitude in regulating later abortions. The wide range of responses by the states to this regulatory situation, combined with other factors such as local political climate, the receptivity of the local medical community to abortion, and the willingness of some government officials to circumvent the Supreme Court decision, has resulted in a great deal of variability in the way abortion services developed throughout the United States (Goldstein, 1984, 514). In 1980, for example, 2,759 facilities in the United States reported that they performed abortions. But three-fourths of all the abortions were performed in 459 (16.5 percent) clinics and hospitals (Henshaw, et al., 1982). Thus the availability of abortion services is a major predictor of their use (Borders and Cutright, 1979). For many women, the local option implies that abortion is unavailable, or at least available only with out-of-town travel and additional costs, regardless of its formal legality.

The paradox of this abortion policy manifests itself in three ways. First, because of the government's connivance with official and professional circumvention of the law, a professional monopoly in abortion has emerged. Berlant (1975) describes a medical monopoly as one that creates a saleable, scarce commodity with fixed prices that are above market value and that eliminates all external competition by developing group solidarity and cooperativeness among physicians. The paradox here—and the book makes this clear—is that abortion reform specifically aimed to widen the health network, by incorporating nonprofessional occupations and even volunteer women, into an enhanced, woman-centered experience. The monopolization of abortion effectively shuts out the amateurs.

A second related paradox is that the High Court's decision to invalidate criminal abortion laws grew out of a strong sense of equity—if only affluent, connected women were receiving abortions, this left out the poor, teenage, and disconnected women. But concentrating abortion in only a few facilities throughout the United States (and sometimes these are difficult to find in local communities unless someone points them out), where market price, not professionalism, prevails, perpetuates the class and age discrimination.

Still another paradox of abortion—one less apparent perhaps—is that women must now actually *make* reproductive choices instead of accepting the drift into motherhood. Whether individual women personally choose abortion is irrelevant to my argument. Its mere legal availability alters women's understanding about their reproductive choices—indeed, it now forces choice with all its agonies and resistances. Under this ethical arrangement, *not* to choose abortion is as much a determined choice as making a decision *for* abortion.

This book, then, is not really about the women's movement, although the abortion issue reinforced it by making it the imperative symbol of women's freedom. But it is about the abortion movement and how primarily male officials and professionals coped with changing demands of women's sexuality, including their demands for abortion. It is not about how abortion is regarded by its detractors, but how abortion was gradually altered from a thing of evil to a necessary, if sometimes distasteful, medical practice. By documenting the changes in the social control of abortion, the book shows the origins for the ideological cleavage that now threatens to undo the constitutionality of abortion.

Because so much of our understanding of abortion has been formed by experts—doctors, lawyers, psychiatrists, social workers, reform clergymen—who often lacked sympathy with women and the women's cause, a study of the abortion movement tells us about how groups in power only reluctantly serve subordinates. Many of the professionals' accounts of their involvement with abortion focus on the preoccupation of maintaining respectability and invisibility, rather than on providing desperately needed services. I rely heavily on what professionals say about abortion because it was the day-to-day struggle with women's rising abortion demands that began to erode the old order of professional arrogance. So, it wasn't feminism per se that changed the way doctors related to their women patients. It was also the millions of women putting immediate pressures for opening up abortion as a standard reproductive service and for generating new systems of health delivery to relieve the onus of involuntary pregnancy and childbearing for all women, regardless of class, race, age, marital status, or region of the country.

I often use the term "therapeutic" when referring to medical control of abortions before the law changed and by it attempt to delineate the social conditions of abortion when only a minute fraction of women could secure hospital terminations. Anyone with the slightest knowledge of hospital organizations knows how inherently conservative these institutions can be. Hence the elaborate methods of screening out doctor-referred candidates for hospital terminations turned abortion into a power tool for medical gatekeepers and an instrument of subordination for abortion seekers. The paradoxical nature of "therapeutic abortions," of course, is that the "therapy" was primarily for providers; patients often paid dearly for these arrangements.

The law functioned between 1870 and 1973 not as a blanket condemnation of abortion, but as the signal for medical discretion: The doctors provided "justifiable" abortion and made themselves custodians of it (Luker, 1984, 33). And I do not mean that hospitals or doctors personally confronted women, demanding that they justify their abortion request. Rather, women were totally excluded from participating at any level of hospital committee action. Quota systems, ideological preferences, even the whim of an individual committee member could decide a request one way or the other. And because of inevitable delays—abortion committees in many hospitals met only sporadically—many women had their cases rejected and were forced into the "black market" to secure the more available, but often far riskier, illegal abortion. The basic rule of the therapeutic abortion game was: The patient waits and accepts the consequences of the higher order's decision, even if by delaying intervention it maimed or killed her. The lesson, then and now, is that legislating morality did not make women more "moral," but it did expose them to greater risk of sickness and death.

THE ABORTION MOVEMENT

I also focus steadily on the evolution of the abortion movement, originally as a conjunction of forces—middle-class women, reform doctors, population-control partisans, and public health advocates—and later as a concentration of state and professional experts. After all, it wasn't women who served as Supreme Court consultants when the judges sought information about abortion—it was doctors. And it wasn't exclusively consumers who pushed to get abortion out of expensive hospitals into freestanding clinics—it was primarily doctors who found abortion far more profitable away from the immediate censure of their medical colleagues (see Goldstein, 1984, 514–529). Where some abortion reformers went wrong was in their staunch belief that they could "turn over" the abortion responsibility to physicians: "doctor knows best." But as James Mohr (1978) points out, it was doctors who used abortion as a smear campaign against midwives in the nineteenth century for their own professional aggrandizement that led to criminalizing it in the first place. In effect, doctors paved the way to Comstock's successful battle against cheap, available, neighborhood abortions.

Doctors often serve the interests of the state in defining normality and deviance (Davis and Anderson, 1983). And this book is a first effort to reconstruct how the profession took it on itself to regain control over a criminally stigmatized procedure by playing within a new set of ground rules: mental health and public health regulations. By 1970 what many doctors realized was that the law had become an unpredictable competitor in controlling the abortion market and that local prosecutors could not necessarily be trusted to look the other way (although they did almost all the time).

Getting safe, low-cost abortions in a humane environment wasn't actually the doctors' ideological preference as much as the reform clergymen and women's groups who fought for abortion as a woman's personal right, not a doctor's duty. While I am critical of the moralistic fervor that inspired these clergymen's pro-abortion efforts, I am only too aware that these mainly Protestant churchmen helped to strip abortion of its old criminal associations. And by introducing what has since become a standard counseling service for almost all abortion patients, at least in the more enlightened freestanding clinics, they took a first step toward publicly recognizing the essential link between a woman's informed abortion choice and her personal autonomy.

I pay special attention to the years just before the Supreme Court decision because it was between 1967 and 1973 that the traditional abortion system became unraveled. This was the period that first opened up some states' limited, and for New York and California, eventually massive out-of-state abortion traffic. In reporting on Michigan women who traveled to unknown clinics in New York City to receive the still-experimental vacuum aspiration abortion, the book documents more than the social psychological process of women's coping. It also details the structure of the quasi-legal network, which later became the model for today's abortion delivery system.

By the late sixties it was clear that abortion was involved in a major legitimation crisis. There was a persistent questioning of the norms underlying the criminal abortion law and not merely a demonstration that these norms were violated in practice. Like slavery in the nineteenth century, the state had become not simply the institution that conditioned the struggle, but an object of struggle itself. Both within and outside official quarters, people raised questions about the appropriateness, clarity, purpose, equity, and consequences of the criminal abortion laws (see Packer, 1968; Schur, 1965). And for every firm supporter of the old Comstock law, there were thousands of informed citizens and reformers who were finding it an onerous, obsolete, and empty symbol of Victorian ethics. How pro-abortion forces mobilized legal resources and transformed the legitimacy issue is recent history—a history I tell from the point of view of partisans.

As any student of social change can understand, the abortion movement has a complex ideological context. If it were simply the women's liberation movement that provided the impetus for legal change, we would not need a separate examination of the anatomy of abortion. Coming to grips with the thought and actions of feminism would be sufficient to understand the origins and evolution of legal abortion. But biological politics, the ideological framework for abortion change, as the next chapter shows, is a conflict arena of fiercely contested, often polarized, issues. State and professional management of abortion does not necessarily offer humane reproductive services, as the book repeatedly makes clear. A woman-centered abortion service has an uphill struggle to undo the legacy of centuries of reproductive neglect and abuse. The first question becomes control: Who controls women's reproductive capacities, under what social conditions, and for what purposes? While the book offers no final solution—indeed, the issues revolve around the future of gender roles and revaluation of outworn gender ideologies—it does show why feminist advocates continue to celebrate abortion. Emerging from centuries of silence, abortion represents the essential feature in reproductive self-determination and for many women, a radical idea whose time has come.

ABORTION AND SOCIAL THEORY

Examining abortion as the emergence of a new discourse about women's reproductive choice places the phenomena in the center of the political, historical, and moral changes of our time.[3] In one sense, abortion provides a glimpse of the social fabric in a state of collapse: the signaling of the end of the epoch of patriarchal control and the beginning of a new, yet unknown era of gender relations.

It would oversimplify and reduce the complexity of social change to

speak of this transformation as unilineal, or as an inevitable progression. To avoid simplistic interpretations, we need a social theory that enables us to look at abortion as a process, as a continuum which is bound to be broken. Analyzing the institutional breaks, not only in knowledge but in practice, confronts us with a far more relativistic and vulnerable picture of society than its more traditional sociological image as a seamless web or as a system of moral consensus (Parsons, et al., 1965).

Michel Foucault, perhaps the most imaginative "non-historian" to write about history and the most institutionally astute "non-sociologist" to analyze the social transformations of modern social control, offers such a perspective of social discontinuity. In the considerable body of work he accomplished before his premature death at the age of fifty-seven, Foucault provided a structural framework for examining juridical and medical practices in relation to modern power structures and belief systems.[4]

To understand social order, Foucault said, concentrate on process—change, eruption, alteration, evolving organizations—not ostensibly fixed and completed social structures. This enables us to uncover modern repressions and their impact for creating deviance and social change. The social theory of transformation entails three interrelated components of institutional life: language, power, and professional practices.

Language, derived from an amalgam of social forces—deviance and history, social needs and political expediency, ideologies and scientific beliefs—reflects changing political, social, and economic relations. In the twentieth century the new rights and obligations related to women as distinct legal entities, separate from family and extended kingroup, cast abortion as part of the new codes of legal equality. At the same time, historical precedents of women as the "second sex" and male control over reproduction weakened reformers' impetus to recast women as wholly free to choose their reproductive destinies. In this book I clarify how legal, medical, and scientific knowledge about women's needs continue to be produced by male-oriented institutions and ideologies, which define the terms and limits of women's choices.

Power, a second component proposed by Foucault, involves the social sources of repression and its consequences in bringing about change. In fact power and knowledge form an interconnected whole. Whoever controls the knowledge has virtual power over their subjects. The study of medicine's historical relationship to abortion demonstrates how professionals created the knowledge and language of control, giving them the power to implement and to perpetuate the very deviance they set out to eradicate. Under therapeutic regimes women denied abortion on grounds of its deleterious consequences for life and health instead sought relief at the hands of non-specialists, for whom death and illness were simply an unpleasant part of business practices. Throughout the book, I focus on the evolving structure of medical, legal, and religious authority and the growing relation between medical knowledge about abortion and legal power to restrict abortion that constrain women's fully determined choice.

Third, Foucault focuses on how professional practices in modern society both create moral boundaries and serve as gatekeeping functions, demarcating good and evil, deviance and normality, insiders and outsiders. Because professionals police the social margins, as it were, they often control values, beliefs, and their related social practices that are in turmoil. From these professional ranks we can thus expect to see the emergence of change agents and power brokers.

In the abortion case, both in the nineteenth century and more recently, doctors played an ambiguous role in abortion, both as crusaders for social reform and as advocates for medical power. Similarly, legal structures vacillated for decades before moving toward changing the abortion laws, and only then as a result of sustained social movement pressure, including defection of lawyers.

In this book, I question the validity of medicine and law to have final control over women's bodies. I also delineate the chaos of moral values and beliefs as new knowledge and innovative practices emerged over the struggle for women's reproductive rights, a chaos we have not yet eliminated.

A RESEARCH NOTE

This book bears the markings of thousands of hours spent in the field over a three-year period, from 1970 to 1973, working primarily in Michigan, but with additional field trips to New York, Chicago, and Washington, D.C. More like an investigative journalist than a traditional sociologist, I gathered most of my information from the likeliest, but often least visible, sources—private physicians, public health professionals, legal officials, reform clergymen, and women who negotiated the tenuous new abortion delivery system. In 1970 abortion was a dirty word for nearly everyone. Other information came from the persistent pursuit of undercover leads: abortionists who managed to escape enforcement and make a profit; reform doctors who ignored or flouted the state law and became heroes; and feminists who used their own funds to secure abortions for sometimes confused, and invariably needy, young women.

Not all the information came from interviews. Organizational documents provided enormous insights into the erosion of the old law and the attempt by various agencies to contend with abortion as a kind of liminal object: neither clearly good nor evil. For six months I played an "insider's" role in the abortion movement, an exhausting period, as I recall. In the beginning I did not succeed in juggling the sociologist's traditional credo of value neutrality with the feminist's new version of value-committed research. I found that I could only do one or the other. So, my involvement in the movement effectively stopped my sociological thought processes. For a time I became an activist only. As feminist research matured and I reached beyond my original goals of completing a doctoral dissertation (Davis, 1973), I discovered that the apparent oppositions were not so polarized after all.[5]

There are concessions, of course, and this book reflects them. Involved in the pro-abortion movement, I could not ethically nor logistically study the Right-to-Life movement, as the pro-life groups were called in the early seventies. So the dialectic, unfortunately, is missing. And while I try to represent the various professional points of view fairly, it's also quite clear that without taking a feminist perspective, as I have, this book would be the doctor's story of the capture of abortion, or the reform clergy's confrontation with the new morality, instead of the larger history of the changing social control of abortion. In abortion, as in many other morally charged issues, the matter of good and evil dwells in the observer, not the object. It is this clash of traditional, legal, scientific, professional, abortion consumer, and feminist perspectives that constitutes the anatomy of modern abortion.

NOTES

1. For a review of medical control over reproduction, consult Barker-Bensfield (1976); Folbre (1983); Gordon (1976); and Oakley (1979).

2. Abortion as an international social movement is analyzed in Francome (1984); Humphries (1977, 205–266); Jaffe, et al. (1981); Potts, et al. (1977); and Simms (1981, 168–184). Abortion as a major form of birth control in preliterate societies is analyzed by Devereux (1967).

3. Sociological theory has contributed extensively to analysis of institutional processes and social change from a variety of political perspectives. For a review see Davis (1980).

4. Foucault's contribution to the human sciences is examined in Kurzweil (1980, 193–226). For representative works that were influential in shaping my version of abortion, see Foucault, 1976; 1977; 1978; 1980.

5. I discuss my abortion fieldwork experiences as evolving stages of research in Davis (1982).

2

Biological Politics

Abortion has the distinction of being the only "crime" that is essential to the well-being of all developed societies and is a key element in dealing with the erosive effects of population growth on economic development and individual welfare in the Third World. In this respect, it may ultimately be a factor in the very survival of the human species as we know it today.
>—Malcolm Potts, M.D., et al.

In this country, the real issue is not an unmanageable surplus of peoples, but a basic maldistribution of the resources.
>—Reverend Jesse Jackson

We are, especially in developed and affluent countries, facing a crisis of values and priorities that will destroy us much more quickly and far more efficiently than a crisis of population.
>—Reverend Theodore Hesburgh

Effective birth control is both more fundamental to our struggle for equality and part of a larger struggle to control our bodies and our lives. In the population control movement today, both here and in the third world countries, the very group of people who control governments and economies also seek to control who has children and how many.
>—The Boston Women's Health Collective

Four statements—each espousing a distinctively different version of the population issue—offer conflicting policy guidelines.[1] These conflicts initially set the ideological conditions for the abortion struggle, beginning in the early seventies. What kind of alternative policies do these positions represent? One position stipulates the need for abortion to maintain human progress. The second, a radical approach, states the need for economic redistribution, especially among minorities. The third spells out a failure in human values, not population control, and stresses the ultimate goal of seeking a drastic reorganization of our social and political priorities. And the fourth statement focuses on women's right to control reproduction as part of the larger issue of social equality and long-denied political partic- ipation. Abortion is essential in the first proposal, irrelevant in the second, categorically rejected by the third, and viewed as an individual option by feminists in the fourth.

In the last third of the twentieth century, the population issue—in some versions only slightly updated from Thomas Malthus's agonized beliefs about the biological and moral perils of overpopulation—forms the bedrock of the abortion question: Is abortion to be legally available, and to whom, and under what social, economic, and political conditions? That this ques- tion is still being raised twelve years after abortion was legalized by the Supreme Court has as much to do with opposing conceptions of population and family planning—if, what, how, when, why to control the number and social distribution of births—as with the reactive anti-abortion movement.

We should make an initial distinction between family planning as an institution and family planning as a personal choice. As an institution, family planning is linked with the so-called population-control solution, itself largely a state- and elite-directed activity. In this case, decisions about the number of children and their social distribution (race, age of parents, region, and other factors) reside with bureaucrats and professionals. Family planning as choice emerged out of the early abortion debate and was shaped in opposition to what partisans believed was a takeover of birth control by experts. Proponents of choice attacked institutional structures of popula- tion control by:

1. Questioning historical and contemporary claims of population experts, especially those who couch population theory in "natural law" terms, such as the as- sumptions that there are strict upper limits to population or that some "races" are preferable to others.

2. Refusing to restrict the questioning to the level of technology or societal needs and posing individual choice as the essential element of family planning. In some technological versions, they noted that population becomes a "disease," re- quiring eradication at its root, including attacks on fertility, especially "exces- sive" fertility of the "lower classes."

3. Willingness to consider the possibility that individuals and couples may choose "nonrational" and less effective means to achieve value-related ends to family planning, such as "natural" contraception. Or the opposite may occur—abortion may be used as a fairly standard form of limiting births. This stance implies the priority of voluntarism in planning, regardless of techniques used, number of births, or specific size of the completed family.

4. Offering a politically valid critique of official versions of family planning, when these are expressed in elitist, bureaucratic, or technological language. Such

discourse confuses and intimidates people. Examples of such elitist orientations include scare tactics focusing on the alleged overfertility of poor and minority groups, anti-women versions of the zero population growth movement (blaming women for the problem), the monopolization of women's health care by a nearly all-male medical profession, and the anti-pregnancy arguments that focus solely on fetuses, not women and women's preferences.

5. Rejecting the universalistic solutions to population offered by state-mandated family planning institutions. For example, the doctrine that "all large families are bad," regardless of the social-economic conditions of the family or society, poses a kind of official tyranny over family life. Rule by experts, namely, the family planning bureaucrats and practitioners, replaces the personal decision making about fertility by the family. Conversely, the idea that every married couple must have children is equally objectionable.

The family-planning institution, by contrast, offers a set of well-developed doctrines, expert-based practices, service delivery schedules, and accounting procedures that are often unrelated to individual or family choice. More correctly termed the "population control" institution, it is one of a complex of social organizations that constitutes the social control of reproduction. The anti-poverty ideology that pervades these state-initiated efforts to curtail fertility, or control it in the interests of preferred social distributions, certainly relates to Malthus's early horror of a population explosion that would outdistance the capacity of the land to produce food. The updated version is equally mechanistic. Rationality is a key theme; the mastery of nature lends itself to the policy of dominance over humans in the most sensitive areas of life: sexuality and reproduction. Here are some key strategies of the population control model:

1. There is a procedure of *objectification*, turning sexuality and births into statistical abstractions. Thus officials analyze sexual practices and their reproductive outcomes, not as human preferences, choices, or failures, but as social distributions and characteristics. This means that population trends—births, deaths, and migrations—can be tracked as a myriad of social indicators, such as age, sex, social class, ethnicity, religion, region of the country, and others. In and of itself, the information is neutral and technologically correct. How these data are *used* by government and business groups is the problem. Planning, organizing, and changing social behavior, often outside the consciousness and context of our everyday lives, reduces citizens to passive spectators in social areas that deeply concern them.

2. The general knowledge of population held by demographers, economic planners, public health personnel, and others involved in managing the family-planning institution is vastly different from the knowledge held by those in the field of medicine. Physicians deal with the science of bodily functioning or the conditions of health or illness. Instead, family-planning knowlege is gained by the technological survey. People are counted as "things" in a kind of dehumanizing process, whereby randomized surveys document birthrates; age at marriage;

legitimate and illegitimate births; frequency of sexual relations; nature and extent of contraceptive practices; rate and frequency of miscarriages, stillbirths, and criminal abortion. Here the truth about reproduction is not expressed in human values or experiences, but in impersonal numbers, stripped of human significance.

3. The entire population-control enterprise supports a cluster of occupations, including demographers, epidemiologists, psychiatrists, nurses, public health bureaucrats, gynecologists, obstetricians, pharmacologists, drug companies, hospitals, nutritionists, family-planning counselors, and abortion clinics. The dominant metaphor of this occupational ensemble is perhaps best expressed in the statement "control by technology," whether by "the Pill," sterilization, I.U.D., abortion, caesarean delivery, hysterectomy, or tranquilizers. What such heterogeneous entities share is a narrow belief in the salvation of rationality, of limiting births as a necessary and sufficient tool of progress.

HISTORY OF THE FAMILY-PLANNING INSTITUTION

To understand the paradox of abortion both as a tool of population control and as a reproductive choice, the early debates on population must be understood, beginning in the mercantilist period of Europe (1450–1750).

Asserting that the progress of nations is the result of the growth of a society's population, mercantilists laid the groundwork for a pro-natalist policy. Among state experts, the effects of the fourteenth-century bubonic plague on population, a desire for increased economic output, the rise of military conscription, and the need for a large labor force all supported their belief in a large-family policy (Overbeek, 1977, 3).

Opposed to the simple mercantilist's teachings of universal marriage and childbearing, late eighteenth- and early nineteenth-century thinkers emphasized three components: cultivatable land, food production, and birth rates. Malthus (1803) was not alone in his then-enlightened view that people would eventually outstrip food production, but he was the first to state this on the basis of natural law. The principle of population, Malthus said, "has this constant tendency to increase beyond the means of subsistence." Malthus warned that the "positive checks" to population entailed vice and misery—"the whole train of common diseases and epidemics, wars, pestilence, plague, and famine." Late marriage and celibacy were the only defenses, Malthus argued, against this dismal array of troubles.

No doubt Malthus and his followers set the stage for the late nineteenth-century views of population and state building, but there were differences in emphasis among later followers of Malthus's doctrine.

First, the neo-Malthusians stressed that progressive, technologically developed societies needed to limit births so that population would not increase beyond food production. The choice appeared to be either population *or* development, never population *and* development. Despite the efforts of a few critics who pointed to the leveling of population growth with economic development, the "natural law" advocates insisted on the inevitability of an accelerating population unless death-dealing restraints occurred.

Second, neo-Malthusians asserted that technological advances and foreign food imports helped to improve real living standards but held to the idea that such improvements would be lasting only if the preventive checks of moral restraint (and among modern neo-Malthusians, birth control) were universally adopted. Among this group there was little hope that technology without population control could save the world from the pressures of overpopulation.

Third, the law of diminishing returns that lies behind Malthus's doctrine of the arithmetical increase of food production (1, 2, 3, 4 . . .) compared with the geometric increase in the population (2, 4, 8, 16 . . .) stipulated that beyond a certain population density, society cannot benefit from advanced specialization and division of labor. Instead, unemployment, crime, war, and social disorganization prevail.

Fourth, although vigilance, restraint, and self-denial were essential for proper control of the population, these were likely to be inadequate checks. For many early and latter-day Malthusians, the sex instinct was believed to be too strong for voluntary regulation. As a result, these prophets of doom predicted that social problems and retrograde behavior would accelerate until increased death rates balanced the birth rates and available food. At such times of imbalance, Malthus said: "Vicious habits with respect to the sex will be more general, the exposing of children more frequent, and both the probability and fatality of wars and epidemics will be considerably greater; and these causes will probably continue their operation till the population is sunk below the level of the food." For Malthus and others, this was a cycle of infinite regress. With a leveling of the death rate, there would be an increase in fertility, eventually evoking a new crisis of overpopulation.

By the twentieth century, the "law of population" dominated social scientists' thinking. Economists, agronomists, biologists, demographers, sociologists, population planners, and public health groups emphasized the urgent requirements for rational control over individual reproduction. Many were not particularly fussy over the forms that population control would have to take for what was believed to be an issue of planetary survival (Handlin, 1968).

Demography, using the decennial census, flourished and became the chief tool for defining, interpreting, and forecasting the population problem. Between World Wars I and II, population theory shifted emphasis. With stabilizing, and even stationary, populations in Europe, economists, long the chief population spokespersons, argued against pro-natalist policies designed to increase the birth rates. Leading British economist John Maynard Keynes (1922) endorsed various measures that promoted economic prosperity for stable populations and achieved other socially valued ends. Low birth rates, Keynes argued, would contribute to a more equitable distribution of income, reduce nonproductive savings, increase private consumption and low interest rates, enhance borrowing for investment, and accelerate government spending for enlarging aggregate demand.

Professor John Jewkes (1939), a member of the Manchester School, held that population forecasting was an unreliable tool and should be abandoned because basing future population trends on a simple extrapolation of current behavior often yields inaccurate predictions. Unforeseen events—the sharp rise of fertility after World War II in the Western world, which declined again after 1957—showed Jewkes to be correct, contrary to the dire warnings of the classic, or Malthusian, position. By the late 1950s the same small-family trend that first appeared in the 1920s and 1930s reappeared. In addition, economic practicalities and birth control were critical elements in couples' decisions to limit family size. Finally, a new wave of neo-Malthusian thinking played a significant role in shaping policymakers' thinking.

New political commitments—foreign aid in the 1950s and the War on Poverty in the 1960s—by the U.S. government contributed to the development of an elaborate ideology about the hazards of an exploding population. Although foreign and domestic aid programs were separated by continents, both used the well-established Malthusian principle (but selectively applied) that population was a problem of poor people. Excessive numbers of children, policymakers believed, was a direct outcome of the "subculture of poverty," resulting in generation after generation of impoverished masses in developed and underdeveloped countries alike.

"Breeding Ourselves to Death," announced Lawrence Lader (1971) in a book sponsored by the Hugh Moore Fund. The book summarized top government and business leaders' efforts to control population. Among alarmists, population growth was tantamount to *the* deadly sin: an inexorable plague on the earth that accounted for *all* the major social problems of our time. As early as the 1950s, the Hugh Moore Fund had published a pamphlet, *The Population Bomb*, by Stanford University biologist, Paul Ehrlich (1954), that asserted the horrors of overpopulation. Ehrlich warned: "The population bomb threatens to create an explosion as disruptive and dangerous as the explosion of the atom and with as much influence on prospects for progress or disaster, war or peace" (1968 edition).

During the 1960s, when fertility rates in the United States dropped, *The Population Bomb* booklet expanded into boardrooms and classrooms and by 1960 had run through thirteen editions, with distribution to 1.5 million persons. The overt intention of this tract was to alert people to human misery and offer technological solutions, using the moral argument of the early Malthusians to push for scientific intervention. The latent message was its use by elites for selective population control at home and abroad.

The Hugh Moore Fund that distributed the booklet listed among its sponsors distinguished Americans in various policymaking, government, business, and communications circles: John D. Rockefeller III, Chairman of the Population Council; Robert S. McNamara, President of the World Bank; General William Draper, former Ambassador to NATO; Charles E. Scripps, Chairman of Scripps-Howard Newspapers; Marion B. Folsom, Secretary of Health, Education and Welfare; Clare Booth Luce, writer; Dr. Linus Pauling, scientist and Nobel Prize winner; Francis T. P. Plimpton, Deputy U.S. Representative to the United Nations; Charles P. Taft, Mayor of Cincinnati; and Dr. Jerome B. Wiesner, Massachusetts Institute of Technology, among others. The booklet invariably spoke of imminent crisis.

In one of their 1971 pamphlets, Zero Population Growth, a social movement based in well-heeled Palo Alto, California, quoted Margaret Mead, who saw the population crisis as a universal problem:

We are facing one of the great crises in the history of man. There are, almost everywhere, too many people. Too many people in affluent countries stumbling over one another as they scramble for amenities. Too many in poor countries living in growing misery and dying of long drawn-out hunger and disease. Too many old people for whom there is no place; too many children for whose future no provision is made. . . . Yet within 30 years, if we do not act immediately, the world's population, already so dangerously large, will have doubled.

In the 1960s, public advertisements promoting a panic view of the situation appeared in *Time*, *Newsweek*, *Fortune*, *Harper's*, *Saturday Review*, the *New York Times*, *Look*, and other popular magazines. Headlines shouted:

"The Population Bomb Keeps Ticking."

"Good Morning. While You Were Asleep Last Night 3,336 People Died from Starvation."

"Population Explosion Nullifies Foreign Aid."

"Whatever Your Cause, It's a Lost Cause Unless We Control Population."

"Massive Reductions in the World Rate of Population Growth Must Be Made."

"Pope Denounces Birth Control as Millions Starve."

"Population Growth Is a World Problem Which No Country Can Ignore—President Richard M. Nixon"

A full-page spread in the *New York Times* featured an infant in diapers with the heading "Threat to Peace." Contest prizes were offered for slogans relating environmental troubles to "Popullution" (Lader). Merchandising techniques used so successfully for selling products were applied extensively by the leading population-crisis crusader, Hugh Moore. According to Lader (1971, 83), the success of this campaign was evident:

Most intellectuals now held overpopulation to be a precipitating factor in war, famine, resource exhaustion, pollution and many of the world's ills. Congress was now approving larger (though still far too small) budgets for family planning at home and abroad—$218.3 million budgeted for fiscal 1971 against an expenditure of only $29.2 million for 1967. And passage of the Tydings-Scheuer-Bush legislation in November 1970, gave hope of far larger federal funding in the future. The man in the street was beginning to be bombarded with TV discussions of population, with bumper-sticker messages ("Trouble Parking? Support Planned Parenthood"), with invitations to join organizations that plan political action, and with a plethora of magazine articles.

The dominant population myth assumed a reductionist's position—economic and social problems are caused by overpopulation—which helped pave the way, or at least softened the ground, for the pro-abortion movement. Implicit in the neo-Malthusian discourse was a basic fear of poor people, reinforced by the "culture of poverty" notion.

First proposed by anthropologist Oscar Lewis, whose research on urban Mexicans showed the extent of poverty-induced pathologies, the "culture of poverty" idea was soon preempted by the population control group. The basic notion was that the poor had their own "culture," a self-perpetuating, often defeatist mentality that maintained poverty from one generation to the next. This interpretation helped to assure policymakers that those victimized by poverty only brought it on themselves. Such a view encouraged callous policies, such as the ruthless, if politically ineffective, effort to reduce population by Prime Minister Indira Gandhi's vasectomy policy in India, or, for some governments, a do-nothing approach. The implicit policy—and we have no way of knowing the extent to which governments use this as a conscious strategy—of death control, especially among infants and the elderly, continues to decimate rural people in large parts of the world.

Social scientists adapted their own scientific weapons for the battle on population. Polls, scientific articles, and textbooks hammered readers with highly sophisticated analyses of the population crisis and what could be done about it. No longer seen in the simple terms proposed by Malthus, the problem was described by new population advocates as a combination of effects that produced worldwide and systematically destructive environmental conditions. Overpopulation and industrialization were seen as contributing in a variety of ways to the deterioration of the environment. The "Small Planet" concept, one of a myriad of environmental ideas developed in the 1960s spanned research on air pollution, water pollution, solid waste pollution, radiation pollution, and heat pollution. The energy crisis, now a common topic of daily conversation, was also beginning to be recognized

even before the oil crisis that began in 1974. Many highly reputable thinkers, such as Julian Huxley (1963), remained as fundamentally pessimistic
as Malthus earlier had been about the final outcome. Voluntaristic measures, such as individualized family planning, were not seen as workable
options for saving the world and preserving the highly technological life-
styles preferred by affluents in the Western world. Voluntarism, it was
believed, could no longer be reconciled with the current pace of environmental destruction. Garrett Handlin (1968), a biologist and one of the
early pro-abortion advocates, asked, "Where do we stand?" His answer
is emphatic.

Population control is inevitable; the question we ask is: by what agency—Nature
or Man? What we call—for want of a better term—"human dignity" can be preserved only if man takes charge of population control. Technology and education
can help in the task, but since we are not willing to forego the human arrangements
of the welfare state, coercion also must ultimately be used—"mutual coercion,
mutually agreed upon," by a large majority of the population. . . . The choice facing
us is not freedom versus restraint but restraint in breeding versus all other restraints.

Scientists had become ideologists in the service of population control.
    Dennis Wrong, a sociologist and author of *Population and Society* (1967),
criticizes "alarmist" writers on the population problem in *Commentary*
(1964). Their depressing picture of a future in which the entire surface of
the earth has been converted into a human anthill is overdrawn, he says.
This does not, however, imply that the population explosion poses no
problem to the world. Wrong puts the issue into perspective. "The population explosion remains a monumentally serious problem even though
some of the fears to which it gives rise are groundless, and even though it
is the result of a technical revolution that is beneficial in other respects."
    Wrong and other social scientists who advocate government birth control
policies do not see such policies as an alternative, but rather as a prereq-
uisite to economic and political development. Conversely, a runaway population undermines development, these scientists stress.
    More recently, demographically trained sociologists have begun to assess
some of the many unexamined assumptions of the family-planning institution (Westoff and Ryder, 1977). The first distortion is that the studies
report the contraceptive behavior of couples, but only women are
interviewed.
    The assumption that future populations can be determined by current
trends is a second error. Many experts now realize that we do not have
techniques to make long-term predictions, nor would we wish to do so as
long as the democratic process enables social members to make voluntary
adjustments.
    False assumptions about human rationality also cloud demographers'

findings. Although it is true that some people do assign economic calculations to their sexual behavior, many do not. Rationality also implies that
choice is based on adequate knowledge and equal distribution of resources.
Teenage, older, and minority women may lack contraceptive information
for rational family planning and receive such information in myth form
(e.g., abortion sterilizes).

Language may be an obstacle to, rather than the basis for, a meaningful
choice regarding birth control. When birth control information is expressed
in medical or bureaucratic jargon, it is often incomprehensible to the average user.

These research limitations have prompted a few critics of the alarmist
school to disengage from the rationality argument, with its emphasis on
numbers, and pose issues in quality-of-life terms. This produces a wholly
different emphasis: Children by choice becomes the crucial human issue
in democratic policies of family planning (Ryder, 1979).

THE ANTI-MALTHUSIANS

The Nationalist Perspective

If family planning represents a "revolution by the Establishment" (Wolfson, 1978, 31), it was never a unanimous victory. Counterforces—nationalism, socialism, Roman Catholicism, the New Right, and pro-family
groups—have exerted a prolonged attack on the population-planning theories of the family-planning institution. Although separated by disparate
ideological styles, these anti-Malthusian forces have recently combined in
their joint attack on legal abortion.

From Adam Smith to the New Right, population is viewed as the crucial
element in the growth and power of nations (Overbeek, 1977), a reverse
hypothesis to the Malthusian principle. While agreeing with the Malthusians that development is determined by population laws, anti-Malthusians
insist that the steady growth of the population is what has brought wealth,
prosperity, happiness, and progress to a nation. H. C. Carey (1858, 1865),
an early American economist, dismissed the Malthusian doctrine "by virtue
of which man is rendered more and more the slave of nature as wealth
and population grow." It made no sense, Carey argued, to say that increased population causes individual misery and national decline when the
reverse is actually the case: Wealthy and powerful nations invariably have
growing populations.

The nineteenth-century nationalists held that the nation served as a vital
link between the individual and the world. With each nation an island,
population must expand to produce the food, clothing, and shelter required
for an "increased power of combination." In this way, humans gain control
over nature. Carey's essay "On Human Fecundity" proposes a more basic

population principle, the biblical injunction "Be fruitful and multiply, said the Lord, and replenish the earth, and subdue it." Carey and others took this as an article of faith and a basic economic law.

Dupreel (1922), a French sociologist, reflected the pro-natalist's nationalist philosophy that emerged as a result of the relatively low birth rates in France after 1920 and the heavy losses suffered throughout Europe during World War I. High demographic rates are advantageous, Dupreel said. Otherwise, we confront "race suicide." For Dupreel and other post-World War I thinkers, population growth stimulated social and economic progress because it tended to "upset social barriers and formal inequalities." By contrast, a stationary population slowed down upward mobility, induced pessimism about the future, encouraged class and caste rigidity, and produced low motivation. Small families are sociologically retrograde, Dupreel insisted, because they "limit themselves to activities that scarcely do more than maintain and reinforce the existing institutions and structures of society."

Dupreel's thesis did not fall on deaf ears. With American industry still at the take-off stage, the ideology of population growth was an appealing alternative to the dismal picture of social development proposed by the Malthusians. Nearly a half century later, Dupreel's theories were evident in American economic analyses. Rapid population growth was shown as the chief stimulus for economic development because it gave rise to social repercussions and counterpressures that offset the initial economic disadvantages.

Nationalists pointed to other advantages of demographic acceleration. One is the steady growth of demand for goods and services. Instead of closing schools and factories, we expand the gross national product to meet spiraling needs.

Another advantage of an increasing population, say growth advocates, is that manpower will be available to build and maintain military strength. A reduced birth rate could seriously jeopardize the number of military combatants available. With the rise of fascism in the 1930s, empire building and manpower concerns promoted policies of demographic nationalism (Overbeek, 1977, 5). Fascist regimes in Germany, Italy, Japan, and Spain encouraged increasing population by prohibiting emigration, suppressing birth control practices, imposing taxes on bachelors, and subsidizing marriages and large families.

A third advantage is related to the population ratio issue. In 1970 the United States had 6 percent of the world's population (1970 census). If current trends persist, the pro-growth groups say, this ratio will decline to between 3 percent and 4 percent, or less, by the year 2000. Russia, China, and the Third World countries already far exceed the U.S population, and pro-growth advocates believe that to dip below this 6 percent level would seriously threaten the balance of power.

The fourth consideration is a racist issue related to the higher growth rates of minority populations. Earlier rhetoric used to describe minority groups as "yellow peril" and "black hordes," for example, has been transformed into a "wave-of-the-future" rhetoric. Black, Indian, and Hispanic groups have far higher birth rates, which some nationalist groups feel will lead to serious racial imbalances. For instance, at current fertility rates, some population planners propose that 40 percent of America's teenagers will be members of a minority group by 1990. These racist arguments are used by both family-planning managers and the anti-Malthusians. Where the pro-natalists differ is in their solution, which is to keep white fertility high in order to offset the higher rates of minority births. I recently encountered graffiti—"ZPG [Zero Population Growth] is white genocide"— scrawled on an interstate highway retaining wall in Portland, Oregon. The fear of being racially engulfed is a genuine, if secret, shame in white society.

Among pro-natalists, who undoubtedly composed the largest proportion of the American public in the 1960s, population policy was an embarrassment, and state intervention was considered to be immoral. J. Stycos (1968) observes:

The public reaction to family planning in the United States has varied between disgust and silent resignation to a necessary evil. At best it was viewed as so delicate and risky that it was a matter of individual conscience. As such it was a matter so totally private, so sacred (or profane), that no external agents, and certainly not the state, should have anything to do with it.

Like President Eisenhower, nationalists took a strong anti-birth control stance. Capitalism, imperialism, and high fertility were all part of the same equation for a strong America.

Socialism and the New Left

Socialists disagree with the idea that population determines social development. Economics is the chief culprit, they say, especially capitalism, with its systematic exploitation of workers, consumers, and natural resources. For socialists, social harmony is not achieved by individuals pursuing their self-interests. Collective efforts must prevail, beginning with drastic modification in the production and distribution of income and other economic resources.

Marx's (1919) original argument laid the foundation for the socialist's attack on the anti-growth mentality. Marx considered unemployment a systematic device by capitalism to eliminate workers and replace them with lower-costing and more predictable machines. As a competitor of the worker, the machine creates "the dead weight of the industrial reserve army." And the greater the wealth of the capitalistic nation, the greater this reserve army. Surplus populations are created as laborers fall into the ranks of the "supernumeraries," the rejected and the alienated. Marx was explicit about the despotism of this inhuman process.

All means for the development of production transform themselves into means of domination over, and exploitation of, the producers; they mutilate the labourer into a fragment of a man, degrade him to the level of an appendage of a machine, destroy every remnant of charm in his work and turn it into a hated toil; they estrange from him the intellectual potentialities of the labour-process . . . they distort the conditions under which he works, subject him during the labour process to a despotism the more hateful for its meanness; they transform his life-time into working-time, and drag his wife and child beneath the wheels of the Juggernaut of capital.

Marx quotes the Reverend Townsend, a Church of England prelate who was opposed to the "poor laws," as a typical Malthusian capitalist. Hunger and misery fuel the capitalist state to society's advantage, Townsend approvingly said. A law of nature [exists] that there may always be some to fulfill the most servile, the most sordid, and the ignoble offices in the community. Herein lies "human happiness," the prelate stressed. In the final insult to a free laboring class, Marx bitterly retorted, hunger becomes the chief incentive to work.

For Marx, the only solution for workers was to voluntarily limit their fertility to reduce their own labor supply. Following the market principle, once labor is scarce, wages will rise, ensuring workers a decent living. But Marx was dubious about the outcomes of human reproduction. Under capitalism, workers are reduced to the "boundless reproductivity of animals individually weak and constantly hunted down." In this vision, pauperism and enforced idleness would be the lot of workers as more and more labor displacement occurred: skilled workers replaced by unskilled, male by female, and adults by youth and children. Only through the combined efforts of employed and unemployed could positive social development occur.

Herbert Marcuse (1970), spokesperson of the New Left and highly influential among students in the early 1970s, reconstructs Marx's concept of alienated labor. The old argument about food deprivations and accelerating human misery is simply not the issue, says Marcuse. He maintains that productive forces do exist that make possible the abolition of hunger and misery, and that what is happening today must be attributed to the global politics of a "repressive society." Why is the quality of life in modern capitalist societies so impoverished, so oppressed for almost all citizens, Marcuse asks? Only by liberating and gratifying needs through "creative experimentation" can the "fetters of capitalist production" be thrown off. For Marcuse and other socialists, this begins with absolute negation of the capitalist's social principles of life: competition, imperialist wars, profits, maldistribution of resources, alienated labor, and a destructive production system. Human freedom, not population control—a capitalist contrivance—is the question. And the answer is found in promoting a meaningful quality of life.

Among black leaders, the population issue is often seen as coercion against minorities. "Population control is subordinate to wealth control," states the Reverend Jesse Jackson. "Forced sterilization or any compulsive directive is anathema to the human spirit," says Shirley Chisholm. More than 20 percent of the nation's population, in Dr. Martin Luther King's words, "languish on an island of poverty in a vast sea of affluence."[1] The fear of racial genocide is real and prompts some minority leaders to reject family planning altogether, especially abortion and sterilization (Sarvis and Rodman, 1974).

For many concerned minorities, the Marxian paradox continues to impede unified efforts for organizing economic and social equity. Excessive fertility creates numbers, the basis for a strong political bid for resources. But high fertility, accompanied by high illegitimacy, high infant and maternal death rates, and poverty life-styles, degrades the quality of life. Thus minority groups may reject the family-planning institution while recognizing the family-planning question: Can minority groups gain access to voluntary, humanistic family planning? Legal abortion cannot resolve this question as long as issues of economic deprivation persist and continue to dominate the political discourse in the black community. And as long as the fertility problem is proposed as a population control issue, primarily aimed at poor minority women, the Marxist paradox will remain unresolved.

Roman Catholicism and the New Right

Traditional forces, such as the Catholic Church and other fundamental religionists, often combine nationalism, religion, and traditional views of women in their opposition to established versions of family planning. For the Catholic hierarchy, sex for procreation is a cardinal principle. Beginning with St. Bonaventure, the church ruled that marital relations were good only if motivated solely by the desire to have children. From this doctrine, the church developed its position that artificial birth control devices were wrong because they frustrated the primary aim of marriage. Pope Pius XI, in his 1930 "Encyclical of Christian Marriage," termed birth control "intrinsically vicious" (*Newsweek*, 6 July 1964: 35).

In Rome, Vatican-watchers prognosticated that the problem of family planning would be part of the church in the modern world. Despite the efforts of a few progressive American theologians and Catholic physicians to influence the birth control issue, the "Marriage Question" (Newman Press, 1963) hinged on an absolute rejection of contraception. According to Jesuit theologians Ford and Kelly, "the church is so completely committed to the doctrine that contraception is intrinsically and gravely immoral that no substantial change in this teaching is possible. It is irrevocable" (*Newsweek*, 6 July 1964: 36).

Not so surprisingly, the official anti–family-planning view is characteristically found among the American church hierarchy, not the laity. The National Council of American Catholic Bishops began organizing against legalized abortion a few months after the Supreme Court handed down the decision in 1973. At about the same time, white fundamentalist pastors began to react negatively to the various cultural changes of the 1960s, including the changes in sexual mores. The anti-abortion movement was, thus, the offspring of two major forces: the Catholic Bishops' crusade through its impact on Congress and the laity, and the Protestant fundamentalists, the Moral Majority, and their appeals to politically neglected status groups (e.g., white working class). The Right-to-Life and other pro-life groups generated from this nucleus took as essential two concepts: dominance of the woman's reproductive role and the overriding rights of the fetus. The Reverend Hesburgh (1972), president of Notre Dame University and a liberal on civil rights matters, takes the biologically restrictive view of women:

As a priest, I have known of nothing that so shatters a woman psychologically and morally as the destruction of human life within her. One of her greatest assets is life-giving, not life-destroying. Cast her in this latter role and you ultimately destroy her. All too little has been said about the rights of a life, but yet an unborn human being is often, for the most frivolous reasons, denied his or her most fundamental human right, the right to life which precedes liberty and the pursuit of happiness.

There is a growing gap between the canonical church, comprised of laws, and the ecumenical church, typified by everyday faith practices. That 90 percent of American Catholic women in the childbearing years approve of birth control casts serious doubt on the overall impact of the formal canonical church doctrine (*New York Times*, 28 October 1971). The fact that Catholic women oversubscribe to abortion—a larger proportion get abortions relative to their numbers in the general population—could be downright embarrassing to the Church. But the Church is not consistent in the family-planning area.

Church progressives, especially in Latin America, recognize the need for birth limitation, citing Pope Pius XII's statement that strong economic and social reasons can relieve Catholic couples of the obligation to have children. Dialogues between priests and family-planning groups in Latin America created a compromise among clerical spokespersons, and the word came down: "We aren't going to approve it [birth control], but we aren't going to oppose it" (*Congressional Record-Senate*, 1964, 16022–23). With the realization that Uruguay produced three abortions for every live birth in 1964, and that 26 percent of 1,890 women surveyed in Santiago, Chile, had criminal abortions in the same year, Latin-American clergy opposition to family planning melted. The American Church, though, remains officially opposed to artificial contraception and abortion. Rhythm, or "Vatican roulette," the ovulation temperature chart method, remains the only approved contraceptive technique.

The picture of the"positive woman" presented by pro-family advocate Phyllis Schlafly and other anti-feminists (Felsenthal, 1981) is that women are the sole upholders of the American home and personal morality. Schlafly insists that sexual freedom dissolves the bonds of the society, leaving nothing but a quasi-criminal anarchy in the home, the workplace, and the school. Where Schlafly departs from earlier versions of the pro-family–religious alliances, such as in Victorian America and England, is in the promise that if women behave themselves sexually, men will be obliged to marry and take care of them. Frances FitzGerald (1981), writing about Schlafly and the New Right in *The New York Review*, explains:

That there exists a trade-off between sexual propriety and financial security for women is in fact the underlying theme of all the "pro-family" groups from the Right-to-Lifers to the fundamentalists. It is hardly a new message but a look at the divorce statistics and the gender of most white people below the poverty line suggests why it might have particular appeal at the moment.

The STOP-ERA movement, the Born-Again Christian movement, and the anti-abortion movement all treat the family as an endangered species, threatened by homosexuality, abortion, divorce, and nonmarital sexuality. President Carter's 1980 Commission on the Family was generated, in large part, from this pro-family faction, which, for Schlafly, means being a "patriot and a defender of the Judeo-Christian civilization." As the New Rightists became more involved in anti-abortion committees, the appeals for support were expressed in almost totally negative terms. Legalized abortion became analogous to the Nazi Holocaust or infanticide, the murder of newborns. Congressmen's jobs were threatened or they were defeated in the polls if they supported abortion legislation or voted against pro-life measures. Pro-woman legislation was attacked because it undermined the family, enabling women to be independent of men. Instead, these New Right proponents believed that legislation should eliminate welfare in order to force women into marriage so that men would have to support the children.

The anti-feminist themes of Schlafly and the New Right hearken back to nineteenth century American nativism with its conspiracy theory of the world. Examined by Hofstadter in *The Paranoid Style in American Politics* (1965), nativists rejected the city, despised foreigners, and attacked liberal politics. The morality arguments generated by the extreme Right may well have their appeal among those classes and status groups—white workers, urban Catholics, unskilled homemakers, and others—left behind by mainstream politicians.

Feminists and the Family-Planning Question

"The gynecologist is our society's official specialist on women," begin Diana Scully and Pauline Bart in their critical article on the male gynecologists' monopoly over women's health (1973). Feminists have organized a women's health movement that attacks a host of evils: sexism in medicine, health-care providers' control over reproduction and contraception, excessive hysterectomies, normalization of cesarian sections as a standard delivery procedure, forceps deliveries, drug-induced labor, and other unnecessary obstetrical interventions. Feminists say that such procedures are often dangerous to women and their babies. As Barker-Bensfield points out (1976), like the nineteenth-century pelvic surgery and genital mutilations on slave and lower-class women imposed by Dr. J. Marion Sims, the "father of gynecology," contemporary medical intervention both in childbirth and on the organs of reproduction promotes exploitative practices. It is the "miseducation of obstetricians-gynecologists and their unilateral, often brutal control over women's bodies," says Scully (1980), that has generated this latter-day women's health movement.

Among feminists, the sexuality and pregnancy choice is a radical necessity for women to control their own bodies. Their view of the family-planning question is: How to avoid the culturally mandated and unconscious pressure for women to have sex and babies against their will? To cope with this, feminists propose five strategies.

First, feminists reject patriarchal control over reproduction, whether this is represented by male or female physicians. The entire health-care industry is at fault, they believe, for promoting the false ideology of medical specialization over women's reproduction. The reasoning is essentially Marxian: Women have become the unwitting tools of the male patriarchy for reproducing labor power and serving as unpaid labor to socialize the young (Mitchell, 1966).

"Self-help" is the term today's feminists adopt for their advocacy version of health care: women helping women to take over their own bodies without the dependencies incurred by the old-line service delivery model. This idea of "medicine without doctors" is a nineteenth-century invention and part of a larger female moral reform movement that occupied many middle-class, native, white American women.[2] It provided a vehicle for feminists' statements. Opposed to the sickly, corset-bound, and frail lady image was the concept of salvation through nutrition, personal hygiene, and changes in dress codes and eugenics. Organizing into physiological societies, these early women's study groups fostered a sense of community against the isolation of the home (Peterson, 1976). But by the twentieth century, the birth control movement, an offshoot of these women's groups, had been co-opted by physicians and middle-class organizations, the most notable being the Planned Parenthood Federation. Entrance into two world wars profoundly altered women's isolation through the increased participation of women in economic and political institutions, and emphasis shifted away from self-help. The movement waned.

"Self-help demonstrations," publicly initiated by Carol Downer in 1971, represent a revival of the early feminine body consciousness. At an all-women's conference, Downer inserted a plastic speculum into her vagina and viewed her cervix in the company of other women. The response to this self-help initiative was intense and ignited a national movement that combined the elements of self-help with a communal ideology. Feminist health care was defined as a collective project for affiliating women with one another, promoting the idea that every woman is her own doctor. Self-help became a broadly defined program to educate women in the anatomy and self-care of the reproductive and genital organs. It emphasizes women learning from other women with minimum or no intercession by professionals.

Second, unmasking the population-control movement as an elite ideology reveals the profound, if often unconscious, prejudice against the "lower classes." Planners seek to control the growth of minority groups and the indigent through enforced birth control, abortion, or sterilization. *The Boston Women's Health Book Collective* (1979),[3] which assembled the best-seller *Our Bodies, Ourselves*, consider the arguments about the dangers of overpopulation as a convenient rationale for certain contraceptive techniques that entail considerable risk to women. The *Collective* asserted:

Fear of overpopulation has led to some extreme suggestions, such as contraceptive medication in the water supply. We have already seen cases of involuntary sterilization of welfare mothers or poor women with more than a certain number of children. These trends violate the right of each of us to choose voluntarily whether to have children. Methods with substantial risks and side effects are tolerated, even espoused. (p. 181)

According to feminists, in the so-called interest of "societal needs," individual choice becomes muted, irrelevant, or impossible.

Third, birth control is not merely an isolated technical act. Instead, the choice of contraceptives is dependent on public knowledge of their attributes and risks and a woman's relationship with herself and a man (or men). Women who use what population-control advocates believe are "ineffective" or "inappropriate" birth control methods, such as rhythm, foam (without a condom), or withdrawal, are ridiculed by the health profession. But there are personal reasons and values why women have trouble using birth control or do not use it at all. The *Collective* summarizes what these might be:

We are embarrassed by, ashamed of, confused about our own sexuality.

We cannot admit we might have or are having intercourse because we feel (or someone told us) it is wrong.

We are romantic about sex—sex has to be a passionate, spontaneous sharing, and birth control seems too premeditated, too clinical, and often too messy.

We hesitate to inconvenience our sex partner. This fear of displeasing him is a measure of the inequality in our relationship.

If we are using natural birth control we sometimes have a hard time abstaining during our fertile days because we fear our partner will get angry and find sex elsewhere.

We feel, "It can't happen to me. I won't get pregnant."

We have questions about birth control and sex and don't know whom to talk with.

We hesitate to go to a doctor or clinic and face the hurried, impersonal care, or if we are young or unmarried, the moralizing and disapproval that we feel likely to receive.

We don't recognize our deep dissatisfactions with the method we are using and begin to use it haphazardly.

We want a baby and can't admit it to ourselves. Or we feel tempted to get pregnant just to prove to ourselves that we are fertile, or to try to improve a shaky relationship. (p. 183)

Even when women are protected from pregnancy, birth control raises other questions. Women may wish to feel confident in not choosing sex, which takes a measure of strength and self-esteem many feel they do not have. Women who wish to limit their sexual availability may feel apologetic or fearful and that they may threaten or insult their partner, or believe that the man may seek sexual gratification elsewhere. In the event of an unplanned or unwanted pregnancy, individual choice entails the abortion option. For a few women, abortion may be a regular substitute for other contraceptive techniques. The women's health movement does not presume to judge the individual woman's decision but emphasizes that, through self-help knowledge and practice, the reproduction decision can be more appropriate for the individual woman's or couple's life-style.

Official institutional views of reproduction may be suspect if they contradict women's experiences. According to Diane Scully (1980), the "surgical mentality" of gynecology-obstetrics includes performing unnecessary surgery on the poor in order to get experience. But it is not only the poor who receive unnecessary and life-threatening medical treatment, insist Barbara and Gideon Seaman in *Women and the Crisis in Sex Hormones* (1977). Incautious use of supplementary hormones for women contributes to med-

ical complications and even death. The worldwide literature on hysterectomy—called euphemistically "prophylactic hysterectomy" by doctors for
their menopausal patients—shows many non-benign results. Scully (1980,
147), a feminist sociologist, quotes Newton, an authority in the area:

Repeated or controlled studies indicate that hysterectomy may yield problems for
some women in the following areas: rejection by male partners, hot flushes after
conservation of ovarian tissue, severe hot flushes after ovariectomy, long-term
psychourinary problems, weight changes, lingering fatigue and prolonged conva-
lescence, painful intercourse, depression, sleep disturbances and other psychiatric
symptoms.

Perhaps one of the more blatant anti-women statements to issue from
the no-growth school is the proposal to alter drastically the sex ratio by
limiting the birth of females. Women would leave one "breeding" daughter
among her descendants and plan to produce an excess of male children.
Garrett Handlin (1968), who applauds this radical policy, concedes that
there will be some social complications:

If women can control the sex of their children and if they wish to improve the
bargaining power of women in future generations, they should produce an excess
of male children. But with a large male-to-female ratio, monogamy would leave
many men out in the cold and dangerously dissatisfied. It would be hard to create
a stable state from such explosive material, so a shift to polygamy would be required.
(p. 217)

Feminists consider such proposals ludicrous and dangerous. For instance,
there is no guarantee that men would not simply prefer homosexuality to
the constant infighting over available females. War could be a very real
alternative in a numerically superior male world. In either event, women's
social status is more likely to decline than improve under such policies.

The anti-juvenile pregnancy argument is more complex. On the one
hand, family-planning managers do not believe it politically feasible to
propose effective prevention such as teaching sex education and birth control in elementary school (where they believe it should appropriately begin
if it is to be effective). Yet, by junior and senior high school, family-
planning managers realize that the reproductive misinformation has already
distorted teens' sexual views and laid the framework for unprepared
sexuality.

On the other hand, pregnancy rates among teens are increasing, with
only about one-third of those pregnant opting for abortion.[4] The others
deliver babies who are underweight or who are more likely to die in the
first few weeks after birth. Among the 80 percent of teens who decide to
keep their babies, child neglect and abuse are rampant. The adolescent
mother herself is at serious risk. She is more likely to have toxemia or

septicemia or other pregnancy-related diseases and to lack the prenatal care that is necessary for monitoring diseases during her pregnancy. Pregnancy among teens produces multiple psychological and social risks as well. Personal development is stunted; the younger mother becomes isolated and cut off from peers and sometimes her family. She has few opportunities to develop job skills and is likely to be consigned to poverty for the rest of her life.

Feminists confront these data with some apprehension. It is difficult to talk of choice when society offers so little support to the adolescent for building self-esteem, the foundation for responsible decision making. Maternity, as the predominant sign of adult womanhood, may be sought by young women or imposed by a society that ignores or denies the prevalence of teenage sexual activity, accepting customs and laws that view it as deviant and immoral behavior (Cutright, 1972, 25). Magnifying this problem is the lack of other nonsexual coping skills that limits the adolescent mother's perspective.

Choice, then, has substantive limits and needs to be redefined. Like Planned Parenthood groups who have adopted many of the woman-centered contraceptive notions, feminists emphasize "responsible choice." But they go beyond Planned Parenthood in demanding that the society produce the necessary economic and social resources to make responsible choice a real possibility for women. This begins with educating physicians and health workers, who are among the more resistant forces for a deliberate and unencumbered sexuality.[5]

Finally, the feminist health movement challenges population-control advocates on the issues of state-mandated family size. Social scientists have long observed the self-adjusting process of the "demographic transition" in North America, Europe, and Japan. As wealth and opportunity increase, fertility declines. Radical measures to coerce smaller families are thus unnecessary. "Natural contingencies in the contemporary world," say psychologists William Wiest and Leslie Squier (1974), "make it disadvantageous for most individuals to bear a large number of children." They enumerate the changing social factors in the United States that contribute to voluntary fertility reductions:

Changing social factors in the U.S. include social security, Medicare, greater mobility, young married couples living alone, greater acceptance of cohabitation, easier divorce, more jobs for women, the rising demand on limited resources, urban housing shortages, rising costs of child care, education and services, the control of disease, a vast amount and variety of consumer goods, availability of travel, entertainment, and leisure time. The care and cost of children now has to compete with many more interests and diversions than ever before. (p. 239)

Few feminists would advocate disincentives for the large family (such as taxing the third child or more) because such negative incentives primarily affect the poor and uneducated. Most believe that birth control, including abortion, is a woman's right but not a duty, and they carefully examine policies of medical sterilization, hysterectomy, contraception, and drug prescriptions. For feminists, the real issue is not population—pro or con— but the creation of a political and social environment that promotes the health, education, and welfare of all the living regardless of age, gender, race, social class, or other categorical distinctions.

The women's health movement realized a rare victory when the Commission on Population and the American Future submitted its Final Report to President Nixon in 1972. Family planning and abortion were part of a woman's individual freedom that the state must concede, the Report stated. A population policy must involve "the freedom of women to make difficult moral choices based on their personal values, the freedom of women to control their own fertility and finally the freedom from the burdens of unwanted childbearing."

The abortion issue includes aspects of both the family-planning institution and the family-planning question. Abortion can be a power tool used by managers for a "balanced" population. Or abortion can serve as part of the choice process for individual women and their families. The progrowth, traditionalist groups reject abortion in either of these policy roles. They believe that abortion is anathema because it offends Nature, God, and Country.

Those interviewed for this study—physicians, nurses, hospital administrators, family-planning staff persons, lawyers, police detectives, judges, and others involved in policymaking and practice—have confronted the various issues proposed by these factions. In the transition from pregnancy as a "law of nature" to a personal choice (or a state-mandated regulation), it is not surprising to find otherwise knowledgeable informants who become inconsistent, mystified, and contradictory about family planning and abortion. Abortion appears to threaten the comfortable status quo of these professionals and throw their commonsense understandings into disarray. In the late 1960s, in fact, the idea of a coherent abortion policy was an impossibility.

NOTES

1. "Population: The U.S. Problem and the World Crisis," *New York Times Supplement*, 30 April 1972.

2. The women's health movement is further examined in Davis and Anderson (1983).

3. *Our Bodies, Ourselves* was originally published in 1971 and has been revised in 1973, 1976, 1979. This chapter draws on the 1979 edition.

4. The issues of teenage pregnancy are summarized in Worthington, et al., 1977.

5. The medical institution has been a chief source of mystification and misinformation about birth control for teens. For instance, in 1970 the University of

Oregon Medical School reported that one of every twelve babies born in that state was illegitimate. In 1950 it was one out of fifty-three. More than half of these unwed mothers were teenagers. In that same year a not-untypical professional in that period, Dr. Daniel G. Morton, chairman of the Department of Obstetrics and Gynecology at the University of California, said flatly: "I am opposed to offering birth control information to unmarried girls under 18 years in most circumstances" (*Look*, 28 July 1970). Such attitudes have prompted Mary Daly (1978), a radical feminist, to call American gynecology a "gynocide by holy ghosts of medicine."

3

Abortion Law: Theory and Practice

This chapter describes various stages in the collapse of religious-legal control over abortion and shows how legal perspectives in the modern epoch have rarely been consistent or stable.[1] Instead, sharp conceptual shifts have characterized social control over abortion.

FROM CUSTOM TO LAW

The concept of "ensoulment," originating with the Greeks and differentiating male and female growth, provided the first systematic theory about abortion. Aristotle believed that the embryo did not become formed and begin to live until sometime after conception—at least forty days for a male and eighty days for a female. Aristotle's thinking derived from a three-stage theory of life: the vegetable phase, associated with conception; the animal phase, coinciding with "animation" (or what we now term "viability"); and the "rational" stage, occurring after birth. Animation was the key concept and referred to the period between conception and birth, after which there were clear indications of "motion" or life. Greek philosophers advocated limitation of offspring on eugenic grounds, providing the fetus was not animated (unformed). According to Aristotle, "if it should happen among married people that a woman, who already had the prescribed number of children became pregnant, then before she felt life, the child should be driven from her" (quoted in King, 1969).

The forty day gender distinction for animation was adopted by the early church and persisted until the nineteenth century. The ensoulment principle, though, remained ambiguous. The twofold distinction between embryo inanimatus and embryo animatus was disputed by Augustine, who may have drawn on Exodus 21:22, in expressing the view that human judgment cannot determine the exact point of fetal development or the moment in which movement actually occurs. For this reason, Augustine and other church fathers outlawed abortion at any stage.

The early church had an additional ally in Hippocrates, the physician who represented a small segment of ancient Greek opinion known as the Pythagorean ethic. This ethic specified that animation proceeded from the moment of conception. Hippocrates stated: "I will neither give a deadly drug to anyone if asked for it nor will I make a suggestion to this effort. Similarly, I will not give to a woman an abortive remedy" (quoted in Edelstein, 1967).

With the emergence of Christianity, a doctrine in essential agreement with the Pythagorean ethic, the Oath became the nucleus of all medical ethics. Under Christianity, the abortion rule signified the merger of two austere theories, apparently out of step with the more tolerant ethos and practices of Roman law (which accepted both abortion and infanticide). Christian doctrine arose largely in opposition to this moral laxness. And except for a few marginal theologians, abortion remained a serious sin, punishable with excommunication, from the time of the early church fathers until the recent Vatican II Council, which asserted individual conscience in moral matters. The official church doctrine, though, remains strongly anti-abortion.

The Christian epoch reveals a dual movement: an inconsistent and ambiguous basis for restrictive abortion and a pronounced doctrinal antipathy toward abortion, especially since the nineteenth century (see Figure 3.1 at end of chapter for characteristic church doctrines governing abortion).[2]

Animation formed the basis of Thomas Aquinas's concept of fetal life, defining movement as one of the most basic principles of life. Generally, canon law regarded the fetus as part of the mother, and its unwilled destruction was not considered homicide. Apparently, quickening (animation) was the only feature of the ensoulment doctrine that remained undisputed in the canon law of the late medieval period. Once the fetus was "formed," or took on a human appearance, its destruction was considered murder; punishment was excommunication or extensive penance, including fasting and sexual continence for up to a decade.

Next to traditional Christianity, English common law was the most influential ideological source shaping legal thought. The intent of the common law was solely to protect the unborn child. "It recognized the child's *separate and independent existence* at quickening and so used this event as a dividing line" (Grisez, 1970). Theoretically, the mother could be as guilty as anyone else who attacked that life. In frequently cited passages, English jurists Coke and Blackstone are reputed to have viewed abortion as a misdemeanor, not as a felonious act. Coke was said to be reluctant to assert secular jurisdiction to assess penalties for an offense that traditionally had been an exclusively ecclesiastical crime. The paucity of common law prosecutions supports this rendering of Coke's interpretation. In light of new evidence about the English ecclesiastical court's indifference to the problem after 1527, critics are more willing to attest that even post-quickening abortion was never established as a common law crime.

The English statutory law introduced in the nineteenth century (1831) treated abortion as a capital crime, although the statute preserved the quickening distinction by providing lesser penalties for the destruction of the pre-animated fetus. But the 1831 abortion statute was abolished, along with the death penalty in Britain in 1836, and did not surface until the 1861 Offenses Against the Person Act that formed the core of English anti-abortion law. This act lasted until passage of the reform acts of 1967. In the 1861 law the intent to take the life of a child "capable of being born alive" was a felony, although there was one significant provision. A person was not guilty of the offense "unless it proved that the act which caused the death of the child was not done in good faith for the purpose only of preserving the life of the mother." With this statement, social control of abortion entered its third epoch with a murky canon law giving way to a more restrictive secular law, which effectively turned over abortion control to an ambitious medical profession. After this point, the "quickened/unquickened" distinction faded and was replaced by the "therapeutic/criminal" demarcation.

This conceptual shift becomes clear when reviewing the American law prevailing in all but a few states from the mid-nineteenth century until the 1970s. Said to be a version of the old English common law, the 1828 American abortion law that emerged in New York served as the model for all early anti-abortion statutes. It was a highly repressive law, as it barred almost all legal abortion, except for a "price."

What was the impact of the nineteenth-century law? First, by maintaining the distinction between the unquickened abortion, defined as a misdemeanor, and the quickened abortion, counted as a felony, it opened the way to a series of medical-legal jurisdictional disputes. Second, this theoretical hole would later make the crime of abortion not only unenforceable, but also by subjecting the law to a dual authority system—legal and medical—provide an opportunity structure for both legitimate and illegitimate entrepreneurs. Third, because of its duality, abortion became a "customer's institution," the affluent buying a medically controlled, expensive, high-quality product and the poor and unsophisticated purchasing severely defective services.

Common law arrangements and a hard-law/soft-penalty situation gave way during the post–Civil War period to more stringent criminal abortion codes. These reflected the shift in public morality in the so-called Comstock era. Such laws also represented the establishment of organized medicine's claim for recognition as official gatekeeper over women's reproduction. Abortion was condemned in the 1817 American Medical Association (AMA) Report by the Committee on Criminal Abortion as a sign of general public "demoralization," and offending physicians were accused of such transgressions as "criminal carelessness." Some Committee members believed that defects in the law encouraged physicians to commit the abortion crime. Critics of the Committee countered that this was an "exploded medical dogma." In a final attempt to quell illegal abortion, the AMA stated that all abortions were "unlawful and unprofessional," a stance that became mere lip service by the twentieth century. Thus abortion remained a divided and divisive medical reality.

TWENTIETH-CENTURY LEGAL THEORY

With the disintegration of church control over secular matters, the legal institution became the logical source for abortion regulation. Its makeshift structure, however, was inadequate for the task. As the law shifted from reflecting the common culture (abortion acceptable before quickening, with prosecution aimed at protecting the woman's life and preserving the family) to focusing simply on punishing violations, the theory of control over abortion became detached from both accepted custom and the problems of enforcement. What this meant was that the abortion law was not a product of the will of the people nor a method for human protection. Nor was restrictive abortion, after the discovery of modern antiseptic surgery in the nineteenth century, a health measure. Instead, the criminal abortion law was a symbolic law that embodied the differential status of doctor versus patient and the male professional's total control over decisions regarding women's reproduction. The abortion law became a closed system, a law seemingly responsible only to itself.

A survey of the Michigan abortion laws from 1886 to 1970 reveals four conceptual shifts that dramatize this movement. First, there was an increase in legal clarity regarding what constitutes an abortion; second, there was a decrease in material proofs that a crime had been committed; third, the law shifted from a substantive law to a conspiracy law; and fourth, the view toward the woman changed from that of willed actor to passive victim. In this process, legal control became *sui generis*, a closed system divorced from both changing social practices and enforcement issues.

The movement toward theoretical clarity was undoubtedly part of a larger trend that involved increased legal regulation over socially objectionable conduct (Packer, 1968). Certainly, the common law was neither sufficient nor clear enough to warrant intervention on the scale that legal agencies were beginning to perceive as their natural domain. Compare the Michigan 1886 law—a simple statement affirming ensoulment and its common law underpinnings—with the more elaborated code that prevailed from 1967 to 1973, when the Supreme Court negated all states' abortion laws.

1886:   A common law abortion could not be committed until the woman was quick with child.[3]

1967–1973:   M.C.L. 750.14. Any person who shall willfully administer to any pregnant woman any medicine, drug, substance, or thing whatsoever, with intent thereby to procure the miscarriage of any such woman, unless the same shall have been necessary to preserve the life of such woman, shall be guilty of a felony and in case the death of such pregnant woman be thereby produced, the offense shall be deemed manslaughter.

In any prosecution under this section, it shall not be necessary for the prosecution to prove that no such necessity existed.

M.C.L. 750.15. Any person who shall in any manner . . . advertise, publish, sell or publicly expose for sale any pills, powder, drugs, or combination of drugs, designed expressly for the use of females for the purpose of producing an abortion shall be guilty of a misdemeanor.

M.C.L. 750.322. The willful killing of an unborn quick child by any injury to the mother of such child, which would be murder, shall be deemed manslaughter.

M.C.L. 750.323. Any person who shall administer to any woman pregnant with a quick child any medicine, drug or substance whatever, or shall use or employ any instrument or other means, with intent to thereby destroy such child, unless the same shall have been necessary to preserve the life of such mother shall, in case the death of such child or of such mother be thereby produced be guilty of manslaughter.

In any prosecution under this section it shall not be necessary for the prosecution to prove that no such necessity existed.

M.C.L. 767.72. An indictment or information for manslaughter may contain also a count for procuring or attempting to procure an abortion and the jury may convict for either offense.

M.C.L. 338.53 (6) (7). (6) The board of registration in medicine may refuse to issue or continue a certificate or registration or license . . . to any person guilty of grossly unprofessional or dishonest conduct. The words "grossly unprofessional or dishonest conduct" as used in this act, are . . . declared to mean:

(a) the procuring, aiding or abetting in procuring a criminal abortion.

(7) It shall be a misdemeanor for any person to be guilty of "unprofessional and dishonest conduct" as defined in this Act.

> The creation of such misdemeanor . . . shall not be construed
> to supercede any existing remedy or punishment, whether civil
> or criminal . . . but shall be construed to be in addition thereto. [4]

In the latter case, the law covers not only the specific content of the abortion crime and conditions for its prosecution, but also accessory offenses as in advertising and sales, aiding or abetting, and unprofessional medical conduct.

The issue of proof also underwent substantial change, from unambiguous, objective physical signs to questions of operator's competency, and thence to putative signs of intent. The court made two rulings in the last quarter of the nineteenth century: one, a declaration by a dying woman must specifically refer to abortion if it were to be accepted as proof of a crime; and two, a witness could not refer to diagrams in a medical textbook as evidence of a crime. The court records often reveal a trace of the heartrending materials that must have been proferred as proofs by relatives and friends after a woman had died as a result of illegal abortion. This statement by the Michigan appellate court, 1874, shows what was inadmissible:

An exclamatory declaration—"Oh, Aleck! What have we done? I shall die!"— made without any indications as to its purpose, or that it was in expectation of death, or that the deceased knew to whom she was speaking or that she meant to speak to anybody, or that she was awake or unconscious, is not admissible as a dying declaration [in an abortion case].

Instead, the court demanded precise material evidence: the sights, sounds, and smells of an abortion-related death, or a statement made by the abortionist before witnesses clearly stating criminal intent.

Michigan, 1874:	Evidence of one who was with the woman and bathed her and changed her clothes, the day before she died, as to the appearance of the bed and clothes, and as to observing a peculiarly offensive odor, is competent [evidence in an abortion case].
Michigan, 1886:	Evidence is admissible that accused had before the commission of the alleged abortion, told other persons that she had the necessary instruments, and had offered them her services.

As these personal and commonly shared signs of guilt became more difficult to procure, legal proof shifted into technical, rather than substantive, evidence. The issue was not the woman's observed death by abortion, or the practitioner's known guilt, but whether the accused was competent to commit the crime. In this judgment, competency and intent become twin hinges on which the prosecutor must hang his case.

In a Michigan appellate case of 1944, it was a technical decision as to whether certain of the prosecutor's questions were "proper"; the substantive issues of the woman's death, witnesses, and material proofs had been all but banished in the subtleties of legal theory.

Probably the ultimate departure from customary norms in criminal cases is the use of circumstantial evidence. This is evidence not bearing directly on the fact in dispute, but on various attendant circumstances from which the judge or jury might infer the occurrence of the disputed fact. This situation provides the widest berth for discretion by the court, leading to "lost cases" and ambiguous directives to law enforcement groups. By 1970 prosecution of abortion cases was based on *intent* to commit abortion or on a *conspiracy* charge linked to criminal abortion activities. Originally, the prosecution was required to show that the woman was pregnant when the operation was performed, inasmuch as she served as the key witness role for the prosecutor's case. In the torturous language that sometimes characterized these cases, though, a lower court was exonerated for its failure to instruct the jury as to the actual condition of the woman or fetus involved in an alleged abortion case. In a word, pregnancy was no longer at issue. The Michigan appellate court ruled in 1970 that the "Court's refusal to instruct jury to effect that in order to find defendant guilty of abortion and conspiracy to commit abortion, jury must find there was living being within uterus of complainant at time of alleged act of abortion was proper." By 1963 the crux of the proof problem involved the court's determination that the aborted woman was a victim, not a participant or an aider or abettor.

Michigan, 1963:   Woman could not be held for commission of crime
                               of abortion upon herself, and consequently could not
                               be held as aider or abettor thereof.

COURT DECISIONS CLARIFYING LEGAL QUESTIONS

In court decisions, incremental changes in the statutes attempted to clarify the legal questions raised by difficulties of the prosecution in sustaining a conviction. Such questions revolved around the problems of (a) *evidence*, or proof required to justify a verdict of guilty, and (b) establishing *intent* on the part of the accused to commit a crime, rather than simply the facts of the crime itself. In both questions the court resolved the issue so as to simplify prosecution and conviction of abortion cases.

For instance, the question of evidence focused on the type of proofs required, as in showing the defendant's tools of the trade, actual observation by police agents of the defendant performing the abortion, and establishing certainty that the woman was pregnant. In practice, police apprehension of the abortionist necessitated that enforcement agents move with extreme caution in arresting the practitioner, lest evidence be lost that would prevent the prosecutor from establishing a "clear cause and intent" to commit a crime. But if police were to delay for too long, the woman could be injured by the catheter, chemical substance, surgery, or other abortion technique.

Under the original law, use of policewoman decoys in abortion enforcement was declared invalid because proof of pregnancy was required. Evidence was often dependent, then, not on police statements of evidence as witness to a probable crime, but on the woman's testimony. Even with expert testimony from legitimate physicians declaring that certain telltale physical signs could be detected—instrument punctures, scraping traces, and chemical damages—the court could not accept this as material evidence unless corroborated by statements of the aborted, or would-be aborted, woman herself. Evidence thus hinged on the woman as the key witness, the main prop supporting the prosecutor's case.

In the event of the woman's death, the court had long held that testimony from her lover, husband, or attending relatives was admissible if there was also sufficient evidence that the defendant (i.e., the abortionist) had told other people of the intended crime. For the aborted, or would-be aborted, woman who refused to testify, the court could arrest her for contempt. But jailing the woman served little purpose; in fact, prosecutors might lose the case because of irate relatives and friends. Subsequent decisions reduced the problem of "reluctant witnesses" (i.e., the aborted woman and her relatives) and at the same time circumvented the thorny issue of proof that a crime had been committed.

To summarize, in a series of decisions made between 1941 and 1970, the court ruled that:

1. The woman could *not* be held for commission of the crime of abortion, nor as aider and abettor. Thenceforth, she would be defined as a "victim" and could therefore serve as "willing witness" without violating the Fifth Amendment by providing evidence against herself.[5]

2. Conspiracy to commit a crime was an indictable offense by common law, and such conduct was made a felony in abortion cases.[6] Conspiracy to commit abortion was both an easier charge to sustain and required simply tracking the third parties to the agreement such that evidence "showed" agreement, understanding, plan, design, or scheme to abort a pregnancy.[7]

3. The conspiracy decision also stipulated that Michigan did *not* recognize abortions for the benefit of the psychological health of the woman. The court rejected the doctor-defendant's claim of the threatened suicide of his patient and in doing so emphasized that legal abortion be restricted to saving the "physical life" of the mother.[8] In the opinion of the court, most unmarried women who were about ready to have children are inclined and frequently tell their physicians

they are ready to take their own life. This does not in my opinion justify any type of an abortion.[9]

4. The viability of the fetus no longer was required for proof of crime. "Intent" to commit an abortion, regardless of whether the woman was pregnant or not, was sufficient to convict on a conspiracy charge.[10]

5. The "intent" clause further stipulated that procuring a miscarriage "unless the same shall have been necessary to preserve the life" of the woman did not require the prosecution to prove that no such necessity existed. The burden of proof in abortion convictions is on the practitioner to prove his innocence, not the prosecutor to present material evidence showing lack of medical necessity.[11]

In short, the legalistic interpretation of the abortion law was to warn that any "*intent* to procure a miscarriage" was in violation of the letter of the law (italics mine). The Michigan Medical Society, for example, used this interpretation of the law in stipulating to members that abortion referral under present legal conditions was both illegal and unethical (April 1971).[12]

Despite the legal and medical constraints on abortion, abortion-related activities during the same time period paint a startling picture of the actual practice of abortion:

1. An estimated 1,000 "therapeutic" abortions were given in Michigan annually (1970).

2. Metropolitan Detroit hospitals admitted as many as three to four patients a day into emergency rooms to "clean up" "incomplete" or septic abortions, many of which were criminally induced.

3. Michigan physicians provided an estimated 30,000 pelvic examinations confirming pregnancy for women planning to get legal abortions in other states or illegal abortions in Michigan (1970). Many physicians actually referred patients directly to friendly practitioners in New York or elsewhere.

4. A few physicians gave abortions in their offices and were known both to the police and to other physicians, who referred patients to them directly.

5. Some counseling clergymen referred women in need of abortion to illegal sources, both inside and outside the state. Although less frequently used, the "local" resources served a stop-gap function for ailing or poor women unable to withstand the costs of out-of-state travel.

6. An elaborate, although tenuously linked, counseling and referral system spread throughout the state, incorporating a variety of agencies that connected women directly, or indirectly, to legal abortion sources in other states.

7. A plan to open an abortion clinic was developed with a view toward satisfying the local prosecutor's expectations of appropriate site and situation for thera-

peutic abortions, as well as facilitating "scenery" for participation by prestigious physicians.

By 1970 these rule evasions were multiplied in states across the nation and characterized the growing contradictions that had become an integral part of the abortion order. Rules and sanctions existed, to be sure, but their nature and applicability remained uncertain. Not only did different law firms interpret the law differently for various physicians, hospitals, and local referral services, depending on the firm's degree of respectability, perception of risk, and personal knowledge of the parties and situation, but also local variations in professional arrangements contributed to a crazy-quilt pattern. Within the same state, permissive rules dominated in some jurisdictions and prohibitive ones were in force in others.

The mere fact that the abortion law had been upheld by repeated court interpretations did not explain these variations. Nor did appeals to medical ethics or hospital censure laws describe the actual operations of how the law was applied in specific criminal abortion cases. Despite two cases on the docket charging conspiracy—in one instance against a doctor and in the other against a counseling clergyman—the rules-in-use guiding abortion prosecutions became increasingly difficult to process. The organization of the criminal abortion system revealed an enforcement structure in which abortion detection, apprehension, and conviction were increasingly onerous and low pay-off activities.

DISCRETIONARY ENFORCEMENT

Appellate court rulings in abortion cases showed an increasing effort by the criminal court, as rule maker, to shore up the prosecutor's requirements. The bureaucratic goals of prosecuting and convicting abortion conspiracy cases were facilitated by complaints initiated by police officers instead of citizens, by the gathering of information and, eventually, the chief evidence from "willing witnesses," and by circumventing material proofs of pregnancy (or the fact that a crime had even been committed). Still, law enforcement agents often expressed frustration and dismay in the criminal court procedure itself, which some believed bogged down at crucial procedural points. Other court observers believed that the most significant legal problem with abortion was a matter of power: "The favorable ground rules are all on the other side" (i.e., defendants). Abortion enforcement was obviously seriously eroding.

Detroit police informants (Homicide Section) emphasized that not only had the rates of successful abortion convictions declined over ten years (no numbers were provided), but also that the number of complaints in which warrants were issued (a more adequate indicator of abortion case processing) had dropped to negligible proportions. Some pending cases, extending over two years, showed little sign of moving from the pretrial arraignment to a court hearing. One state police officer stressed the legal problem in this way:

This is the problem you're confronted with. They [prosecutors and Court] do not use the substantive charge, but they use the statute charge, which is conspiracy to commit abortion. You don't have to prove that the woman was pregnant in this case, but simply that there was a conspiracy or an attempt to commit abortion. The statutory provision takes care of punishment, but the definition of the crime is not spelled out. This is in the common law which is considered adequate and so is not written up in the statute. Here only the punishment is stipulated by law.

Detroit policewomen (Women's Section) pointed to the low incidence of reported abortions among minor women (five for 1971). They said that this figure was probably closer to 100 five years ago. A few informants attributed this to the availability of legal abortions in New York.

Enforcement agents presented various reasons for these changes, including loss of respect for the law or for life itself. Closer inspection of the facts suggests that women were steadfastly reluctant to press charges against an abortionist, regardless of the form of treatment received. If a warrant was issued, the case was likely to be terminated at one point or another in its process through the criminal courts.

THE "SIEVE EFFECT" MODEL IN ENFORCEMENT PROCEDURES

The "sieve effect," or sifting and sorting out of abortion cases—crime reports to initial complaint, to pretrial, to arraignment and eventual conviction and sentencing—shows the constraints on legal agents at various phases of trial and conviction of abortionists. The procedural engine that pushes the accused from one point to another shows in rough fashion how cases get terminated because of technical problems, administrative muddles, value conflicts, or public opinion. Figure 3.1 describes the "sieve" process (from Blumberg, 1967, 50–51).

The problems of abortion investigation and prosecution thus served to prevent effective enforcement, while also blocking systematic legal change. In this way, enforcers created a risk environment. By maintaining a continuous threat of legal action they warned organizations of the penalties for flouting the law and effectively forestalled long overdue medical and social reform by putting pressure on legal and medical professionals. As for law enforcement officials, the law stood intact until changed. The business of enforcing it, though, was more problematic. The pragmatic rule of "hands off" usually applied. Lacking complainants, witnesses, and unified community support, enforcement agencies learned shortcuts: routinizing surveillance and dropping investigation to a bare minimum.

Figure 3.1
The Sieve Effect

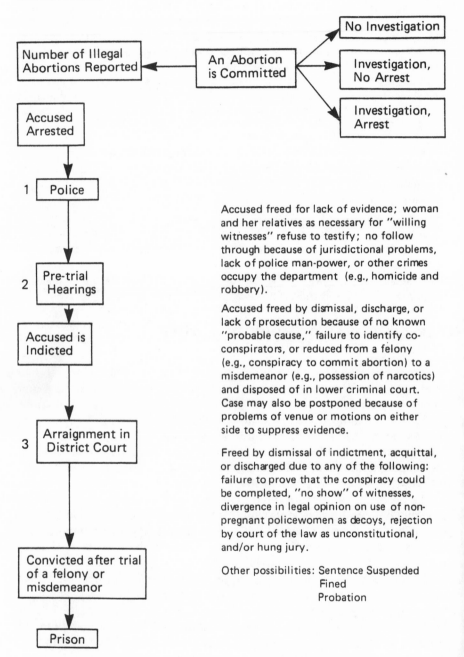

Number of Illegal Abortions Reported ← An Abortion is Committed →

No Investigation

Investigation, No Arrest

Investigation, Arrest

Accused Arrested

1 Police

Accused freed for lack of evidence; woman and her relatives as necessary for "willing witnesses" refuse to testify; no follow through because of jurisdictional problems, lack of police man-power, or other crimes occupy the department (e.g., homicide and robbery).

2 Pre-trial Hearings

Accused is Indicted

Accused freed by dismissal, discharge, or lack of prosecution because of no known "probable cause," failure to identify co-conspirators, or reduced from a felony (e.g., conspiracy to commit abortion) to a misdemeanor (e.g., possession of narcotics) and disposed of in lower criminal court. Case may also be postponed because of problems of venue or motions on either side to suppress evidence.

3 Arraignment in District Court

Freed by dismissal of indictment, acquittal, or discharged due to any of the following: failure to prove that the conspiracy could be completed, "no show" of witnesses, divergence in legal opinion on use of non-pregnant policewomen as decoys, rejection by court of the law as unconstitutional, and/or hung jury.

Convicted after trial of a felony or misdemeanor

Other possibilities: Sentence Suspended
                              Fined
                              Probation

Prison

Law enforcers believed that "good abortion cases are rare" despite "lots of abortions going around." This suggests that most criminal abortions reported by staff in hospitals and in doctors' offices and by school administrators and hotel or motel managers were never investigated in the first place. And if cursorily investigated, the report seldom resulted in a warrant. In theory, any physician or health officer who strongly suspected that a patient had an induced abortion was required to notify police. In practice, few hospitals ever contacted police unless the woman appeared to be dying. (In this instance, the hospital acted expediently to ensure itself against legal liability, whether from officials or from relatives charging malpractice.) By failing to notify police of a possible crime, the hospital also avoided police harassment of sick patients. Because few patients actually died of septicemia or hemorrhaging with modern medical technology, the hospital routine was preserved without the interference of third parties. Thus police were unable to make a complaint in the first place.

In jurisdictions with a heavy proportion of black citizens, there was mutual reluctance by police and populace to interfere in abortion traffic. For example, one Detroit police department complaint against a black defendant and all-black clients (1971) never went beyond an initial warrant, although the police secured signed statements from all the participants, including attending physicians. Interviews with Detroit police suggest that shortage of money and manpower accounted for this withdrawal from active enforcement. Only strong pressure from the county prosecutor, who was known to be an adamant Right-to-Life supporter, prevented this big-city police system from effectively closing down all of its abortion surveillance and investigation.

In one mid-Michigan city a black police officer informed me that the black community was "left alone" as not "worth bothering about." As long as suspected abortion activity was confined to the ghetto, there was little or no enforcement. Instead, ghetto policing concentrated on narcotics investigation. The cost of prosecution, the low priority of abortion enforcement as compared with other crimes, few or no citizen complaints, and fear of tampering with medical prerogatives were involved in this decision.

Even when police strongly suspected a conspiracy case, follow-up may not have been feasible. One police officer informant said:

I've been told on three different occasions that there's a doctor from _____who refers to an abortionist, a physician abortionist. But we couldn't get a case on it. Three different occasions, but we haven't been able to do a thing. Doctors aren't going to burn him on that. The administration in hospitals support him in doing this. I'm sure that's correct because there are three independent reports here. There's no way for us to follow up on this. Police view this as simply not being worth going all the way on it. It's just not worth doing. These doctors can afford the best lawyers. We can't fight this.

As for the "local ladies" who depend on illegal abortionists, the department policy is hands off. In this informant's words:

The police could detect the local ladies, but they don't care. They—I mean the establishment—don't care about the poor. They're less educated, less capable of testifying in court. The police are much less likely to care about prosecution in these cases. The girl has probably had negative contacts with the law, and she's not interested in getting involved either. It's an area we just don't like to touch.

Other urban settings had different enforcement patterns. A black woman gynecologist practicing in Detroit emphasized that black women had little incentive to report an abortion, or even to enter a hospital emergency room for treatment of uterine bleeding or infection that frequently followed an illegal abortion. Fear of police harassment and investigation of the woman's assumed criminal statuses or connections kept black women who had received a "bad" abortion from becoming involved with legitimate institutions. Instead, a "neighborhood" physician took care of the incomplete abortion without notifying police.

A few black physicians who practiced gynecologic medicine in Detroit reported that police interference was pervasive. These physicians not only refused information but also drew the line at referring indigent patients through the slow-moving hospital abortion boards. In their experience, the poor black woman suffered undue humiliation in her request for a therapeutic abortion. One common practice used by hospital abortion committees was involuntary sterilization for the woman requesting the abortion. This was viewed by dissident physicians as the ultimate "price" for an abortion. Mutual distrust between police and blacks, together with the often prohibitive costs of legal abortions, usually meant that the illegal abortion route was the only resource available for most ghetto women.

A black woman gynecologist described the police *modus operandi* as harassment and humiliation for both physician and patient. In her experience:

The prosecutor's office makes a lot of noise. You're forever aware that these guys can move in on something. All the incompletes that come in [to hospitals] are reported as criminal abortions and admitted as such. The hospital administration makes the report. There are very few patients who will go into the hospital and say they've had an abortion, however. In the case of a septic AB, that is an infected abortion, we used to do this regularly [i.e., report septics as criminal abortions]. But we have run into problems with the police. The inhumane manner in which detectives question patients is very bad. You certainly haven't scared the patient. She's not going to tell. They're going to protect the illegal operator for their own daughter, sister or what have you. Why should they tell the police where they had their abortion? This just shows you how desperate women are to have abortions. The really appalling thing is that the detective comes into the ward where there are a lot of women, and they hassle the woman. They spread her business out. They just tell what her business is on the street. Everybody knows about it. It's inhumane. Just because society has forced them to do something illegal, I'm not going to go to the detectives.

Police interference, particularly against black practitioners, leads to withdrawal by many of these physicians. In the same informant's words:

The homicide squad is coming to me. They were looking for a Negro woman who gave an abortion [in which the patient died]. They're just fishing around. We all know licensed physicians are doing it. I've never seen this other woman who's doing it, though. Some things you just don't delve into. It isn't what you want to do, but it's one of the things you have to do so you don't get involved. One of the reasons that the police don't have information is that we don't feed it to them. So they must suspect a lot. But they really don't have any information to pin down.

One twenty-one-year-old black woman who had three criminal abortions and was in jail for heroin possession said that she and her friends avoided the hospital situation altogether. "When you go to the hospital, that is, through the emergency room, the police come in on the case. The detectives come in and ask a lot of questions. They bug you a lot and try to get something on you. They try to clean the books on you."

If police could not depend on respectable physicians or hospital emergency room victims for information, to whom did they turn? One police practice was the surveillance of known abortion sites as a source for "getting a good pinch." Yet the dubious activity of observing and subsequently tracking down frightened or sick women who leave these premises resulted in few successful warrants. Most women, investigators stated, were unwilling to testify against the abortionists, even in such extenuating circumstances as severe bleeding or other abnormalities. According to officers, the aborted woman was either too ashamed of the act or too grateful to the abortionist to report the crime. Police investigators tended to stereotype the aborted woman, which was probably the greatest shortcoming in successfully pursuing a case. There was angry resignation in the words of this Michigan state detective, as he described the problem of securing abortion witnesses:

In terms of getting abortions you're dealing with a moral degenerate who's an unwilling witness. She's probably a swinger or a prostitute or some kind of promiscuous person. . . . Even if the girl is knocking on death's door at the local hospital, we try to get the girl to give you the guy's name so that we can get a complainant and a witness, and then you're set up. But you end up afterwards with a hostile witness because if she recovers, then there's no witness. You lose both ways. If she recovers there's no witness, because she no longer wants to provide information, because she just wants to get out of there and not be involved. If she dies, there's no witness either. So it's a very difficult case to prove.

In most jurisdictions, abortion cases never appeared on the docket because evidence simply melted away. In the absence of concrete information about abortion activity, stereotypes of abortion seekers flourished. One county prosecutor recognized the ethnic differences in abortion but took a grim view of the clients:

Among blacks and Mexican-Americans, abortion is not very frequent. They have a different outlook. Children are wanted in this case because they can make money off the welfare system. Abortion complaints, generally, have decreased over the last ten years. Sometimes a situation is reported, but we have no idea of how many self-abortees there are. There are so many better ways of eliminating the fetus now with the garbage disposal. Also, people are not as nosy as they used to be, and so they're giving fewer reports. There's a live and let live attitude. The people are self-centered now, and they don't report these things. They don't want to be involved. There's a difference in the moral characteristics today. I think it's a very serious problem.

Still another approach is to treat the issue professionally, that is, abortion investigation as a specialty. In this detective's words:

Know your victim, in this case, what kind of woman she is, whether she's a prostitute, a middle-class woman or what have you. An awful lot of technique is involved. We try to get her to come along with the program so that she'll be willing to talk . . . treat her like a lady, kill her with kindness kind of thing. Abortion is a very difficult case to make. The success or failure is dependent on the officer. This is an investigative specialty.

If witnesses were a continuous problem to the police, an even greater problem was the assumption by police departments that public opinion would not support prosecution if the physician-abortionist was tied into a medical network or had "clean hands" (i.e., no patient deaths). In the case of one well-known Detroit physician, even with active police surveillance and numerous complaints charging him with abortion, the department was either unwilling or unable to shut down his operation.

LEGAL MORALISM

Where law is conceived as a tool for educating the masses or for achieving social order, there is a tendency to extend boundaries of social control. When so conceived, the law may become a ready instrument for the achievement of state morality. (Skolnick, 1967, 58)

Although Professor Skolnick has properly identified the basic political character of legal moralism, he neglects an equally important issue: At what point does public consciousness about a law or cluster of laws shift from acceptance or tolerance to suspicion, rejection, and intolerance? What kind of "data" are necessary and sufficient to convince professional and public opinion that the law is bad, or an overreach of appropriate state function, and hence requires change? And how does the political character of the social problem covered by the law in question undergo fundamental change?

The criminal abortion laws represent the last underpinning of the Victorian purity doctrine—abortion only to save the woman's life. By 1971, two years before the Supreme Court acted to make abortion legal, evidence against repressive state control was accumulating within professional circles. Lawyers pointed to the lack of public consensus as the primary reason for failure to uphold the law. In their view, how could a law be enforced when the definition of what was criminal continued to change? Then, too, doctors were seen as being "above the law." One state assistant prosecutor emphasized:

Physicians who give hospital abortions are above the law, in that they are protected by their colleagues, the community, and by women who receive the abortion. This is a situation in which the police are virtually ineffective. They [police] must bring the case in. There must be a complainant. It's difficult to do in the present milieu of changing and contradictory attitudes. On the other hand, the prosecutors who must do their jobs and who are ambitious, are not limited by the physician's judgment. If they think they have a good case, but not enough sufficient evidence that a crime has been committed, they may still move into the situation and prosecute. Generally, though, there is a very low probability of prosecution occurring.

The live-and-let-live attitude most police departments took toward abortionists, unless they were confronted by a woman's death, was viewed as the only realistic policy. The dilemma in abortion law enforcement was summed up by this former state assistant prosecutor:

The police can't operate unless the community is reasonably cohesive in this matter. Abortion is a crime today and not a crime tomorrow. People must be convinced in the community that something is a crime in order for it to be prosecuted. How can you get a prosecution when the defense attorney can point to legislators who support abortion reform? You can't touch it. That is prosecution-wise. No prosecutor would operate in this area. No attorney-general would prosecute. The problem here is the problem of consent. Until the people at the legislature know what they want, no prosecutor is going to want to touch this. The prosecutor has to be very careful that he doesn't step on the legislator's morals and other functions. You shirk the function that belongs to the legislature. Even a freshman law student wouldn't handle a case like this.

Exasperated law enforcement officials, in turn, accused physicians of neglecting an area that was really their responsibility. By forcing what was really a medical choice onto enforcement officials, doctors and hospitals helped to maintain the legal impasse. Physicians who gave hospital abortions for "health and welfare" reasons operated properly within their discretionary power, these officials argued. The counterrecognition that physicians who used judgment where "absolutely essential," as in medical, psychiatric, rape, incest, or rubella cases,[13] were probably assuming some legal risks if operating in jurisdictions with "ambitious prosecutors." But, said counseling attorneys, to deny physicians their medical prerogatives strips the profession of rightful power to make judgments in its area of expertise.

By the early 1970s officials operated in an area of increasing ambiguity. Not only had many states—Arkansas, California, Colorado, Delaware, Kansas, Maryland, New Mexico, North and South Carolina, Oregon, and Virginia—liberalized conditions for abortion, including legal abortions for physical and mental health, rape, and incest (see Appendix A), but also the national legal picture was clouded by different, if not competing, professional reforms. While the American Law Institute Model Abortion Law allowed abortion for a broad range of mental health, rape, and fetal conditions, the American College of Obstetricians and Gynecologists opened the door even wider to include unspecified conditions. Their 1968 abortion law recommendations stated: "In determining whether or not there is a substantial risk to the woman's physical or mental health, account may be taken of the woman's total environment, actual or reasonably foreseeable." (See Appendix B for an overview of permissive conditions for abortion.)

Rather than prosecuting practitioners and humiliating women involved in abortion, questions were being raised—in and out of law courts—as to whether restrictive legalization of abortion was not the real problem. The *New York Times Magazine* featured an article entitled "How California's Abortion Law Isn't Working" (Monroe, 1968) and took a position opposing any barriers to legal abortion. The article pointed out that sharp increases in the number of women whom psychiatrists diagnosed as mentally ill in order to meet the key provision of the new law made hospital abortion hypocritical, unfair, and burdensome, putting it beyond the reach of many citizens.

State courts were given little incentive for creating order out of their legal chaos because appellate courts began issuing contradictory or vague rulings. For instance, in *U.S. v. Vuitch*, the Court upheld an indictment of a physician for performing abortion in violation of the law. At the same time, the Court accepted the plea of expanding the mother's "health" to include mental as well as physical health. Thus the burden of proof shifted from the defendant to prove his innocence to the "government to prove that an abortion was not performed to preserve the mother's life or health" (*Citation*, 1971, 65).

Deformed infants' lawsuits emerged in which parents claimed that doctors legally bungled when they failed to inform the woman of the possible birth defects caused by rubella in the early months of pregnancy. The courts dealt with the issue of the physicians' responsibility by declaring— no responsibility. The discussion surrounding deformed infants often had a strong note of unreality. Physicians could not be sued if they failed to recommend abortion because it was illegal; and once the fetus was aborted, the legal issue was nonexistent. If the baby was born with severe birth defects, there was no proof linking physicians' error to this medical situation. Thus the court reasoned: It is impossible to determine the child's damages for failure to recommend an abortion (*Citation*, 1971, 66). The *Minnesota Law Review* (November 1970, 55, p. 58) surveyed the fetal deformity cases and took exception to this decision. The editors insisted that physicians had a clear duty to inform the parents of possible defects in the same way as in any other medical procedure or treatment.

While the courts were protecting physicians who operated within the hospital sanctuary—for example, California and New York passed statutory requirements that abortion could be performed only in hospitals— lawyers were being disbarred for even arranging abortions (*Citation*, 1971, 10). It was obviously a new set of rules and no jurisdiction could adequately sort out the legal entanglements.

Other issues tested in the courts: Did abortion violate the old abortion manslaughter law (New York)? Was a psychiatrist who did not perform abortion entitled to a suit challenging the constitutionality of the Colorado statutory restrictions? Could an unmarried pregnant minor obtain a therapeutic abortion without parental consent? Was the restriction of legal abortion to hospitals constitutional? Did the criminal abortion laws violate the woman's privacy? Is the state's interests in affording a fetus an opportunity to survive superior to the right of a pregnant woman to destroy the fetus? On the whole, these legal questions were almost always answered conservatively, that is, to protect the status quo.

The fact that the law was increasingly out of step with medical and public opinion encouraged reaction. Harriet Pilpel demanded "The Right to Abortion" in a June 1969 article in *Atlantic Monthly*. The author cited the statement of scientists Tietze and Lewitt's in *Scientific American* (January 1969) that "abortion is still the most widespread . . . method of fertility control in the modern world." Pilpel also noted that in a United Nations Conference on World Population in Belgrade in 1965 findings showed that "abortion is indeed the chief method of birth control in the world today.

... About thirty million pregnancies are purposely terminated by abortion each year. Of these, studies indicate that almost one million are in the United States." Other feminists attacked the idea that the abortion law protected women. Their retort: Until a contraception is devised that genuinely provides women with rational choice, legal abortion will be a necessity. The New York chapter of the National Organization for Women asserted:

There is no perfect contraceptive. The U.S. Food and Drug Administration reports that the intrauterine devices, one of the most effective contraceptives available today, have a failure rate of 1.5 to 3 percent. This means that if all married women in the United States could and did use these contraceptives, there would still be about 350,000 to 700,000 unwanted pregnancies a year among married women alone. Even sterilization is not a 100 percent effective method of contraception; some operations fail. Therefore, in order to insure a complete and thorough birth control program, abortion must be made available as a legal right to all women who request it. (quoted in Pilpel, 1969)

Feminist groups had an ally in Mr. Justice Goldberg, whose defense of privacy in the 1965 Connecticut birth control case (*Griswold v. Connecticut*) was based on the assumption that compulsory pro- or anti-birth control laws are equally "totalitarian" and "unconstitutional" and represent "cruel and unusual punishment." Right-to-life advocates countered this approach by describing abortion "as a lynching in the womb" (quoted in Pilpel, 1969).

De facto practice was actually more permissive than the medical indications recognized *de jure*. This was true in the United States and in Europe. Tietze's (1977) survey of abortion laws and abortion practices in Europe showed that only two countries, both Catholic, Belgium and Ireland, absolutely outlawed any abortion, whereas fourteen nations recognized medical, social, eugenic, or humanitarian conditions in their abortion law. In seventeen nations the practices of the medical profession were either liberal or very liberal. That *de facto* practice tends to be more permissive than *de jure* stipulations is not unusual in legal circumstances; discrepancies between the formal and informal law are common (Skolnick, 1966; Ross, 1970). For the volatile abortion situation, the gap between abortion law and practice triggered powerful social reactions. The belief in the apolitical nature of the law, for long a basic tenet in social thought (see Davis, 1980) was shattered.

Various court decisions were seen as examples of the deterioration of the old legal order and with it the traditional social control over women's bodies. Here are some examples of nationwide court decisions that were cited during this conflict period of the late 1960s and early 1970s:

- *Foster v. State* (1923)
  —the court asserted the right of a New York physician to terminate a pregnancy to save the life of the woman or to prevent serious impairment of mental health.

- *Griswold v. Connecticut* (1965)
  —the law prohibiting contraceptives was ruled unconstitutional.
  —decision extended to encompass women's right to abortion.

- *People v. Belous* (1969)
  —court ruled California's abortion law unconstitutional because of vagueness.

- *Ballard v. Anderson* (1971)
  —unmarried minor doesn't need parental consent for a therapeutic abortion.

- *Doe v. Bolton* (1973)
  —court denied a motion to appoint a guardian for a fetus in Georgia.
  —fetus doesn't have constitutional rights during gestation.

In this rapidly changing legal climate, pro-abortion partisans manipulated the language of the criminal statute, which in its original intent limited abortion only to "preserve" the woman's physical life. The language of "preserve" came to be variously interpreted, such as "to keep alive or in existence," "to keep safe from harm or injury," "save," "keep," or "maintain the mental and bodily health." In other words, the precise legal meanings of the word became redefined and were used to renegotiate the abortion order by reform physicians, hospitals, and counseling clergy.

The legal facade for long had been maintained by reference to "health" as a medical and mental phenomenon, with most abortions in the 1960s given under psychiatric, not medical, orders. Again, inconsistency in hospital interpretation of the language resulted in decisions to perform abortion made on a hospital-by-hospital basis. Medical decisions were made less in keeping with the strict letter of the law, though, than with conditions of local enforcement and medical politics. In this context, the American Law Institute proposed national liberalization of abortion. Their proposal took account of what many hospitals were already doing under a medical-legal disguise.

Clergy broker arrangements, discussed in later chapters, grew out of this ambiguous law and lax enforcement. The rhetoric of "patient need" served both to supplant and to transcend the statutes by appeals to a "higher law," a rationale developed through experimentation within the softened legal structure. Clergy brokers operated correctly on the premise that the criminal justice system's hands were tied. Abortion referral would not be prosecuted. Counseling could legally be performed in one state and referral for abortion to another. In Michigan, for example, as long as counselors routed clients to non-Michigan sites, they could carry on their shadow referral system without fear of prosecution in Michigan. Partisans were now set for massive civil disobedience of the state's criminal abortion law.

Figure 3.2
Doctrinal Perspectives

SOURCE	PERIOD	DOCTRINE
Old Testament (as interpreted by the early Church)	A.D. -- early church	Abortion not condemned as a "capital offense since the fetus was not regarded as possessing a soul within the Sixth Commandment restriction.
New Testament	A.D.	No specific reference to abortion.
Dicache	c80	Abortion is a sin ranked in importance with the Ten Commandments.
Epistle of Barnabas	c138	"You shall not slay the child by abortion.
Pedagogus by Clement of Alexandria	c150-c2T5	Abortion is compared with homicide and the destruction of an attitude of love for humankind.
Apology Tertullian	c160-c230	"For to prevent its (fetus) being born is an acceleration of homicide."
St. Basil the Great	c374	"Whoever purposely destroys a fetus incurs the penalty of murder (whether) it is formed or not formed."
St. Augustine	4th-5th century	Condemns the whole spectrum of acts from birth prevention, sterilization, abortion through infanticide.
Roman Catholic Church	5th-12th century	A distinction is made between formed and unformed fetuses. Abortion is condemned in the former; ignored in the latter case.
Si Aliquis	10th century	Applied the penalty for homicide to both contraception and abortion.
Decretum by Gratian	1140 A.D.	"He is not a murderer who brings about abortion before the soul is in the body."
Jesuit, Thomas Sanchez	1550-1610	If the fetus is not ensouled and the woman die without a completed abortion, then the abortion was lawful since the fetus is an invader (based on the doctrine of self defense).
Affraenatum	1588	Pope Sextus V. announces that all abortion is homicide.
Pope Gregory	1591	Papal edict rescinded all penalties specified in the Effraenatum with the exception of those that applied to an ensouled fetus.
Apostolic Sedis Pope Pius IX	1869	A distinction between formed and unformed fetuses is eliminated by assigning the penalty of excommunication for any abortion.
New Code of Canon Law	1917	All references to Aristotle's analysis of gestation referring to the forty-eighty days for female and male ensoulment, respectively, are removed.

Figure 3.2 *continued*

SOURCE	PERIOD	DOCTRINE
Casti Connubii	1930	Pope Pius adopts an Augustinian principle that the lives of mother and fetus are equally sacred and may not be destroyed for any reason.
Mater et Magistra	1961	Pope John XXIII, the ecumenicalist, states that whatever is opposed to life in any form violates God.
Humanae Vitae	1968	Pope Paul VI asserts that "Any direct interruption of the generative process already begun, and, above all, directly willed and procured abortion even if for therapeutic reasons are to be absolutely outlawed as a means of regulating birth." Two exceptions: (1) ectopic pregnancy, (2) cancerous uterus. The doctrine of "secondary effect" justifies abortion in these two instances on grounds that the direct intention is to remove the fallopian tube or cancerous uterus to save the woman's life. If such an act also kills the fetus, it is recognized as a side effect and, thus, not a sin.

NOTES

1. Data for this chapter include analysis of crucial court decisions on abortion (1886–1970) from *Michigan Compiled Laws* and *Michigan Appellate* (appealed laws), and intensive interviews with professional staff persons and former abortion patients. Staff persons include public health officials, prosecutors, lawyers for the defense, law enforcement persons, Detroit physicians and hospital administrators, and two days' fieldwork with the Detroit Police Department, including the Homicide Section and the Women's Section. In addition, I drew on documents from medical, police, and counseling clergy sources.

2. Historical treatment of abortion adapted for this section include partisan viewpoints on both sides of the abortion issue. See, for example, Callahan, 1970; Noonan, 1970; Hall, 1970, Grisez, 1970; Lader, 1967, 1973; and Connery, 1977. Callahan (1970) and Grisez (1970) provided the material for the doctrinal survey.

3. *People v. Sessions*, 26 N.W. 291, V. 58 (1886), *Michigan Compiled Laws* 594.

4. The following statutes are taken from *Michigan Compiled Laws* (1948), as amended, and Michigan Public Health Law, Section 338.53. *Note*: I include the reading of the abortion laws, *as amended*, which brings all court decisions up to 1972. However, the subsequent discussion of legal clarification treats persistent problems that characterized *older* versions of the law. To present both earlier and amended versions seemed awkward and often redundant.

5. *Petition of Vickers*, 123 N.W.2d 253, V. 371 (1963), *Michigan Compiled Laws*, 114.

6. *People v. Smith*, V. 296 (1941), *Michigan Compiled Laws*, 176–180.

7. *People v. Wellman*, V. 6 (1967), *Michigan Appellate*, 573.

8. This was the interpretation of this case in an undated legal opinion by a Detroit law firm (in a Clergy Counselling Service document).

9. *People v. Wellman*, 580.

10. *People v. Marra*, V. 27 (1970), *Michigan Appellate* I: 1.

11. Ibid., p. 5.

12. This interpretation was offered by the Judiciary Committee, Michigan Medical Society, and was circulated by letter to members (April 1971). Such a narrow interpretation did not necessarily represent the views of the majority of physicians in the state. The letter did serve, however, to reinforce a conservative orientation among most physicians regarding their participation in abortion service.

13. Only medical indications were legitimate. Psychiatric, social, and fetal (i.e., genetic) conditions for abortion were illegal under Michigan law.

4

The Medical Establishment: Resistance and Adaptation

Mrs. Frank Jones, a 41–year-old Catholic woman with six living children, is 18–weeks pregnant and requests a therapeutic abortion from the hospital abortion committee. Her medical history indicates normal pregnancies and deliveries, although with increasing morbidity in the last two pregnancies. This includes prolapsis of the bladder with some incontinence the last months of gestation, mild to moderate hemorrhoidal condition, widespread varicosities in legs, thighs, and genital area, and a family history of diabetes and heart trouble. The psychiatric history has been normal until this pregnancy. The psychiatric reports show that since the positive pregnancy test, Mrs. Jones complains of deep depression and has threatened suicide repeatedly. According to her attending physician, her husband is an electrician and has been forced to stay home from work the last two weeks because his wife has seriously neglected her household and childcare duties. The Joneses are formerly from Alabama and have no relatives in Michigan. Mr. Jones cannot afford a housekeeper to care for his wife and children. I further understand that the family cannot go on much longer and will be forced to place the children in foster care and the wife in an institution.

If you recall, Gentlemen, this case came up last month but was rejected because it lacked documentation—only one psychiatrist's letter had been received. Now the request has the requisite letters from the attending physician and two psychiatrists. The Committee cannot postpone the case further because Mrs. Jones is well into her second trimester and any additional delay contributes to increased surgical risk. What is this Abortion Committee's determination for Mrs. Jones?[1]

For more than twenty years, hundreds of thousands of such petitions were read by sponsoring physicians or psychiatrists to hospital abortion boards all over the United States and Canada. Initially, the patient who sought therapeutic abortion needed strong medical indications—evidence that the pregnancy could in some way be life-threatening. As obstetrical skills increased and the abortion procedure itself became less dangerous, psychiatric, rather than medical, indications became paramount. The woman was required to testify to psychiatrists about the facts of her breakdown and mental incompetence. The "psychiatrization" of abortion proved to be an effective method for excluding the majority of women who requested abortion. This method was also economically advantageous for psychiatrists and politically useful for obstetricians. The restrictive state abortion law enabled 2 percent to 3 percent of the more dramatic pregnancy cases to be treated as *bona fide* medical problems, while ignoring or denying the others. Psychiatrists also held a kind of disciplinary coercion over physicians who might otherwise have treated abortion merely as "cosmetic surgery"— treatment at the patient's convenience. Psychiatrization was originally intended to reduce abuses. But over time there was widespread administrative recognition that psychiatric indication had little or nothing to do with standard medical diagnoses, and this led to the decline and disappearance of therapeutic abortion committees, beginning in the late 1960s.

FROM CONSULTATION TO COMMITTEE

Until legal reform, almost all physicians accepted as a matter of course the illegality of abortion. Yet part of their medical training required technical mastery of various gynecologic procedures, some specifically adopted for abortion. Patient pressure, especially in smaller or less medically sophisticated communities, stimulated a fairly vigorous abortion trade, especially on evenings and weekends. That abortion was highly lucrative and fairly difficult for outsiders to detect in a regular medical practice enabled doctors to circumvent the law with near impunity.

Throughout the 1930s and 1940s, "private consultation," or informal agreement between two physicians, became a routine method for dealing with requests for hospital abortions. The chief of staff of a university-affiliated hospital in Detroit was asked how the private consultation method worked, and the answer suggests its weakness as an effective control over physicians: "There's one other physician that you contact. Unfortunately, it doesn't do any good because I help my friend and he helps me. For all intents and purposes, consultation really doesn't have any means of control. It just permits men [the doctors] to diffuse responsibility somewhat."

In some hospitals, formal protocol was waived altogether. A nurse might function as the go-between, securing the physicians' signatures with no words exchanged. "We always did abortion, but we didn't talk about it," said a former obstetric nurse with twenty-five years' hospital experience. Saturday morning was the "special operating" day in one city hospital. In other surgical facilities the D & C (dilatation and curettage) was a cover term for abortion. In this way physicians avoided legal and administrative intervention. Often the medical language associated with such surreptitious abortions evoked images of "spontaneous miscarriage," the natural termination of a pregnancy because of congenital irregularities from fetal or maternal causes. When medical records indicated a diagnosis of "incomplete abortion" that was "allegedly bleeding" and a D & C administered "as required," insiders often translated this into abortion, if they were at all familiar with the operating physician's style of practice.

The simple consultation—"You just get a friend," lamented the president of one Detroit hospital—invited flagrant abuse of rules. Regulations subsequently were tightened, requiring two qualified staff physicians to approve a therapeutic abortion. Although this security measure failed to reduce the number of hospital abortions, it served to delay the procedure somewhat because of the additional time required to seek approval from colleagues and, in some hospitals, to complete excessive paperwork.

A gradual shift away from the *laissez-faire* consultation to a more centralized scheme occurred in the late 1940s. Federal grants-in-aid programs and hospital accreditation committees demanded more rigorous record keeping, which usually entailed sending all surgically removed tissue to the hospital's department of pathology. Earlier, the D & C procedure made no mention of the removal of fetal tissue. This change in record keeping required tissue review of fetal residue, and this made abortion an explicit procedure. Consultation, an inadequate control at best, was replaced in most hospitals with the abortion committee.

The abortion committee became part of an elaborate control mechanism in the 1950s. Hospital chiefs of obstetrics-gynecology, senior obstetricians, hospital governing boards, and hospital lawyers and administrators worked with or against the executive committee that made the actual abortion decisions. While satisfying no party completely, legalists were the most sanguine about the shift of abortion from a free-lance to a highly regulated practice. A medical leader in the development of the hospital abortion committee observed:

In view of some, it is liberal. In view of others, it is too conservative, too restrictive. Historically, the policy dates about 20 years ago. This institution was giving many abortions. The trustees rejected this and tried to get a system going that would cut down on this. They decided to have a trustee on the board (i.e., Abortion Committee). They were fearful that the hospital would become an abortion mill. That policy has been variously supported and criticized. We're also concerned about the legal rights of the unborn.

Essentially, the committee existed to quell rumors of actual practices of excessive abortion. The commentator went on:

I get complaints that too damn many abortions are done and they're taking up beds for sick people. Some OB-GYN [obstetrics-gynecology] people see abortions as a threat. They see the hospitals as taking up too many slots for abortions. We get a lot of demands from all over the state . . . and now we've limited the number of persons who can come in.

The hospital abortion committee represented one organized response to the built-in medical repugnance to abortion. Not all doctors opposed abortions, though. Whereas white, male obstetricians generally were hostile to abortion, abortionists were often recruited from among the ranks of black doctors, some of whom may have been persuaded by lack of legitimate professional opportunity. Female obstetricians/gynecologists took a different approach; neither hostile nor willing to play the abortionist's role, they perceived abortion to be the patient's responsibility.

Some physicians opposed abortion on the moral grounds that it is taking life and is an irrevocable act. More frequently, though, the legal situation was paramount—it involved too much risk to doctor and patient. And the nearly ubiquitous fear of malpractice continued to provoke hostility toward nonmedical abortion. But for most medical leaders, the newer concepts of abortion on "convenience" or "demand" circulating in the 1960s were simply not professional medicine. The terms aroused suspicion among medical, administrative, and lay groups alike. Specialists did not wish to become known as "the abortionist." Yet, with only a few facilities in every state providing hospital abortion, the demand for statewide service was inevitably heavy. Doctors from smaller Michigan communities, for example, relied on teaching hospitals for abortion referrals. But after 1970 acceptance of such open referrals abruptly terminated. The OB-GYN chairman of one university hospital explains why the hospital shifted its policy from accepting statewide abortion referrals to limiting service to local physicians and their patients:

From 1964–1970, we and _____[Detroit hospital] were the only ones doing abortions. We were spending hours a day doing abortion. We don't want to only do abortions. This was causing a lot of furor, so we limited it to just our own patients. On the other hand [formerly referring doctors] were in a furor because they thought we should do their abortions. Doctors reported, "I can't do mine, they're illegal. But you have a state facility and you can handle this." Basically, abortion is all work, no challenge and violates the doctor's sense of appropriateness.

Most physicians socialized in medical school regarded abortion as both dangerous and unethical. As late as 1969, medical students were using the standard Williams's *Textbook on Obstetrics*, which espouses extreme caution for physicians undertaking therapeutic abortion:

Since therapeutic abortion entails destroying the fetus it is a grave undertaking and must never be considered unless there is imminent danger of death of the mother as the result of pregnancy, or of great bodily or mental harm. Neither the law nor medical ethics permits the procedure for sociologic reasons, i.e., illegitimacy, poverty, or rape.

This restrictive stance had been liberally revised by the 1971 Annual Clinical Meeting of the American College of Obstetricians and Gynecologists. Abortion was permitted "to safeguard the patient's health or improve her family life situation." Nevertheless, most practicing physicians were trained under the earlier repressive regime, making them ill at ease with the newer professional ethics.[2]

In a significant sense, the abortion committee system served physicians well. Committees often performed a dual role: They screened cases that included requests for therapeutic abortions as well as "requests" for physician-recommended or patient-elective sterilization. In time, the sterilization procedure came to be inevitably linked with hospital abortions, especially in metropolitan and teaching hospitals. By requiring sterilization as the "price" for abortion, especially for poor women or for those who had had multiple pregnancies, committees drastically eliminated most appeals. In addition, committees (a) regulated the number of women admitted to abortion service to fit available resources—operating room, gynecological staff, anesthesiologist, and so on; (b) served as a check on overly "liberal" physicians; and (c) presented a united front that protected participating physicians. Prosecutors faced with a body of medical experts, some of whom included the most respected obstetricians in the state, were unlikely to cause trouble. In Michigan, for example, there was no record of a prosecution of a hospital abortion.

During the 1950s the committee system effectively curtailed most smaller hospitals from providing abortion service. These facilities lacked specialized personnel (e.g, obstetricians or psychiatrists) to staff screening committees. Close surveillance by local influentials, hospital administrators,or other staff opposed to abortion also kept smaller community hospitals from offering abortion service. Eventually, abortion services tended to be concentrated in larger hospitals with obstetric-gynecological departments. Teaching hospitals, which often lacked a community hospital board of trustees, supplied the greatest proportion of abortions for state residents. In fact, at one time, referrals into these facilities were statewide without residency restrictions. By contrast, Catholic hospitals never served abortion patients.

By and large, hospital committees took a conservative reading of the law, that is, abortion to "preserve" the mother's life. "Severe" medical problems were the only medical indications honored, or at least recorded. Social, economic, psychiatric, or fetal conditions were *not* acceptable grounds for an abortion. In limiting the rationale of abortion service to medically ill patients, committees kept the number of hospital abortions to a mini-

mum. For instance, in one large Michigan hospital with an abortion committee, only ten abortions were given in 1966.

Measurements of the total number of hospital abortions per year differ
depending on whether the source of the data is *reported* abortions or
estimated actual abortions. To cite a typical situation, the only available
report on the number of hospital abortions in Michigan is in a 1970 State
Department of Public Health survey, conducted by Johan W. Eliot. Out
of a total of forty-five distributed questionnaires returned (representing 29
percent of Michigan hospitals), only seventeen hospitals indicated that they
had performed any therapeutic abortions. Together, these hospitals reported 387 therapeutic abortions. Estimates by abortion reform physicians,
by contrast, ran as high as 1,596, although most insiders repeatedly used
a 1,000 figure as the "typical" number of legal abortions for the state.
Whether this included the undercover procedures masked as D & C remained uncertain. What is clear is that hospitals reported few abortions
in the mid-1960s, that there was a peak in hospital-performed abortions
by 1970, and that a steady decline took place thereafter because of the
availability of legal abortions in other states.

The hospital abortion practice was consistent with traditional medical
values. Because most physicians were convinced that abortion was more
dangerous to the woman's health than a full-term delivery, they ignored
well-established international data published for more than a decade that
showed abortion to be safer than childbirth. While almost all doctors reported that they believed prosecution to be only a remote possibility under
the committee system, they hesitated to become involved in "abortion
mill" operations. A Michigan Medical Association-sponsored poll of practicing physicians in seven Michigan cities and towns revealed other reasons
why hospital abortions were so rare:

1. fear of loss of reputation for hospital and staff physicians;
2. threat of community sanctions, e.g., loss of hospital privileges, loss of license;
3. lack of adequate surgical technology or know-how, epecially for late abortions,
   which kept the postoperative complication rate high; and
4. limited commitment by hospitals to expand services, despite increased demand.

Because American physicians lacked experience with large-scale abortion
practice, many had little confidence in their own capacity or that of existing
hospital systems to provide abortion in the mass numbers that now appeared to be demanded. Under these circumstances, legal abortion was
not an option for most women.

The hospital procedure for an abortion was the same as that for a standard gynecologic operation, including the requirements that patients remain
in the hospital for two days and have general anesthesia, a board-certified-

obstetrician-gynecologist (OB-GYN), and attendant physician. Ability to pay the costs for this major surgical procedure eliminated most abortion seekers and confined abortion service to the few who could afford it. In 1970, private patients paid from $500 to $800 for an abortion in Michigan hospitals with full surgical services. By contrast, clergy-referred abortion patients reported that clinic abortions in New York City, after the state liberalized its law, cost $125 (1971).

What was the standard routing into this physician-controlled network? First, the patient contacted her own physician, who had to agree to "work with her in securing a therapeutic abortion." For many patients, this was a hurdle in itself.

Second, the patient's physician had to have hospital privileges in a facility with an abortion service or know a colleague who did. If the physician had no lines into the therapeutic abortion service, chances were slim that his referral would be honored.

Third, the patient must have secured one (and in some cases, two) letter from a psychiatrist indicating that the pregnancy would "put the woman over the brink." Suicide letters, while recognized as "exaggerating" the woman's mental disability, were preferred.

Fourth, the request was forwarded from the patient's medical advocate to a member of the abortion committee, which often included one or more hospital trustee members. Physicians conceded that trustees tended to be far more conservative than physicians but considered this an asset in a situation where demand was potentially limitless. As one physician gloomily commented about the future role of the hospital in the event of legal change, "How are we going to handle the swarm of women who are [already] climbing in the second-story window demanding abortions?"

Fifth, a hospital social service professional interviewed the patient. This was usually a *pro forma* matter, having to do with method of payment. But it also served as an additional screening device to determine the economic and psychological feasibility of abortion for each patient.

Sixth, the woman had to have the husband's consent, even if he was not the father of the fetus. If the husband had deserted, moved to another state after a divorce, or was in prison, consent requirements could cause weeks of delay or prevent the therapeutic abortion altogether. A tragic case reported by the head of one abortion committee involved a woman with eight children who was in extremely poor health and had had a leg amputated. Medically, she was the "perfect" candidate for a therapeutic abortion. But the committee had to turn her down because she was unable to locate the deserting husband for his consent. In the case of a pregnant fourteen-year-old who had been raped, "no justification was needed." An abortion committee chair reported: "[Rape] is in itself enough for aborting the kid. Although it's against the law, we take care of it. We take a bet in this case that the prosecutor is not going to turn against us." Only hospitals protected by elaborate screening machinery and a benevolent administration could take such an open stance.

PSYCHIATRIZATION OF ABORTION

In a classic sociological essay, "Mistakes at Work," Everett Hughes (1972) pointed out that in the learning and doing of one's work one often encounters unavoidable risks. Such risks may be psychological, physical, legal, social, or economic. In some lines of work, including medicine, the probability of making a serious error is high. In such situations, people who are subjected to the same work risks will construct collective rationales and defenses against the lay world. In therapeutic abortion, where multiple risks and potentials for mistakes existed, the construction of collective rationalizations centered on the patient's mental state. If the committee system constrained physicians and spread responsibility across the medical institution, psychiatrization went one step further. It blamed the victim at the same time that it exonerated participating physicians.

Bringing the psychiatrist into the abortion decision fit into the ideology and organization of abortion services. Abortion was perceived as a dangerous, "bloody" enterprise that threatened the patient's life as well as the good name and legal standing of the hospital. An extraordinary rationale had to be designed to justify the service in the first place and to rationalize errors, such as the patient's death, injury, or adverse psychological reaction. Suicide was especially favored as a psychiatric indication. Letters from psychiatrists that were the most meritorious and received the most careful attention from abortion committees were those indicating that the pregnancy in question might provoke suicide or was likely to cause a successful suicide. And in using psychiatric grounds for therapeutic abortion, the risks of patients or their families suing for medical errors or punitive treatment (such as sterilization) were greatly diminished. Abortion could also be legally justified as "saving" the mother's life—a fair exchange in the fetus versus maternal health issue. What prosecutor would intervene in the case of a psychotic woman who had already demonstrated her incompetence to raise a child? Most abortion committees gambled on the odds that none would interfere. They were right. There were virtually no prosecutions for illegal abortion in accredited American hospitals, despite the frequently brisk business in therapeutic abortions.

The comprehensive psychiatric evaluation took into account the total life history of the woman: family background, sexual and pregnancy history, religion, relations with the father of the "baby," career and future goals, previous psychiatric treatment, emotional and behavioral problems related to the pregnancy, and the patient's likelihood for inflicting self-harm or seeking an illegal abortion. With all these precautions, once the applicant had been accepted for abortion, it was unlikely that the woman would be interviewed or counseled by the physicians actually performing the abortion.

Patients actually had little or no contact with the operating physician and often learned, only well after the fact, that the abortion had included sterilization. Because abortion patients were viewed as "psychotic," "hysterical," "depressed," "neurotic," or "guilt-laden," symptoms associated with what psychiatrists Ewing and Rouse (1974) term the "post-abortion hangover," the patient was considered to be in an unfit mental state to evaluate her own treatment. Early supporters of the psychiatric route believed that the aborting woman not only lost her baby, but rejected her own womanhood as well. The belief in woman-as-childbearer, a paramount function, undergirded the entire therapeutic abortion structure. No studies documented the psychic costs for women. Emotional symptomatology included depression, crying spells, anxious feelings, sleeplessness, excessive worry, and guilt. By focusing on patients' problems, especially emotional disturbances after abortion, psychiatrization succeeded in masking its elaborate control order and its structured helplessness for abortion clients. This is substantiated by Jansson (1965), who states that emotional problems were strikingly *more* pervasive after legal abortions than after other abortions or deliveries.

When the state abortion laws changed, the established psychiatric diagnosis became unnecessary. "Is therapeutic abortion on psychiatric grounds therapeutic?" psychiatrists asked (Ewing and Rouse, 1974). As one critic pointed out: "Just a few years ago psychoses probably constituted practically all the cases of therapeutic abortion on psychiatric grounds performed anywhere in the United States" (Partridge, et al., 1971, 135). Another label, "depressive neuroses," soon emerged to replace the old one of "psychosis of pregnancy." Depression became, at least for an interim, the greatest single factor indicating justification for hospital abortion.

In abortion reform circles the preferred diagnosis for abortion seekers became "transient situational disturbance," which eliminated altogether the psychiatric language of psychosis and neurosis. The reasoning was as follows: A psychotic or neurotic patient might be using pregnancy to mask an underlying mental illness that abortion would not treat. The woman would simply become pregnant again. Or abortion might be used as revenge against the woman's family or her husband or lover. Psychiatric indications for abortion do not cure hysterical, paranoid, or masochistic patients. A few physicians involved in abortion service resisted the mental illness category altogether because it denoted patient instability and with this the ever-lurking fear of malpractice. Most abortion patients, especially in the larger hospital abortion services, were strangers and did not form part of the doctors' regular patient load, giving the doctors' feelings of insecurity some basis in fact.

By contrast, the "situational disturbance" category implied that few or preferably no psychiatric consequences would follow a therapeutic abortion. Unremarkably, as labels changed, so did the patients' reported reasons for seeking abortion. Study after study documented social or economic reasons, in addition to psychological reasons, for applying for pregnancy termination. Patients voiced fear of illegality, illegitimacy, social stigma, rejection by family, having a malformed fetus, losing a job, costs of delivery and of raising a child, giving birth to a child of a different race, and other normal responses to the anxiety of an unwanted pregnancy and the agonizing process of remedying it (Adler, 1975).

The psychiatric profession became increasingly uncomfortable in its abortion-legitimating role. A 1969 report by The Group for the Advancement of Psychiatry published "The Right to Abortion: A Psychiatric View" and proposed a radical solution: "We believe that a woman should have the right to abort or not just as she has the right to marry or not." But abortion on demand was rarely attempted by hospital-based physicians, who remained largely indifferent or hostile to the new psychiatric ethic. The committee system remained the primary defense against "promiscuous" abortion. As the abortion movement expanded, a new version of therapeutic abortion emerged. The two examples of hospital abortion services that follow illustrate the differences in hospitals using the older psychiatric diagnosis and the newer "situational disturbance" label. Such differences in the hospitals' orientations grew from special local conditions, as the case studies of "Metro" and "Community" Hospitals document.

Case 1: Metro Hospital

Located in inner-city Detroit, the 550–bed, nonprofit Metro Hospital[3] was one of four hospitals associated with a major state university. At the time of the study, it functioned primarily as a teaching-research center, offering a variety of basic research and clinical programs in obstetric and gynecologic medicine. Here medical departments were centralized and, in medical matters, the accountability structure originated with the department chair and thence moved to the chief of staff, to the dean, then to the president, and finally to the board of trustees. Historically, leading businessmen or their wives controlled the Metro Hospital boards. Most members viewed their board function as a civic and moral involvement and had few reservations about expressing their own opinions. On the whole, they took a dim view of abortion on convenience.

Metro was the only metropolitan hospital exclusively specializing in women's practice. The hospital restricted patient admission by a formal referral system and later by patient residency requirements. Business and political linkages affected hospital abortion policy in subtle and complex ways. While a few staff physicians might have considered board surveillance as an attack on their professional autonomy, top administrators and hospital lawyers looked to board members for policy guidelines.

Different interest groups operated under different conceptions. Administrators emphasized bureaucratic constraints—legal risk, costs, and manpower shortages—as reasons for restricting abortion service. Some physicians who were critical of restrictions pointed to the president of the hospital, whose open hostility to "abortion mills" at whatever quantity of service, was said to reflect his Roman Catholic orientation.

The obstetric department, supported by the dean and younger professional colleagues around the state, stressed that experimental, research, clinical, and teaching functions required an abortion service for training residents and conducting research on maternal and fetal studies. One solution was to integrate abortion into other specialized surgical programs, thereby masking the extent of abortion service. Another compromise was the hospital abortion committee, whose primary duty was to screen out the largest proportion of requests. For Metro, only one of sixteen screened applicants was admitted.

The screening of abortion patients reflected the conservative political structure. A seven-person medical committee plus an *ex-officio* board observer evaluated all applications, whether from staff physicians or outside referrals. Legally, only a life-threatening condition was grounds for therapeutic abortion. Practically, the committee used a variety of indicators in addition to severe illness: Long-term psychosis, fetal or genetic disorders (e.g., rubella or sickle-cell anemia), poverty or, more chancy, an abnormal mental state, such as hysteria, suicide, or drug-related disorder.

The established criteria were not necessarily hard and fast rules. In an interview, the chairman of the hospital abortion committee admitted that if a physician made a strong appeal for a patient, he could sometimes unlock the gate. The committee was "reasonably flexible," he said, when numbers were down. When the demand was up, though, strict criteria were used.

Medical attitudes played a significant role in keeping a tight system. Staff physicians insisted that abortion surgery was not challenging medicine. "This is not what we're trained for, and we don't like the idea of having our beds full of abortion patients when there are sick people that need medical care," they maintained. Being involved in abortion mills also discredited the hospital and profession.

Negative associations—abortion and criminal activity and the doctor-turned-abortionist-for-profit—were cited as significant reasons for holding down the number of therapeutic abortions. Another reason was the general reluctance of physicians to be involved in any sort of "mill-like," assembly line practices. "It cheapens the enterprise," critics said. And medical school socialization certainly contributed to an anti-abortion ethic. Training for obstetricians focused on the "preserving" of fetal life, not destroying it.

Strong religious opposition by Catholic physicians and administrators contributed indirectly to the low medical view of abortion. But most obstetricians interviewed during this time were reluctant to accept abortion as appropriate therapy for problem pregnancy, regardless of their religious beliefs.

Overall, many physicians concluded that abortion patients were, on the whole, an undeserving patient group. Abortion patients were attested to be mentally ill, irresponsible, incompetent, and promiscuous, and according to one physician, they were using the doctor as a "diaphragm." These negative attitudes were compounded when physicians calculated the legal and professional risks. One opponent expressed the collective rationale as follows: "Why bring in a possible malpractice suit on your head by a confused or irate patient or her relatives, or incur the wrath of the county prosecutor's office?"

Commitment to the status quo undoubtedly supported stiff limits on abortion. Expanding the abortion program had no advantages, one staff physician emphasized:

It's not worth it. Keep the system tight, so we don't have to deal with too many of these people [i.e., abortion patients]. I'm already overloaded now. Besides, we're already taking in more abortion cases than anywhere in town. Let some of the others [i.e., hospitals] do it for a change.

Low commitment to abortion service, together with a program oriented toward "challenging" medical specialization in a university setting, tended to keep all but a few staff physicians from trying to alter arrangements. And while therapeutic abortions had been given in this hospital for more than twenty-five years, the official rationale for the hospital abortion entailed limited service to provide surgical care for the severely ill. The unofficial reason: Abortion provided an added staff service for training OB-GYN residents.

The quota system was rationalized by staff physicians as a necessity for dealing with manpower and operating room shortages. In reality, the screening system used to maintain quotas involved an elaborate referral system that evaluated the woman's medical suitability on a physician-to-physician basis. The woman never confronted the committee, nor was she consulted at any point in the deliberations.

Delays were endemic in the selection process. According to the chief of obstetrics, access to abortion service was limited by:

1. Initially finding a cooperative physician who would be willing to work through the referral and abortion committee;
2. securing a psychiatrist willing to write a "strong" letter of recommendation for termination;

3. waiting for the monthly, or later biweekly, review committee;

4. surgical postponements because of patient backlogs or other staff commitments; and

5. requirements for the husband's consent for married women, or parents' permission for minor females.

Data on 100 cases suggest that women who had access to therapeutic abortions at Metro were the urban, white, Protestant women who were relatively older, married, or formerly married with a completed family. Ability to pay was undoubtedly also a major feature. Legal abortions were confined to patients who could afford the costs of referral and hospitalization and who had the knowledge to understand and use the elaborate network necessary for obtaining approval for abortion. In other words, the clientele was largely well heeled and middle class.

However, Metro Hospital was a significant exception to most hospitals in the state, with black patients making up 31 percent of the abortion clientele, approximately 20 percent of whom were indigent. The reported denial of accessibility for the poor blacks was not apparent at Metro. Vigorous action by medical leaders had opened up a channel, however limited, that provided abortion for this medically underprivileged group.

Delays accounted for the high number of late terminations at Metro. The relatively uncomplicated early abortion (twelve weeks' gestation or under) required early diagnosis of pregnancy and surgical intervention shortly thereafter. Vacuum aspiration, a low-risk technique developed for early terminations, had an excellent record. But procrastinations, typical of this structure, resulted in a statistically larger proportion of risky procedures that carried a higher incidence of postoperative complications. Not surprisingly, two-thirds of abortions at this hospital involved "late" interventions (after twelve weeks) and/or sterilization.

Mistakes were not uncommon. For instance, five suction-type abortions (vacuum aspiration) were performed on late pregnancies (fourteen weeks or over); this procedure should not be performed beyond ten weeks of a pregnancy. A large staff, few of whom performed more than a few abortions a year, contributed to lack of collective experience, and hence there were errors in judgment. Hospital physicians blamed the higher complication rate on their sickly patients. Few examined the structural barriers that blocked early, medically safer abortions.[4]

Contraceptive information and abortion counseling were not part of the abortion program. Instead, the abortion committee evaluated all patients in terms of recommendations for sterilization. Medical grounds for this "final solution" to "promiscuous" abortions were forcefully debated by individual members and typically included the physician's evaluation of the woman's condition and moral character. Most "hospital-recommended" sterilizations concentrated on older women with multiple pregnancies or those with a diagnosis of "mental retardation" or "psychosis."

Records also reveal that patients were *most* likely to receive sterilization procedure if the woman was twenty-two years or older; she was, or had been, married; the patient had two or more children; and the woman had a reported history of a gynecologic disorder, medical disease, or an inherited or congenital condition of mental deficiency (four cases).

Little difference in incidence of sterilization could be shown by race, employment status, or religion. A late pregnancy was somewhat more likely to be followed by sterilization, whereas patients with psychiatric disorders or social-genetic indicators were less than half as likely to be sterilized as cases with reported medical problems. Rubella (German measles), which affects the fetal cellular system, was theoretically a counterindication for sterilization. These records showed, however, that rubella cases were as likely to be sterilized as the psychiatric patients. The only apparent exception was the younger woman whose pregnancy history was interpreted as indicating an abortion to prevent the birth of a possibly malformed child, not to end childbearing altogether.

Postoperative follow-up, a significant factor in tracing abortion complications after the patient has left the hospital, was not part of Metro's program. The woman returned to her family physician, less often to a staff doctor. In neither case was a postoperative history included in the hospital record for staff assessment or to correct the treatment program. Part of the problem resided in the medical histories themselves, which were unsystematic, if not casual, documents. Physicians took little care to standardize their reports. It is also conceivable that the ambiguities and inadequate information that characterized many of these records helped to cover "mistakes" at work. Until the New York abortion law reform, few public health or medical physicians made any effort to treat elective abortion as a serious medical practice. It was left to public health officials in New York City to carve out an entirely new public health research on abortion complications.[5]

On close examination, diagnostic categories were often unrelated to either legal or hospital norms, or to the patient's actual medical or psychiatric status. This hospital's medical records included the following diagnoses: drug abuse, mental retardation, contraceptive failure, a history of miscarriages, rape, rubella, incest, inability to cope, immigrant, broken home, cardiac failure, chronic disease, diabetes, extreme youth, and situational psychosis. Reducing this sundry collection into a single category resulted in nearly universal use of a psychiatric diagnosis; in these records it was "psychosis of pregnancy."

Indeed, in 80 percent of all cases, "psychosis" was cited as an indication for abortion. Nor did this always coincide with patients' actual psychiatric history. Even with a broad interpretation of this condition, only 54 percent of medical histories had any reference to psychiatric illness. The professional myth of abortion service as one confined to medically, or at most psychiatrically, ill women was not borne out.

High costs inevitably limited the number of hospital abortions. With hospital fees for private patients averaging $500, with an additional physician's fee of $300 or more in 1970, few patients qualified economically for service. Inflexibility in payment plans also screened out patients, especially those who lacked an affluent husband or welfare support.

Selecting patients for abortion, then, depended less on the patient's health status than on other nonmedical considerations. Composition of the abortion committee, number of requests at any given time, staff commitments, and physicians' evaluations of the patient's economic status or social worth all influenced which women would be admitted to the abortion service.

Case 2: Community Hospital

Abortion service in Community Hospital was a latter-day reform product, one of many interim abortion programs that emerged throughout the United States in the late 1960s and early 1970s. Unlike the large, urban hospital depicted in the last case, Community, located in a rural, mid-Michigan area, functioned chiefly as a general hospital supported by the local community. Little medical specialization was available, with the exception of one board-certified obstetrician. All other hospital staff were general practitioners or doctors of osteopathy. Physicians consulted with colleagues in this decentralized and nonhierarchical hospital; they were not accountable to them.

A cohesive board, consisting of business and professional men who shared club and recreational activities with physicians, governed the hospital. Hospital control involved a shared enterprise with typically harmonious relations between administration, staff physicians, and board. The medical entrepreneur who wished to create or expand a particular service could readily maneuver himself into a board position. This situation accounted for one physician's single-handed efforts, often in opposition to his obstetrician colleague, to establish a relatively extensive abortion program.

Community Hospital had a fairly large catchment area, serving approximately 100,000 persons, with a capacity of 146 beds, sixteen of which were devoted to obstetrical cases. Pregnancy terminations were reserved for the thirty-seven-bed surgical ward and were available at any time surgical loads were down, provided that the informal physician preference for a "discreet" service was met.

Professional values toward abortion service in this rural-based facility underwent dramatic change over the 1960s. Through the systematic efforts of one physician who promoted a family planning/social therapy conception of abortion, a gradual loosening of restrictions had occurred. Challenging the "straitjacket" medical mentality that limited abortion to the severely ill patient, this abortion advocate convinced colleagues that abortion was "preventive" community medicine. Surgical intervention of an unwanted pregnancy "preserved" the woman's health and "saved" the community the often tragic consequences of rejected children or the extended costs of welfare.

Value changes encouraged the organization of an abortion service for local women. From a primarily one-person enterprise limited to one or two patients a week in the late 1960s, the service expanded to accommodate six to eight, or even more, patients a week. If calculated at a yearly rate for 1972, this facility would have provided approximately three and one-half times more abortions than any other single Michigan hospital.

In this Republican/Main Street area, the ideology of medical practice involved a strong orientation toward private practice in a *laissez-faire* climate. Values of professional autonomy and community medicine (getting to know the patient), combined with an anti-bureaucratic conception of work, helped to generate the rationale for abortion service. Abortion was accepted, or at least tolerated, as a public health measure and recommended by local advocates as a medical responsibility. Although not all physicians adopted the new rhetoric, their disclaimers were drowned out by more vocal partisans.

The medical leader of this program attacked standard therapeutic abortion as both inconsistent and hypocritical, the product of the "tyranny of physicians" and the "tyranny of committees." It was inconsistent because only a few hospitals in the state were willing to treat abortion patients, thus denying service to most needy women. It was hypocritical because abortions had long been given for a variety of nonmedical reasons (e.g., rubella, rape, mental health, and so forth) but had been called by "something else." Further, the language of "preserve" in the law could be interpreted to mean "keep," "maintain," or "prevent harm." Health, then, was a *quality* of human life, he argued, not merely a matter of saving the woman from death.

The advocate-physician waged a one-person campaign to create a model abortion service. A lone crusader, he eventually convinced colleagues, hospital administrators, and local elites that present abortion practice needed to change in the interests of community health. To build up his credentials, he deliberately moved into leadership roles in community, medical, and political organizations. Vigorous volunteer activity on the local mental health board, for instance, provided one channel for his claim that "comprehensive health care" also included "mental" health. This approach permitted abortion to be rationalized on "mentalistic" grounds.

By effectively competing for elected posts in the Michigan Medical Society, he obtained an effective forum for his ideas and legitimated the "maverick" medical values to colleagues back home. By maintaining Republican party leadership at local and state levels, he became relatively impervious to local prosecutors, who needed his support for funds and influential contacts. This situation was reinforced after the local prosecutor brought in a relative with a "problem pregnancy," which the doctor "resolved" by abortion. After this incident the physician had little concern about opposition from the local prosecutor. In making abortion available to a number of wives or daughters of local influentials, he had acquired enough social capital to offset opposition from anti-abortion groups, such as Catholic lay women.

Most important, the advocate-physician had maintained a visible abortion structure in the local hospital. This strategy required his continuous vigilance against possible detractors who could threaten tenuous arrangements with the hospital board, administrators, and colleagues. He justified these efforts on the grounds that a clandestine arrangement could not communicate his message, which was the need for an expanded health mandate in which abortion was one medical option for a problem pregnancy. Anger against the "rubber stamp" psychiatrist also spurred efforts to generate an abortion service free of the "tyranny of committees."

When asked how he got started in this abortion enterprise, he replied,

It was a matter of being open.
Take your [author] case, for example. A woman like you who wants to take care of her children and do her academic work, to give an abortion would be to preserve her life. I show girls that it's not a clandestine thing. We do it so openly.

He then clarified how "open" the system really was:

We walk into the hospital openly, we sign all the forms. The doctor used to do it late in the evening and he called it therapeutic abortion. Sometimes it was just a D and C, but you don't put it on the records like that. Some doctors do it on a liberal interpretation, others just do a D and C and call it something else. This is very hypocritical, and it's very dishonest. As far as the administration is concerned, all of the tissue goes to the pathologist, everything is up and above the board. I acknowledge it's being done, and it's not being done under cover. I don't claim that what I'm doing can be done at _____Hospital, though. As long as I've been here, they've been doing it and for a year for rubella.

As for abortion being a crime, the doctor angrily pointed out:

Six years ago I told them that either what we're doing is wrong or the law is wrong. The more I read, the more radical I become. I made the transition in less than six months' time, that is through my reading and thinking. I was opposed to abortion, but with all the rhetoric we became more open about it. I had a beautiful 19–year old girl who went to Detroit and came back dripping pus. This convinced me. My colleague is getting uptight about it. He is a senior obstetrician. He wouldn't get involved in the decisions. As we pounded and pounded on him he said, "You can do these abortions, too." I didn't do much surgery then; I did anesthesia. Because I was tied up in anesthesia, I didn't want to get involved in anything else. If you'll support me, then I'll get an additional privilege. They won't let any GP do them. Even though I was doing incomplete abortions, scraping, cleaning out and that sort of thing and stopping the bleeding for my own tonsillectomies—really,that's how I got started with the abortion thing. It's that _____[the senior physician] didn't want to do them. He was too damn hung up. I regularly do two to four a week, while he never does more than two a year.

Although willing to concede that most physicians rejected being involved in abortion surgery ("Who wants to be the abortionist?"), he believed that every obstetrician should be willing to do the abortion "thing." "If you accept referrals on hysterectomies and other things, then accept referrals on abortion. Where's the consistency? If you can give a couple of abortions a year, why not give more?" This rhetoric was not accepted by most local physicians. Any acceptance of the service was related to positive regard for the innovating physician rather than to strong approval of his program. Most observers also added that the likelihood of this program working in other community hospitals was almost nil. For most physicians, the advantages of the present legal system were appealing; doctors did not have to make the hard decision.

Patient records at Community Hospital show a substantially different abortion population than that of Metro. Selection favored young women who were unmarried, were students, and were sexually inexperienced and small-town working girls or housewives who lived or went to school in the immediate area. Sixty percent of the group had never used birth control, which was about average nationally for younger women during the time. Early pregnancies only, terminated by vacuum aspiration, were treated in this setting. Intervention as preventive medicine was stressed, and any delays were avoided in order to prevent the need for a "late" abortion. An informal referral network also facilitated early intervention. Overall, the program was a low-risk, moderate-cost enterprise that operated within the constraints of a community hospital setting.

If we can classify these women as "locals" who fit a rural or small-town image of "good girls," then a benevolent medical program performed a dual role: Abortion restored the woman's status from a morally suspect person to a "respectable" or "normal" one and prevented illegitimacy, especially among the young. In this way abortion maintained community "health." As a grass-roots welfare program, abortion also eliminated additional taxes for unsupported women and their children.

Under a one-man directorship, screening abortion patients at Community Hospital was reduced to a single outside consultation. If approved by the directing physician, the patient was referred to one of four or five staff physicians for counseling. The *pro forma* counseling procedure operated less to determine the woman's needs than to judge whether the woman fitted the admittance criteria: local residence, early pregnancy, and legal consent for abortion, either by the husband, if married, or by a parent, for a minor. During counseling, the patient was informed that she was to assume moral and legal responsibility for her choice.

Consultation was multifunctional: (1) It acted to legally protect the operating physician by furnishing him outside collaborators who were also implicated in the act; (2) it provided a process by which patients could be evaluated in terms of their motives for abortion and thus troubled or troublesome clientele could be screened out; and (3) it served to inform patients of the legal and medical hazards involved. Emphasizing patient responsibility for the act, this medical system sought to ensure that risks would be primarily assumed by the patient or her family.

Informal quotas played an implicit role. If the directing physician took in as many as six patients a week, this represented only about 3 percent of the total number of calls for abortion he typically received in the same time period. Management of this potentially risky procedure was handled by limiting the number of abortions to fit colleagues' expectations of "appropriate." Too much demand for hospital operating room, anesthesiologists, and nursing time could create consternation among colleagues or nurses. For the physician who had a viable medical practice to maintain, there was little incentive to expand abortion service.

Hospital intake for abortion explicitly limited patients to those with early pregnancies. Almost all patients (96 percent) had pregnancies between six and twelve weeks, with all terminated by vacuum aspiration. In screening for low-risk patients—those with early pregnancies who were medically, psychiatrically, and morally "normal"—the system limited the number of medical and psychosocial complications that were believed to follow "late" terminations. No responsibility was taken for the referring of high-risk patients who were excluded from service.

As a modified surgical program, abortion represented innovation within standard hospital practice. This meant that the abortion procedure was treated as "typical" gynecologic surgery, requiring an operating room, a physician-anesthesiologist, nurse-attendants, recovery room, and bed rest. Patient use of hospital bed facilities, however, had been drastically reduced. In fitting all aspects of the surgery—preoperative, abortion, and recuperative activities—into an abbreviated period of six to eight hours, instead of the usual twenty-four to forty-eight hours of inpatient care, the hospital could accommodate more patients at less cost to both facility and patient.

Abortion referral and physician "follow-up" were compatible with family-planning rationales. Entry into the system was relatively open, with nonmedical or medical referrals or even walk-ins equally acceptable. To reduce the possibility of abortion "repeaters," patients were carefully coached in contraceptive practice by the directing physician. Although approximately 69 percent of patients reported erratic or no use of contraceptive devices before their pregnancy, almost all (91 percent) of the women had some form of physician-prescribed birth control after the abortion. This included seven women whose husbands received vasectomies (i.e., male sterilization) by the same physician. As "preventive" medicine, contraception became a crucial goal of abortion service at Community. In counseling the patient both before and after abortion, physicians stressed the bottom line of moral behavior—avoidance of repeat abortion. By teaching and administering birth control as part of the abortion program, the directing physician secured approval by colleagues for this questionable medical service.

Once the woman passed the initial screening by two physicians, diagnosis was essentially irrelevant. Almost all patients received "abortion on request," or termination for personal or family reasons (82 percent). Medical or psychiatric problems, when present (18 percent), were usually viewed as complications related to the present pregnancy. For the hospital record, an unplanned pregnancy was translated into the mental health code of "reactive depression." Here the physician followed the conventional usage established in two state university women's hospitals. Legal discovery, if it occurred, would expose not only one relatively isolated hospital system, but a network of hospitals similarly involved.

Even with a relatively simple surgical procedure and a short hospital stay, abortion costs were considerable. The hospital charged a standard $175 payment, plus a physician fee of $150. Almost all physicians agreed that cheap or no-cost abortions would only encourage patients' bad habits—failure to use birth control. In this case, however, flexibility of payment methods, including insurance, cash, time payments, Medicaid (five cases), or mixed payment plans, allowed even the less affluent to obtain an abortion.

Hospitals often complained that abortion patients were poor credit risks. Once the "problem" had been eliminated, the patient reportedly left the scene with no discernible traces. Falsifying names and residences was a standard practice. This situation did not exist at Community. Local residency, gratitude for the physician's willingness to engage in medically risky conduct, and a flexible payment plan all generated a loyal clientele, or at least one that paid its bills.

IMPLICATIONS OF MEDICAL CONTROL

In medical abortion it was not only the application of medical knowledge that was significant for organization of services, but also the stunning assemblage of powers derived from surveillance and regulation. Mastery over women rather than nature characterized this control structure. Medical abortion practice was not exclusively medical, but rather was linked to an entire range of institutions, economic requirements, and social regulations over women's lives. This was characterized by the psychiatric vocabulary used for abortion screening and committee systems, which identified and selected appropriate cases for therapeutic abortion. Especially in its earlier highly structured, psychiatric phase, medicine was profoundly enmeshed in social structures of control. As the control structure loosened, medical experimentation took place. The freestanding clinic, a futuristic model for permissive abortion on a massive scale, offered freedom in two ways: Doctors were free from hospital supervision and patients were free from punishment-centered medical treatment.

In this pre-legal abortion period, though, medical power, for all intents and purposes, was absolute, affecting both patients and physicians. First, formal definitions of power were based on rules of legal rights. The physician's definition of the situation prevailed and contrasted sharply with the image of the physical and mental incompetence of the patient. It was not so much that the woman was deprived of the right to choice, but that the patient did not have *any* rights in the abortion situation. The medical establishment maintained the right to determine health procedures for women in a totalistic way: who, what kind, how much, when, and why abortion would be available.

Even with a less rule-bound system, as in the Community Hospital case, therapeutic abortion was geared to establish the legitimacy of local professional power over the competing powers of church, hostile citizens, or a reluctant medical system. The system of right, in theory a legal matter, centered, in practice, entirely on the medical system and its capacity for selection, exclusion, and subjugation. The production of therapeutic abortion remained totally outside the patient's control.

Second, the overall administrative strategy for hospitals had the effect of politically immobilizing individual abortion patients. Patients experiencing inept or brutal treatment, poor service, enforced sterilization, or psychiatric or mental health labels could hardly bring demands on a system that barely tolerated them in the first place. The system was *laissez-faire* in the worst sense. "Let the buyer beware" implied that the legal system kept hands off the medical system. This left doctors with a high degree of autonomy and patients with none.

Third, medical abortion offered strong punishment-centered rules for patients but weak punitive regulations for physicians. The high cost of abortion service and the psychiatric labeling of patients could be viewed not only as protective medical features, but also as punishments used to limit patient loads or to keep patients in line. Controlling of highly qualified physicians, by contrast, was a more dubious enterprise.

Eliot Freidson and Buford Rhea (1963) emphasize how the professional structure promotes high levels of discretion in medical work. This grants physicians autonomy and privacy but, at the same time, blocks efforts at professional self-regulation. This discretion helps to explain the persistence of the "overeager" or incompetent hospital physician whose abortion practice operated outside the approved context. Punishment, such as "talking-to," reduced case referrals, and diminished social interaction with other physicians, was too slow or inadequate to regulate behavior effectively. And with the support of colleagues, outright dismissal was rare. The administrative fear that abortion tended to attract medical "misfits" remained a troubling undercurrent of concern.

The exclusive medical dominance over the abortion procedure helped to maintain an image of women as being hysterical, passive, incompetent, or immoral. As the institution of abortion evolved, this negative image became a central issue in reform. When the abortion movement finally emerged and created alternatives to hospital abortions, physicians abandoned the therapeutic abortion business. Instead, their role shifted to a "clean-up" committee, or what one physician stated as "patching up" aborted patients returning from hurried, fast-turnaround clinics in New York or elsewhere.

In the overpriced legal market of few abortions marked by punitive and costly conditions, as described in this chapter, the abortion consumer was often forced into seeking an illegal supply source.

NOTES

1. This is a reconstruction of a hospital abortion committee request based on extensive interviews with medical personnel and examination of patients' records.

2. In 1968 an international conference on abortion, attended by 114 participants from nineteen countries, was convened by the Association for the Study of Abortion. Sessions were devoted to the ethical, medical, legal, social, and global aspects of abortion. What is clear from examination of Dr. Robert Hall's two-volume publication of conference findings is that the medical system possessed extensive knowledge about abortion during the 1960s. Little of this information, however, diffused to medical students or practitioners, who continued to operate on the old assumptions: Abortion was a dangerous, life-threatening intervention.

3. Documentation of case studies is based on hospital records of almost all abortion patients for one year—June 30, 1970, to July 1, 1971—from two Michigan hospitals. These comprise 100 cases for each hospital. The proportion of abortions to overall service was low, although approximately similar for both facilities, despite great differences in bed capacity and the total number of patients served. For Metro, abortions accounted for 1.1 percent of total services (with a 550–bed capacity), and for Community, the abortion figure stood at 1.4 percent of all medical services (146–bed facility).

4. In a study of 425 abortions done at the University of Michigan over a five-year period (1970), the medical researcher concluded that abortion-related complications were a "technology problem." Too many physicians with too little abortion experience helped to boost the complication rate. Along the same line, the director of a New York City saline abortion program (for late termination) pointed out to me that physician error in judgment is invariably related to limited expe-

rience. He believed that most practitioners needed to work as apprentices in abortion techniques for weeks or even months before they were ready to practice alone.

5. Pakter and Nelson (1971) were among the first to systematically report on variations in abortion complications by method of termination and by period of gestation. The following two tables summarize their findings.

Table 4.1

Complication Rates per 1,000 Abortions by Type and Method of Termination. New York City, 1 July 1970–31 March 1971

Type of Complication	Total	METHOD OF TERMINATION				
		Dilatation and Curettage	Suction	Saline	Hysterotomy	Other
Hemorrhage	1.5	1.6	1.0	3.4	4.7	0.9
Infection	2.6	1.3	1.2	9.4	16.3	3.4
Perforated Uterus	1.7	2.3	1.8	0.1	5.8	0.9
Anesthesia	0.1	0.1	0.1	0.3	1.2	---
Shock	0.1	0.1	*	0.3	1.2	---
Retained Tissue	2.4	0.6	0.7	12.8	2.3	---
Lacerated Cervix	0.3	0.4	0.2	0.2	1.2	0.9
Failure	0.7	*	*	4.9	---	---
Other	0.6	0.5	0.4	1.1	2.3	1.7
Unspecified	0.1	0.2	---	0.3	---	0.9
Total	10.0	7.3	5.3	32.7	35.0	8.5

*Less than 0.05.

Table 4.2

Complications After Abortion by Type and Period of Gestation, Numbers and Rates per 1,000 Abortions. New York City, 1 July 1970–31 March 1971

Type of Complication	PERIOD OF GESTATION					
	Total		12 Wks. & Under		Over 12 Wks.	
	Number	Rate	Number	Rate	Number	Rate
Hemorrhage	128	1.5	68	1.0	60	3.7
Infection	214	2.6	85	1.3	129	7.9
Perforated Uterus	143	1.7	124	1.8	19	1.2
Anesthesia	10	0.1	5	0.1	5	0.3
Shock	7	0.1	2	*	5	0.3
Retained Tissue	199	2.4	44	0.7	155	9.5
Failure	61	0.7	3	*	58	3.5
Lacerated Cervix	23	0.3	17	0.3	6	0.4
Other	48	0.6	30	0.4	13	1.1
Unspecified	9	0.1	6	0.1	3	0.2
Total Complications	842	10.0	384	5.7	458	28.0
Total Abortions	83,872		67,520		16,352	

*Less than 0.05.

In other studies it was found that the saline method and hysterectomy were estimated to be three to four times more injurious to the patient than the suction technique (i.e., vacuum aspiration). (See Kerenyi, Mandelman, and Sherman, 1974, ch. 12).

5

Illicit Markets

Illegal abortion mills provided two distinct benefits: They were useful in achieving control of welfare populations and in protecting reputations of both unmarried and middle- to upper-class women and their consorts and families. While the medical establishment maintained the official pro-natalist ideology, illicit abortion practitioners met the unofficial yet compelling political and economic needs to discourage large families, avoid illegitimate births, and maintain the facade of public morality. In fact, criminal abortion practitioners were allowed to function in a kind of "enclosed legality" because they supported the established social hierarchies.

The illicit abortion market offered a lucrative field to individuals who were unable to establish themselves successfully in a regular practice (Bates and Zawadski, 1964, 127). Criminal abortionists were often medical rejects—physicians afflicted with alcoholism, drug addiction, mental illness, senility, and loss of licensure from other crimes—who were able to develop a successful practice in a profitable, albeit illegal, field. They took advantage of a strictly defined moral division of labor in which legitimate medical practitioners left the field open for a few medical risk-takers to meet the abortion need. In this way individual gynecologists could remain unencumbered with the "dirty work" of abortion.

Spawned in the mid-1930s, when the profession of midwifery was disappearing, gynecology had absorbed two distinct functions of the midwife: term delivery and abortion. Term delivery, deemed a legitimate function, was handled by the established medical community; abortion, declared illegitimate and criminal, became the province of the illicit abortion practitioners. But while the moral division of labor was strictly defined, the legal status of abortion as an "enclosed legality," and the "quasi-medical" characteristics of its practitioners, allowed the legitimate medical community and other concerned citizens to locate individual practitioners and the police to infiltrate the abortionist group and organize mutual informing.

This created a concentrated, supervised system that disarmed, to some extent, the illegality and rendered the system politically harmless.

Pregnancy, thus regulated by those in political control, produced the gynecologist as well as the illicit practitioner and, more than incidentally, a method for controlling women's entire reproductive lives. Abortion came to be seen as departure from the *norm*, a sickness to be understood, if not cured, by marriage and supervised pregnancies under the legitimate physician's care. The exercise of medical power over women and the perpetuation of an abortionist class with special knowledge are the two sides of a single process: reproductive power exercised almost exclusively by men without the affected woman's consent.

TRANSACTIONS

The managed negotiations, exchanges, and supervised conduct by legitimate medicine over the illicit abortion market kept medical boundaries reasonably intact against legal assaults.[1] In fact, the criminal abortion system could not have been sustained without the entire apparatus of the legitimate structure. Deviants and respectables alike shared the same universe of discourse—the language of control over excessive, inappropriate, and untimely pregnancies.

The moral division of labor was inevitably a tenuous enterprise. Fallouts, or shifting of moral categories, among respectables-turned-abortionists or deviants-transformed-into-liberation-heroes, especially after 1970, when the established order was collapsing, required that special institutional adaptations be developed. Physicians and the medical system generally did not aim to eliminate criminal abortion, but to differentiate between types of abortion, types of abortionists, and types of facilities. The hacks, quacks, greedy, and others who resisted medical supervision were turned in to the police; those who operated "clean" approved settings were protected.

Emergency Room Support for Incompetent Abortion Practitioners

Along with its other functions, the hospital emergency room became a basic support structure that covered up mistakes and failures. Police and medical circles concurred that emergency rooms in large city hospitals served as the chief outlet for "botched" abortions. These were medically serious conditions that doctors' offices were unable to handle. As these victims of "botched" abortions were wheeled into the emergency room, hemorrhaging and in shock, the emergency room staff not only worked to undo the damage, but also to keep track of the number of illegal abortions, as well as serving abortion patients who received medically incompetent operations, either from local or out-of-town sources. This setting thus became a central link between the legitimate and the illicit systems. Law enforcement agents, once demanded by hospitals to assume legal responsibility for an abortion patient, were rarely called on and then only in instances when the patient was dying. Police were well aware of this emergency room function, however. Legally immobilized, they watched a vigorous illegal trade of botched abortions come into the "back door" of the hospital, even while the "front door" of the facility was closed to such traffic.

The harshness of the offense was blurred by nondescript terminology describing obvious criminal or self-induced abortions as "spontaneous abortions" or "uterine bleeding." Diagnoses for "incompletes" were glosses for a variety of abortion-related uterine ailments, while illegal abortion remained an unnamed entity. Some indication of the number of illegal abortions processed in two of Detroit's larger hospitals (with obstetric-gynecologic services) suggests that "septic" abortions or "trauma" was associated with 32 percent of 900 "incomplete" cases in one hospital and 22 percent of 1,200 similar cases in the second hospital (1970). According to the administrator, this meant that there were 522 *known* illegal abortions in that city, with the actual rate probably four times this number. This rate reportedly remained constant from 1966 through 1970. The highest incidence of medical failures was attributed to abortionists without medical training, estimated to be 95 percent of all abortionists operating in Detroit and serving primarily the minority population.

Experienced emergency room physicians kept a "mental file" on type and source of septic abortion. Such hospital detection required an understanding of abortion instruments and their patterns of use by illegal practitioners. In this way the emergency room physicians pinpointed the incidence of illegal abortion (as compared with self-induced or "spontaneous" abortion) and, in a few cases, even the operator. Reporting this information to police, however, was perceived as a "problem." One physician-director of two large Detroit hospital emergency rooms described the strained relationship between hospitals and the police department:

We've had problems here [in reporting to police]. For instance, in 1967 we took pictures of a catheter which was imbedded through the uterus into the peritoneal cavity. Taken from every angle, it was pretty obvious there were holes in the uterus. Uteruses simply don't come with holes in them. This instrument was sticking through. We brought it [pictures and instrument] to the police. We asked them to please investigate. The police would not move because, according to them, there was lack of evidence. . . . We certainly would like to move against the butchers—only the police don't seem to be cooperating.

From the police perspective, selective reporting ("bad" abortionists only) discredited the facility as a reliable source of information. Police preferred to investigate primarily those cases identified by members of their own enforcement staff.

Despite the host of institutional conflicts that gave rise to this communication impasse, hospitals continued to inform police in the event of an abortion death. At one time, illegal abortions were the major source of maternal deaths in Michigan, with the 1970 figure estimated at thirty to thirty-five abortion-induced fatalities that year. Antibiotics drastically reduced the number of deaths from illegal abortion, even though the total number of illegal abortions remained almost constant over a ten-year period.

A few physicians questioned whether "self-induced" abortion was anatomically possible. One doctor stated that he rejected patients' claims of "self-induced" or "spontaneous" abortion as defensive statements protecting a friend, neighbor, or illegal operator who actually inserted the instrument, packing, or chemical. For these reasons—poor or inadequate record keeping, lack of police accounting, and resistance by patients to state the source of an "incomplete" abortion—the actual incidence of illegal abortion remained merely guesswork.

Referral Networks

The business of getting patients from doctors' offices into abortionists' facilities was handled by increasingly elaborate referral networks. Even before the development of a clergy broker organization, a few physicians and agency and lay persons reported they had "lines into" the illegal system, routing patients either directly or indirectly to services. Physicians were often dependent on the "good" abortionist to handle a patient's "problem" that they themselves were unwilling or unable to manage. In turn, abortionists relied on the informal "grapevine" to maintain a constant patient intake. One out-of-state physician-abortionist informed me that Michigan referrals from physicians and clergy constituted more than 15 percent of his abortion practice. This figure reportedly had varied little over a five-year period.

Before the clergy organization emerged as a "visible" structure, referral was secretive and, preferably, indirect. One former Planned Parenthood board member living in a high-prestige university town operated a one-person referral "business" for years, with tacit cooperation from a few local professors, physicians, and the Planned Parenthood state board director. Her referral network, described below, had three components: (1) in-state underworld linkages, (2) out-of-state legal and illegal connections, and (3) clergy contacts.

Phase 1: Underworld linkages. The earliest phase of illegal abortion referral included in this research dates back to 1963.[2] From this period until 1967, private referral persons operated as legitimate contacts in developing a helping network (described in Chapter 7). The referral persons "drifted" gradually into the enterprise. For the Planned Parenthood informant, accessibility to university students and commitment to family planning and sex counseling were primary considerations leading to her involvement.

Her initial problem in setting up a referral practice was identifying "good resources." To secure reliable and safe treatment for clients under hazardous legal and medical conditions, she used the following procedure. All parties remained anonymous. First names only for client and abortionist were used. In some cases the illegal operator was simply referred to as "Doc" or "Doctor," whether he was a physician or not. Abortionists were investigated periodically with information provided primarily by the clients themselves, including reports about the safety of the procedure or the emotional impact of the event on the woman. Clients, however, often failed to report after an abortion. Valuable information about the experience would then be lost. Pooling client reports did sift out bad operators. But there were continuous problems in keeping the good ones.

According to this informant, the abortionist typically presented himself as a doctor. But if she tried to verify this, she could expose herself and her tenuous business to outsiders. If she lost trust with the operator, this might antagonize him and eliminate a good resource. Then, too, abortionists were not reliable. They were likely to move in and out of the situation, depending on enforcement conditions. Negotiating the often complex routing could be a complicated and frustrating job, as this taped interaction suggests: (*Inv.* = Investigator, *PPI.* = Planned Parenthood Informant)

Inv.: Why don't we start with what kind of experience you had in the beginning—whether you were working with other persons in the community, whether you were alone, how you made the kind of contacts with the resource man in Detroit or elsewhere.

PPI.: That's where you are going to have a difficult time because I simply don't remember. It came on kind of gradually, and then somebody told me about this guy and I started sending people to him after I talked to him myself, and then it seemed unkind for me not to make contact with him, so I did.

Inv.: You were sending them through directly?

PPI.: Right. I had his name [illegal organization], but they never knew it. He would call and say, "This is doctor." He would arrange a meeting place. He did all the arranging you know. A motel around here, and he switched around, so he never got caught.

Inv.: He was operating out of motels then?

PPI.: Yes.

Inv.: Now was this a Mafia organization?

PPI.: I think the guy he transferred the gals that got botched to [sic] looked and sounded like Mafia, whereas he did not. I met him finally. He came to the

house and we had coffee and talked things over. He had a very good personality, and the girls would always report back to me. They all liked him.

Inv.: What technique was he using?

PPI.: Curettage, D & C.

Inv.: Was he a physician?

PPI.: He said he was. I found out later that he wasn't. But he was very proud of
his work, proud of his competency. With regards to training, I don't know
that he had any. But he was good. We had no problems. But, once I found
out, I called him on it. I said, you kind of betrayed me [in calling himself a
physician]. Now I can't trust you any more. And he got mad and he wouldn't
take anybody from me. So what I had to do was to go through my listing,
which I had as of 1968, and here, you see, I have underlined in red, those
girls who are willing to act as go-betweens. . . .

Inv.: Did you send any [patients] to Mexico?

PPI.: No. Have you read that listing [list of abortionists, their addresses and quality
of service rendered]? Now if you'll go on through that list you'll see that it is
the actual list of people [i.e., doctors] which meant that the picture changed
so rapidly that if I sent a girl out there she might possibly be picked up looking
for the doctor. But, of course, all the taxi drivers in that area were helpful,
and they'd take them somewhere else without the girl's knowledge of anything.
I thought it was much too risky. With the person I was using, every once in
a while, the doctor would have to go on vacation, because the heat was on,
so we'd send them to somebody else.

Developing referral options when the regular source was unavailable
required this referral person to be aware of possible situations that clients
might encounter. Clients as go-betweens, although relatively effective information sources, were not satisfactory for developing or acting on new
resources. By 1968 this informant used the boyfriend of a former abortion
patient to make the necessary contacts.

The "runner system," which involved an intermediary between referral
person and abortionist, reduced the risk of her being discovered, but costs
for both referral person and client were still prohibitively high. Financing
abortions and postoperative expenses for needy clients, another task referral persons often took on, cost this informant $1,500 in unpaid "loans."
For clients, abortion costs ranged from $300 to $1,000, depending on location and source. Detroit contacts continued to be problematic because
of hazardous medical procedures and illegality of connections (i.e., the
belief that contacts were part of a Mafia ring). Even reputable abortionists
were "difficult" to deal with: They were "harsh" and even "brutal" to
patients. Former abortion patients reported back that the abortionists refused to provide anesthesia, either because of added medical risk in a
nonhospital facility or because of additional trouble and costs. A diagram
of a typical network formation during the early phase is shown in Figure
5.1.

Figure 5.1
Network Formation Showing Direct Linkages Between
Referral Person and Abortionist

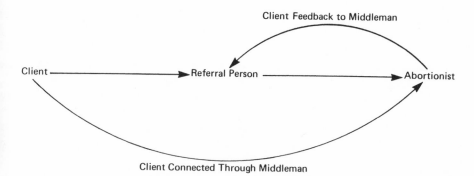

Client Feedback to Middleman

Client — Referral Person — Abortionist

Client Connected Through Middleman

Phase 2: Out-of-state legal and illegal resources. During Phase 1 almost all referrals were to "local" or Michigan abortionists. Later the list included out-of-state legitimate and illicit resources. The "runner-system," which maintained old contacts, was still used locally. Through "underground" sources, lists of abortionists could be bought. These included names and locations of operators, as well as costs, safety features, and technology. Lists could be purchased from an underground clearinghouse for $5.00, but such lists often required frequent replacement because of changes in address or price and quality of service. Contacts, formerly limited to Michigan, could now be made with various practitioners throughout the United States and other countries (England, Mexico, Puerto Rico, and Japan).

Previously, most information depended on client feedback. The new system did not require this because legitimate monitors were available on the scene. Traffic increased during this time, but the system was actually more efficient than in the preceding period.

Now concern focused on "weeding out" high-risk patients or those with medical or emotional problems likely to be exacerbated by abortion. Such persons, it was believed, were likely to end up in a hospital and, once there, to broadcast their illegal act to authorities. This seriously raised the risk of detection. If mistakes were made, responsibility centered on the referring person. Very young "hippie types" or those who were "disturbed," "on drugs," or "morally irresponsible" were perceived as threatening to the referral order. Moreover, a "disturbed" woman was at jeopardy for repeated abortions, a situation viewed as physically damaging and morally degenerating, especially for the teenage woman. "Cooling out" this client type involved referral to a psychiatrist, who, in some cases, furnished the necessary credentials for a hospital abortion. Evidence from this in-

Figure 5.2
Network Formation Showing Indirect Linkages of
Referral Person to Abortionist

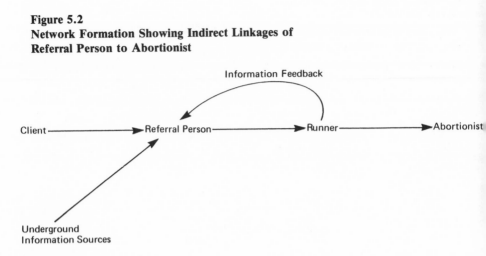

formant, as well as from early members of the clergy group, suggests that "problem" clients constituted an unresolved issue in referral operations.

Figure 5.2 shows the second phase of network formation based on indirect referral contacts with abortionists. Increased information and traffic, together with a perceived reduced risk situation, were standard network features.

Phase 3: Clergy brokers. Up to this time the referral network was only loosely and indirectly connected to legitimate support persons. Moral support from a few family-planning staff members and reform-oriented physicians was helpful but severely limited. For the Planned Parenthood informant, client demands required a full-time commitment to abortion referral. Even though physicians or agency persons were not contacted directly—inasmuch as clients were pushed to make connections on their own—there was a fear that "no one else could or would do this." By late 1968 connections with statewide reform groups and clergy leaders permitted this informant to begin channeling clients to local members of a clergy counseling group who assisted women in obtaining abortions. Despite almost five years of increasingly heavy abortion traffic, this informant was unaware that two clergymen were operating similar networks. Secrecy had been so skillfully maintained that none of the three was aware of the others' referral organizations. (The clergy broker system is more fully developed in Chapter 7.)

Colleagueship

Protection systems are nourished by colleagueship, that is, by those members who share in a guilty knowledge and give mutual support even in the absence of positive sentiments toward their occupation or its erring members. Physicians, particularly, have a highly developed colleague structure. So, it is not surprising to discover that a viable criminal abortion system grew out of and was sustained by these normal relationships.

One type of contact was the "old-school tie" with colleagues-turned-abortionists or with former hospital physician associates who moved into illegal practice. Legitimate physicians either ignored this information or adapted it to political ends. For example, the physician-turned-abortionist became co-opted into the reform circle and became "one of us." Referrals to "our kind," reform physicians said, was how "we helped women who can't afford to travel out-of-state."

In the period before reform, few physicians actually admitted to having a "contact or so" who would "take care of the woman's problem." What most physician informants said was that physician referral was widespread. At the same time they disclaimed their own involvement, for legal and ethical reasons. Fear of disapproval by colleagues and censure by legal authorities were the primary reasons most physicians avoided illicit contacts. A classic statement to an abortion seeker was made by one Michigan physician, who openly stated that he refused to jeopardize his own career but advised the patient "to go find somebody in Detroit. . . . I can't give you any names, but if you get an abortion, I'll patch you up." A few physicians tried making referrals through the hospital route but reported to be discouraged after rejection by hospital abortion committees. After this, they often withdrew from all abortion referral. Others increased efforts, "calling around" to more "friendly" colleagues with wider referral networks who might know about "local" (illegal) abortion facilities. Patients were invariably advised to then contact the resource directly, after the contacting physician provided the name and address.

Professional ties frequently endured long after the physician-turned-abortionist left his circle of colleagues. Former shared activities—student days, shared internships, mutual difficulties of establishing a practice and a reputation—allowed physicians to rationalize supporting their offending colleagues, even when they recognized that their former colleagues had moved "beyond the pale." In one case, only after the abortionist was indicted and threatened to destroy another physician's reputation did a hospital chief of gynecology admit that "he was beyond saving." At this point the gynecologist chief severed ties completely, despite an active interoffice referral that had existed for some years. On the whole, most physicians resisted disengaging from former associates, even when they no longer used them as referral sources. Perhaps this accounted for the belief held by prosecuting attorneys that physicians indicted for abortion could usually rely on former associates as court witnesses to vouch for their medical credibility. By contrast, non-physician abortionists lacked this support and were more likely to be indicted and convicted for illegal abortion.

How did physicians rationalize to themselves and others why some members of their profession become abortionists? There appears to be no single rationale here. The most commonly expressed belief was that the problem reflected personality or judgment deficiencies rather than anything inherent within the medical profession or legal structure. The physician-abortionist was one who had "lost judgment," was "overeager in some areas," "only turned bad as the result of _____[a negative professional situation]," and so on. Abortion as an "excessive" type of practice might be traced to a bad medical experience (e.g., loss of hospital privileges), inability to live by the rules, a deteriorating mental condition, or general incompetency in medical practice. Other physicians were more cynical, citing financial greed as the compelling reason for colleagues leaving standard medicine. They also added that only "fools" would get into this business when their licenses were at stake.

The abortionist's career, physician informants claimed, was relatively easy to slide into. For example, the advantages of an exclusive practice (e.g, ethnic clientele) and relative isolation from hospital-medical groups and legal entanglements (including malpractice suits) might contribute to a physician's decision to begin an abortion practice. Legal risks (lawyers, police payoff, local community "contributions," etc.) required high costs of operation. In turn, expensive legal protection provided a rationale for charging even higher fees. Reform physicians were probably a unique group in that they had a primary professional concern in changing the abortion laws. Such informants were likely to express tolerance of the abortionist role ("after all, it could be any of us"), rejecting, not offenders, but the "bad law" that led to "back alleys" and "butchers." In sum, conditions sustaining exchanges between respectables and deviants included colleagueship, expressed tolerance, efforts to assist patients, opposition to the abortion law, and physician's reluctance to bring legal action against other physicians. Under these conditions, there were few openings for prosecutors to press their claims.

THE ABORTION BUSINESS

Throughout the 1960s, restrictions on hospital abortions required that most demand had to be deflected into illicit channels. Lader (1967) estimated that in the United States only about 8,000 women a year, the overwhelming percentage of whom were white, qualified for legal, hospital abortions. Twenty-five years earlier at least 30,000 hospital abortions were performed annually. Abortion writers and reformers almost universally used the figure of one million abortions performed each year during the sixties in the United States. Even at the modest price of $150 for an abortion, this represents an astounding amount of untaxed income. The abortion business was a profit machine, and abortionists were rich men.

Part of the revenues were also used to improve services; the other part, to insulate the criminal organization from prosecution. Contraband goods and services generally follow this pattern (Sutherland and Cressey, 1969).

Studies by Kinsey and others show that a restrictive abortion policy discriminated most severely against women of lower social-economic status or those in situations that were most distressing, such as teenage pregnancy or poverty (Schur, 1965). Police reported in 1960 that criminal abortion was the third largest illegal enterprise in the United States, surpassed only by gambling and narcotics (Martin, 1961). With only loose medical surveillance, the quality of these illegal services was often poor (Packer, 1968).

As noted earlier, death by abortion was the leading cause of maternal mortality until the Supreme Court's legalization of abortion. Sepsis, punctures, embolisms, and hemorrhage were among the chief causes. Inept techniques and inadequate aftercare swelled the number of fatal cases, estimated at 5,000 to 10,000 a year in a study at the University of California (Lader, 1967, 3). Eighty percent of these deaths occurred among nonwhites (Lader, 1967).

The exact abortion death rate was estimated to be far in excess of this number because the abortion death rate was often shrouded in false diagnosis, as Taussig notes:

The same lack of honesty appears in our mortality records where we find cases of abortion death registered as pneumonia, kidney disease or heart failure. The recent splendid statistical investigations of maternal mortality made in New York and Philadelphia show that in 25 to 30 percent of abortion deaths a false diagnosis was put upon the death certificate. These errors were detected only by a meticulous follow-up of hospital records and personal interviews made by the physicians in charge of the survey. (quoted in Bates and Zawadski, 1964, 79)

Successful abortionists could make few visible mistakes. Unlike legitimate physicians operating under the protection of hospital boards and colleagueship, and who may have been entitled to occasional errors, the errors of the less-than-technically astute criminal operator were easily discovered and the suspect prosecuted. Therefore, competency in the abortion field was both a necessity and a mark of pride. For example, one black physician reported how he had mastered the abortion craft. Shunned by white medical groups, his practice was restricted to poor, rural, Southern blacks. In an interview he said:

I was a top student in my class and passed the boards in 1937. I used to do home procedures (abortion) because I was working with a poor population. I wasn't admitted into the white medical society, and so I wasn't permitted to practice medicine in any of the hospitals in Indiana. Now I've moved into office procedures for abortions up to 8 to 10 weeks. But before the vacuum aspiration, I used an extra-ovulary product which was a paste, a gel product. This is a German product which has the same effect as saline [injection]. It separates the amniotic sac from the embryo. My father was a pharmacist, and we worked to get the paste perfected. By removing the caustic products, all we had to do was insert this [into the uterus] and she [patient] then expelled the products of her conception.

Another out-of-state physician-abortionist bragged that he was "the bridge that carried the Michigan clergy across until the doors were open in New York," referring to his supporting role in helping women to obtain abortions in the pre-legal period. He emphasized shifts in technology over his thirty-four-year history of providing 30,000 abortions as a "master surgeon." In this informant's statement:

I've done abortions since early in my practice and learned the technique by fundamental principles. I've always been a student of anatomy. In the early period, I gave the D & C or paste if it was 12 weeks or above [gestation]. I've used this with tremendous success up to 7 months [gestation]. Now I know they're using the salting-out method in New York. I suppose I've given 20 to 25 percent salines for these later cases, but I'm not sure when labor is precipitated with saline injection. With paste I know that the woman is ready to deliver in twenty-four hours. I'm very experienced. Down through the years, I've learned what works and what doesn't work, and I know what I'm doing. I know what the fetus and placenta look like after they're removed. . . . I know what the uterus feels like after you've gotten everything out. . . . I like to pack my cases. I use a gauze pack with a string [of gauze] five yards long with some [?] inches of packing hanging out of the vagina, so she won't get infected. You pull it out yourself. There's more bleeding with a tooth [removal] case. This controls bleeding. I studied in the best clinics—Japan, England, and New York.

Technology, then, was an intricate part of tradecraft. Another skill was the development of defensive strategies to avoid legal entrapment. One such strategy included acquiring the trappings of community respectability: multiple professional and community affiliations—black medical societies, local hospitals serving primarily a black clientele, and church, school, and civil rights groups. Rapport with patients, too, was essential if the abortionist was to protect himself from discontented or irate patients, who could then inform police. By keeping open phone lines and by making himself available in the event of postoperative emergencies, the abortionist limited mistakes to the spheres of the office or a friendly local hospital.

Anticipating trouble became more problematic when the patient was an out-of-state resident or, for the black abortionist, when she was white in an almost exclusive black practice. Transactions with legitimate physicians who assumed part of the responsibility made this patient type a worthwhile risk. One abortionist reported that to avoid surveillance he occasionally made arrangements to meet the woman in a different section of town. This raised overall costs considerably but protected both patient and abortionist.

Most abortionists had frequent tangles with the law that, for some men, extended over decades. This necessitated regular payoffs to police, which ran as high as $3,000 at a time. All abortionists had to learn to recognize police agents, who were fairly easy to detect since they (a) were white in a black community, (b) came in teams, and (c) were accompanied by a "deputy-woman" acting as a patient but who was "very nervous." One abortionist screened intruders by noting their reactions and then stalling the procedure—keeping the patient waiting in the reception room and delaying the physical examination while on the table.

Even with precautions, abortionists could not always avoid prosecution and, for some, conviction. One black physician reported that *failure* to give a medically contraindicated abortion led to his arrest. When the rejected patient died in the hospital as a result of a criminal abortion given by a non-physician, the woman's husband blamed the doctor for her death and went to the police. A criminal trial followed, resulting in conviction and a fourteen-month jail sentence. The abortionist told me how the court effectively discredited him, even though he had the support of legitimate physicians, many of whom had been referring abortion patients for years. In describing the court scene, he said:

Judge _____, a Catholic judge, was the presiding judge for my case. The trial was a comedy. Doctors verified my character references and my competence. The women [patients] verified this, too. Many doctors had been referring patients to us [team of three physicians and one pharmacist]. They sent their girlfriends, wives, daughters and so forth. They [court] brought in two black girls and one white woman. They couldn't even get the physician to testify against me. But they trapped the white woman. They said to the white woman on the stand, who was a very pretty blonde:

Q: Where were you with relationship to the doctor?
A: I was on the table.
Q: Where were your legs during this time?
A: My legs were on the stirrups.
Q: Where was the doctor in relationship to you during this time?
A: The doctor was standing at the bottom of the table.
Q: Then the doctor was located between your legs?
A: Yes.
Q: The doctor then inserted something up your private parts?
A: Yes.
Q: What was this that he inserted?
A: I don't know, a speculum, an instrument of some kind.
Q: You cannot testify for certain what it was that he put up your private parts?
A: No, I can't testify for certain.

And that was the end of the prosecutor's questions. They charged me with conspiracy to perform an abortion. I had a fourteen-month jail sentence and lost my license.

After release from prison, this informant learned to deal with "legal pressure" by turning to legislators and "police higher-ups," whom "I've helped out in the past." Informal protection was the *quid pro quo* for "taking care" of their women who needed some "local treatment," on a reduced or no-fee basis.

As technology changed, costs conformed to new market conditions. In the 1960s the price for a "late" abortion—packing followed by D & C— ran as high as $1,000, with early procedures averaging $500. By 1971 abortion was still "lucrative," but individual abortionists reported that profits were more modest. But because abortion practice was not reported on the income tax returns, doctors could pocket the difference. One Chicago physician charged $200 an abortion, competitive with the New York market. He claimed his services were actually "cheaper" for Michigan, Ohio, and Illinois women, who saved transportation costs in the bargain. For one Michigan abortionist, "profits" were in the form of service to the black community. A sliding scale with a high of $150 to no-cost operations accommodated inner-city patients, all of whom were black.

Abortion, unlike many surgical procedures, lends itself to a high-volume patient load. Such volume produced large profits for a few entrepreneurs. In the late 1960s one Michigan physician charged only $200 for an early abortion (six to twelve weeks' gestation), but with 100 operations a week, he was able to gross more than $80,000 a month. A large proportion of these revenues must be redistributed as payoffs to police or for attorneys' fees. All business-abortionists retain at least one regular attorney; others may consult three or four because of concurrent pending cases with different charges, such as conspiracy, medical malpractice, and operating after revocation of the medical license.[3] High volume is the goal of criminal abortionists, and it accounts for low use of anesthesia, high patient turnover, and few supervisory staff, with little time spent on the individual patient. Short recovery periods, related to this time factor, were also the leading condition in medical complications after surgery.

Before 1930, midwives dominated the abortion field. By 1958 Kinsey (in Calderone, 1958) reported that nearly 90 percent of the operative abortions were being performed by physicians, most of whom had regular medical practices. An inside look at how the abortionist worked was provided by Dr. Timanus, a Baltimore physician who performed 5,210 abortions over his medical career. Here is a transcript of the dialogue between this abortionist and reform physicians from a 1958 Planned Parenthood Conference on Abortion (Calderone, 1958, 63):

Dr. Rose: You built up a "clientele," you stated, of about 353 M.D.s?

Dr. Timanus: Correct.

Dr. Rose: I wonder what the proportion was of general practitioners and specialists? Among the specialists, if you are able to speak in somewhat general terms, how many of those were, for instance, psychiatrists on the one hand and, on the other, surgeons or obstetricians?

Dr. Timanus: I cannot tell you that. As far as I know, most of the doctors were general practitioners, many of them in the counties of Maryland.

Dr. Kleegman: Did you have to give any rebates to these referring physicians?

Dr. Timanus: No, never.

Dr. Jacobziner: To your best knowledge, how many physicians practiced your specialty in Baltimore, and what was the average charge?

Dr. Timanus: I would say that at the time I was operating, there were two of us who did 90 percent of the work. The charge varied according to people's ability to pay. In the early days, the charge was $25, $50, $75 or $100, depending somewhat upon whether it was before or after the third month. In later years it was $150 to $200. I first retired because of all the furor in Baltimore about abortions. I was never named, but I simply decided to stop. Afterward, at least 20 doctors told me how serious it was that I do some work, and so I started again, but to make the thing more or less prohibitive I charged $400 for a treatment. The most I ever got was $3,000.

Thirty years later, three well-established abortionists informed me that they detected few physicians, or even non-physicians, operating large-scale abortion practices or even entering the abortion market during the early 1970s. Police were well aware of all abortionists, they reported. The careful maneuvering necessary to enter the market restricted most candidates. But, above all, entering the market required enough initial capital "to take care of local boys at the station house" if they should give any "trouble." Reform physicians and abortionists alike asserted that getting into the market in 1971 was less profitable than it was earlier. Medical referrals were "drying up" because of competition from legal sources in New York, California, and elsewhere. This discouraged new operations but apparently had little effect on well-established practitioners.

Legal threats were persistent market features for illegal practitioners. Even so, well insulated black physicians, "respectable" in terms of local black community norms, were unlikely to be prosecuted. If prosecuted, they were less likely than their white counterparts to be indicted. If indicted, jail sentences were token punishments, rarely extending over a few months or years. At the same time "respectable" white physicians were more likely than blacks to have highly competent legal counsel and a battery of mainline professional associations that could enhance credibility. These doctors rarely were prosecuted. Because abortion practice was highly profitable, abortionists could pay for long-term litigation, often extending over many years while the offender continued operations, reaping profits, meanwhile, to pay off costly legal action. Delays and postponements, abortionists and defense attorneys said, benefited their cases because courts were reluctant to sentence because of the growing ambiguity of the law.

The "bad" abortionist was a vexing problem for the profession. From performing competently, dependable in taking referrals, and providing safe operations, an abortionist, it was widely believed, could easily become transformed into an alcoholic or a senile, mentally incompetent, or physically ill person. This created a dangerous situation with few professional remedies. A few physicians recognized that the source of the problem was professional isolation, but turning the miscreant over to police was unacceptable to the profession. Using more subtle approaches was more advisable, such as stopping referrals, preventing hospital privileges, or even threatening the abortionist with legal suits. The profession preferred to police its own as much as possible. Asking the physician to desist operations worked—sometimes—but not very effectively. The doctor usually reappeared in a different community. Stopping all referrals was one control tactic, but reputations of abortionists were not necessarily confined to professional referrals. Word-of-mouth circulation among former patients kept clients coming, often long after the abortionist had retired or even died.

In one story told of a senile physician-abortionist who resisted giving up practice, enforcement came first by way of professional censure and after that failed, direct action. As reported by a former president of a county medical society, intervention occurred as follows:

We had a colored doctor performing abortions in his office, which was in his home. He was picked up by the court [and] sent through the probationary and fining system. They let him go at the time. The Mafia got into this deal. The doctor was seventy-nine. And he was starting to get sloppy. One woman who was given an abortion died in the street on her way to the car of an embolism. The way we handled this business was to negotiate an out for the culprit. We took away his tools, burned down his building and had him legally constrained by putting him under the care of his daughter. There had to be a legal agreement. After all, he was too old to go to jail.

In general, physician-informants and clergy leaders said that conditions under which the profession was likely to *move against* an illegal practitioner included:

1. blatant display of the illegal abortion practice, signifying lack of appropriate professional discretion;

2. failure to link into the ongoing local medical community, as in social or professional relations;

3. personal and social characteristics objectionable to the local medical community (e.g., alcoholism or manifest mental disorder);

4. use of "name dropping" of respectable physicians or associations by an indicted abortionist; and

5. an especially restrictive community milieu forbidding professional tolerance of illicit practice.

Other conditions than those mentioned earlier that physician-informants believed *sustained* the abortion practitioner included:

1. location in a large city with an inactive or tolerant prosecutor;

2. a relatively open referral network, not limited to the local community (one general practitioner in Pennsylvania took abortion patients from a five-state area);

3. a formerly successful practice as a non-abortionist, which builds up "credits" for referral purposes;

4. a preferably long history as a successful abortionist, or one who made few "mistakes";

5. isolation from known underworld figures or organizations (although the myth of the Mafia tended to be a universal one, with any discovered abortionist said to be linked to these suspect persons or groups); and

6. charging competitive prices commensurate with risk and number of alternative suppliers. When cost remained above market price, referral sources evaporated quickly.

NEW ROLES FOR ABORTIONISTS

As abortion reformers moved into a more active public phase, abortionists were asked to assume new roles adapted to changing ideology and practice. In the late 1960s and early 1970s abortion conferences often included abortionists as spokespersons for a liberated abortion law. Some were tottering elders, long banished from professional societies because of their criminal activity, who stated that they were attempting to restore their respectability before it was too late. Others were "marginal men"—so-called "doctors" or unlicensed practitioners, mainly from Southern states—some of whom were trying to "make it" in this new institutional milieu.

Some abortionists reflected bitterly about the past when they saw prestige accorded to planners and directors of abortion clinics and hospital services. Others hoped that an expanding market for abortion would offer new opportunities, if new sources of referral could be developed. Office abortions in New York, free from local public health board surveillance (except in New York City), provided one outlet for formerly prosecuted abortionists.

In some cases the abortionist became transformed from pariah to hero. It was he who forged the chain, making it possible for others to institutionalize abortion as a health service. Whereas other professionals were too timid to rise to the challenge, the abortionist took responsibility into his own hands. Responsive both to consumer need and to public outcry against restrictive abortion policies, he moved forward when others held firm to respectable reputations and status quo careers. The NARAL (National Association for the Repeal of Abortion Laws) Conference in October 1971 featured one Michigan abortionist who openly proclaimed his intention to test the law. Public testimony by a Michigan Clergy Service counselor stressed the heroic proportions of his effort: "Dr. _____has been serving the poor and the black. He has struggled and been agonized in this abortion fight. The abortion law of Michigan discriminates against poor people who cannot even raise money for travel even when the medical fee is waived completely." Another speaker emphasized, even more dramatically, this physician's role in change: "Dr. _____has rendered the veil of discrimination by striving for equalization. This is a constitutional issue, then, and Dr. _____'s decisive act will prove a model for other states to follow."

Subsequent events suggested that the doctor in question, while waging his own legal battles, stirred little significant legal action either within or outside the state. Instead, his national conference role was symbolic. He provided a rallying figure to link the politically scattered state reform units and directed reform into substantive action: building an alternative abortion delivery system.

NOTES

1. Data for this chapter were drawn primarily from interviews with physicians, hospital administrators, police, defense and prosecuting attorneys, and persons formerly engaged in referral activities with abortionists. This includes one Planned Parenthood board person and members of the clergy group, with additional data taken from clergy documents. Three physician-abortionists were also interviewed. Informal conversations with two other former abortionists at a National Abortion Conference (NARAL) in Washington, D.C., in October 1971, provided additional insights to illegal organization. Because of inability to secure interview data as "privileged communication," I was unable to get interviews with two other "notorious" abortionists, then under legal indictment in Michigan. Attorneys for the defense strongly advised in both cases against taking statements from these sources because of legal jeopardy both to myself and the respondents.

2. I was able to identify not more than five full-time physician-abortionists serving Michigan residents in 1970. These doctors were located in Detroit (three), Saginaw (one), and Chicago (one). All but one of these physicians were black. The Saginaw, Michigan resource had subsequently closed down. Most of the so-called underworld connections were with out-of-state doctors brought into Michigan one or two days a week to perform a guaranteed number of abortions. Almost all other "doctors" were either medical technicians or other paraprofessional persons, or someone who had "picked up the trade," perhaps when serving in the Army. A few doctors of

osteopathy were reportedly performing abortion as part of their practice. I was unable to locate these practitioners.

3. Such a large volume of abortion patients would have been more difficult before the widespread distribution of the vacuum aspirator. This instrument can evacuate a pregnant uterus in a matter of minutes.

6

Rupture

The emergence of a new institution requires the destruction of the old one—its values, forms, and functions. Social movements, which carry out this destruction, are often depicted as evolving in a progressive fashion toward a unified goal. The reality is far different. For in attacking the old morality, other movements arise to counteract attempts at transformation, placing pressure on the original social movement to reinterpret and adapt to unanticipated events. When we trace the abortion movement from its origins and development to its eventual impact on American society, it becomes apparent how open-ended the organization really was for the purpose of defense and reaction and the results of successful counteraction. The form was fluid, but the meaning was even more so.

The cultural turbulence of the 1960s gave birth to a wave of liberationist movements, setting the stage for collective attacks on criminal abortion laws. The ethnic, youth, anti-war, women, and abortion movements, although organizationally separate, tended to be mutually interactive, borrowing language, ideology, and political strategies from one another. At the same time, each of these movements was also a distinctive symbol system, involved in radical cultural change and challenging established hierarchies and fundamental social relationships. Each movement also evoked a crisis of legitimacy in its respective sphere in its effort to upset existing arrangements: white power over minorities, adult repression over youth, male dominance over women, medical and legal intervention over women's reproduction. For all these movements, the existing political order was perceived as morally wrong—out of place, disordered, unjust, and oppressive. Despite a common enemy—the so-called establishment—these movements lacked overall coherence.

Observers often wrongly equate the women's movement with the abortion movement because some symbols were commonly shared. But feminists represented a strong reactive element against established groups' attempts to rationalize abortion as a standard medical procedure. Similarly, rebellious youth were often opposed to the technology trend, reacting against the machine solution to social problems. Anti-war advocates were often blatantly sexist; and minorities, especially, were appalled at the prospect of abortion as a state-controlled mechanism, fearing genocide as the "final solution." Hence this wave of movements did not provide a progressive, unified push for abortion reform as much as acting as a catalyst for accelerating institutional crisis—the destruction of common understandings and taken-for-granted roles and statutes.

By the mid-sixties American society appeared cracked, and for many critics, the moral alliance of church, state, and professional medicine that controlled reproduction was believed to be weakened beyond repair. Established groups winced beneath the ideological thrust of reform, envisioning the birth of a new, possibly dangerous, reproductive regime—dangerous because it was out of their control. Elites rose to the occasion, and the abortion movement was launched. The movement's first task: Attack the pro-natalist concept of natural motherhood.

A NEW REPRODUCTIVE IDEOLOGY

For a long time we supported a pro-natalist regime, and we continue to be dominated by it even today. Thus the feminine mystique of the "angel in the house" thrown up annually on Mother's Day is emblazoned on our sometimes guilty and shamefaced national consciousness. On the subject of reproduction and abortion, the pro-birth ideology has entailed these key principles[1]:

- Sexuality is a private, domestic matter and is used primarily for reproduction.
- Woman's basic status and role is circumscribed by pregnancy.
- Laws serve to protect motherhood, but it is strictly forbidden for schools and other institutions to "counsel, discuss, or inform" youth about family planning or spacing of children.
- Religion, law, and medicine have a natural right and social obligation to regulate birth control and abortion in the interest of the woman and her family.
- Women who die of criminal abortion are either insane or immoral and receive their just deserts.
- Therapeutic abortion is exclusively reserved for life-threatening circumstances, and the medical profession has a legal-ethical duty to continue such restrictions.
- Criminal abortion laws reflect the will of the people.

Around these principles, the pro-abortion forces waged their opposition campaign.

First, it was anger expressed by women's rights advocates with their middle-class concern for equal pleasure in bed and an end to alienated sex. The sex "revolution," however, was a misnomer. In an era of sensitivity groups, Masters and Johnson's sex therapy, and the "Joy of Sex," the feminist messages quickly became assimilated into what Christopher Lasch (1979) refers to as the "culture of narcissicism"—an individualistic, socially nonproductive preoccupation. Although a far cry from partisans' original intent that called for radical equality in all forms of relating, the sexual equality message generated strong support for abortion on demand.

Second, it was resistance to the "barefoot and pregnant" version of womanhood that animated active university and community volunteers and professional women to reconsider their "natural" role. "Sexual apartheid," one speaker announced to a rapt audience at Michigan State University in 1969, is "behind and beneath the general conservatism in America and its failure to grant to its minorities and to women its American birthright." The message was radical: Until the masculine culture, the male-centered and directed world, relinquished unshared power, women would be unable to assume responsibility for their own destinies.

Equal pay for equal work, day care for working mothers, equity for women in divorce settlements, and other demands began to surface. Birth control and abortion began to be seen as necessary means for achieving the more difficult goals of economic and political equality. And looming large in this reactive discourse was the ever-present specter of overpopulation: The woman who stays at home, whose entire life is organized around her maternal role, is more apt to exceed the zero population growth ideal of two children per family. Moving the full-time homemaker into new social and economic roles was believed to be the best prevention for unwanted pregnancy.

Third, rather than protecting motherhood, restrictive contraception and abortion laws undermined women's health and family integrity, opposition groups said. The overburdened couple, the raped teenager, the adolescent mother, the abused child, the damaged fetus, and the single mother were all featured in the pathos of an aroused social awareness. For example, family planning, a polite middle-class term for birth control, was introduced into Detroit for teens by Planned Parenthood. Attendance at these educational and talk sessions was mandatory if teens wanted to gain access to "the Pill," the I.U.D., or the diaphragm. Keeping sex a secret from already "sexually active" teenagers, Planned Parenthood leaders insisted, was a guarantee for disaster: an unwilled pregnancy, an abortion, an unhealthy mother, an unwanted child, an abused infant. In actual practice, the enterprise was a hit-and-miss affair. Teenagers "dropped in" but failed to stay long enough to get the necessary information or the physician's referral. Or girls might discover their boyfriend "didn't like the interference"—whether by the agency or the contraceptive itself. Agency intervention, in the absence of an enlightened home and school process, probably failed in its essential socialization mission. Its byproduct, though—informing teens that sex and pregnancy were personal decisions—may have been its greatest accomplishment.

Mindless motherhood came under attack. When women's sole preoccupation is with their role as childbearer and rearer, unintended consequences were said to follow. "Momism"—the overabsorption and control of children, especially boys, by their mothers—became one of the deadly sins attributed to the compulsive mothering complex. Not only was it destructive for children, but also, psychologists warned, there is the "empty-nest" syndrome that awaited such overzealous mothers as the retiring childbearer sunk into depression, anxiety, and despair. Women were told to diversify and adopt more flexible roles if they were to avoid the double indemnity: oversmothering children and undersupporting the self.

Motherhood itself became suspect, unless it was a self-determined act. Lester Breslow, M.D., president of the American Public Health Association, was quoted by abortion law reformers as insisting on the "freedom of each woman to rule out certain times and circumstances for her own motherhood." Some critics went further. In a speech to abortion supporters, Dr. Ethelene Crockett, medical adviser of the Detroit Model Neighborhood Comprehensive Health Program, said that women's struggle for justice was intimately related to the issue of enforced pregnancy. "More than one hundred years ago this country banned slavery. A woman pregnant against her will is doomed to years of servitude by the society which forces her not only to carry a pregnancy but, if parenthood results, forces her to continue this servitude until the child becomes self-supporting."

In a follow-up statement this black physician and a leading reformer in the abortion movement laid out the "new motherhood" platform:

Women must have more control over their bodies, their lives. Adequate financial assistance must be given to every woman who wishes to have children. Day care facilities for children must be made available and cheap enough so the lower income woman can increase her earnings, while knowing her children are adequately cared for.

The role of elective abortion as a means to achieve these goals logically followed: "Planning for one's family is a continuum in which we could logically see abortion as one facet used willingly to control family size."

Fourth, advocates attacked the dominant institutions of religion, law, and medicine that masked control by using the idea of *protection* to limit women's social participation. In the nineteenth century, anti-abortion groups argued that protecting pregnant women from unscrupulous practitioners or unsafe contraceptive procedures appeared necessary and reasonable. In light of today's advances of medical technology, this "protection" represented a clear denial of freedom. Refusing women access to contraceptives and legal abortion really meant consigning them to mandatory pregnancy and, in the case of teenage mothers, subjecting their infants to possible abuse or early death. A letter to the Michigan legislature from a public health nurse in 1968 details some of the abuses of what proponents asserted was a retrograde abortion policy:

In May 1967, a baby girl was reported to the Health Department as neglected and starving. She was found deserted by her unwed mother and irresponsible relatives in a filthy, malnourished, underdeveloped condition. Her sixteen-year-old mother had syphilis at the time of the baby's birth, and the baby, which weighed four pounds thirteen ounces when born, was found at the age of six months to weigh a little over six pounds. This child was made a ward of the Court but it is doubtful that this child will ever be physically and mentally well-developed as she has suffered intensive deprivation of food and maternal care. I am sure that this particular mother would have preferred that she never had this child, and certainly one would feel that this child should never have been born.
A young teenage girl, I should say a twelve-year-old child, delivered her baby at home unattended and threw it out of the window into the snow from the second floor. Shouldn't something have been done about this child's pregnancy?
A mentally deranged mother, released from a mental institution pregnant, delivers her baby alone and drops it in the toilet and drowns it.
A mentally retarded woman becomes pregnant, delivers her baby alone and puts it out on the front porch in the winter.
I think you will agree that we need to make legalized abortion available to these women who need it so desperately.

Religion, law, and medicine, the triumvirate that had long exercised final authority in determining the production and distribution of abortion, were equally dismissed as archaic, hypocritical, and disastrous. Supreme Court Justice Tom C. Clark, writing in the *Loyola University Law Review* in 1969, applauded what he insisted was the right direction for legal change.

The law, lagging behind as usual, began to emerge from its quagmire and rid itself of the archaic restraints on abortion. In 1962, the American Law Institute proposed an affirmative policy declaring that the termination of pregnancy is justified whenever (1) its continuance would gravely impair the physical or mental health of the mother, (2) the child would be born with grave physical or mental defects, or (3) the pregnancy was the result of rape, incest or other felonious intercourse.

Five years after the American Law Institute policy, Clark notes, the American Medical Association reversed its negative policy and adopted the Model Penal Code proposal with only a few revisions.
By the late 1960s physicians, nurses, hospitals, trade union leaders, public health groups, legislative committees, informed citizens—all were speaking out on the urgent need for legal reform. But resistance from traditional

groups meant that the legal change process was slow. Initially, the public had to be educated.

In 1970 a public hearing sponsored by the Michigan State Senate Committee on Abortion Law Reform catalogued testimony presented by 128 persons. In what later appeared as a 461–page volume, different interest groups in the abortion controversy were given a public forum: pro-abortion, anti-abortion, obstetrics, gynecology, radical feminist movement, psychiatry, women's organizations (e.g., Women's Commission, National Organization for Women [NOW]), Zero Population Growth, Protestant churches, public health associations, and social services. Some presenters had no official designation but expressed issues and values that were emerging as part of abortion law reform: battered children; the cheapening of life; high costs of abortion, whether legal or illegal; insurance coverage for abortion; legal restrictions in a revised abortion law; medical risks in abortion; and moral and social reasons for repealing abortion laws. Dr. Molley Lo, a pathologist at Sinai Hospital in Detroit, served as an expert witness, briefing the Committee on medical aspects of abortion. Her appeal for law reform, though, was on other grounds:

Let me hasten to say that the most compelling reason for removing legal restrictions on abortion is not scientific or statistical, but moral or social. Complications of an unwanted pregnancy are frequent and cruel and may result in permanent damage to the life of the mother or the child. They range from the discomforts of pregnancy to the brutal psychologic and physical abuse by an illegal unqualified abortionist; from the subtle rejection of an unwanted child to the violent assaults and even murder of the defenseless child; from the inconvenience of an unnecessary trip to Britain or Japan for a safe abortion, to twenty or more years of burden of raising a child as a punishment for failure of the contraceptive or for one's mistake in life.

Religion was not ignored. The Senate Committee heard a wide variety of Right-to-Life arguments—respect life, the Nazi menace, destruction of human life, playing God in therapeutic abortions, adverse affects of abortion on the mental health of the mother, sacredness of human life, ethical need for physicians to preserve life, and denial of civil rights to the fetus. But the orthodox religious arguments found few supporters among pro-abortion partisans.

Counterarguments were tendered that temporarily silenced religionists: separation of church and state, arbitrary enforcement of abortion laws, and medical control as immoral and in violation of human rights. Because there was an essential lack of public consensus on the matter of personal morality, the orthodox position was interpreted as an attempt to impose a selective set of religious values and thereby uphold women's oppression through the capricious acts of hospital abortion committees who played God over women's bodies. But in imposing a selective set of religious values that supported the traditional triumvirate in its regulation of abortion, religious zealots were, in effect, turning over the decision for motherhood to male legislatures, hospital committees, and theologians.

Not all public debates were as well mannered as the Michigan Senate Committee. The Reverend Howard Moody, senior minister of Judson Memorial Church in New York City and pro-abortion advocate, wrote an angry rejoinder to Terence Cardinal Cooke's abortion policy letter to the Catholic bishops. In light of the Church's decision to banish to "immediate excommunication any Catholic who deliberately procures an abortion or helps someone else to do so," Moody declared an end to the ecumenical movement. Writing in the *Village Voice* (13 May 1971), Moody said:

Now the Catholic position on abortion, as on other social and moral issues, has been known for some time and is not new. What is new is the Church's decision through its Cardinals and Bishops to drop rational discourse and theological debate and go for emotional outbursts and frenzied labeling of the opposition as "baby killers" and "wanton murderers"—what is new is the call for *all-out* religious warfare on those who do not share their religious beliefs concerning abortion. It is shocking that the highest spokesman of the church in this state should use and encourage in his followers the vicious name-calling and despicable sloganeering unworthy of the Christian name.

It was Moody who organized the clergy problem-pregnancy counseling groups, eventually distributed throughout fifteen states, that referred hundreds of thousands of women for legal abortions. As spokesperson for this organization, Moody retaliated against the Catholic position of the protection of the fetus with a counterproposal:

Why does the Cardinal become excited and stir up his Church followers about aborted fetuses when he has never been known to have raised his voice in compassion for the sufferings and deaths of women who, before the law was repealed [New York], were victims of ignorance and malpractice? The Church would hound those women again down the dark alleys of illicit abortions in defense of the fetus and in the name of the sanctity of life.

Whereas Moody defined the abortion issue as a religious crisis—Catholics against all other people—a Michigan clergy leader in abortion reform, the Reverend David Abbot, rejected the religious interpretation and, instead, pronounced abortion to be a privacy issue. "The State should not be in the business of making individual, personal decisions," Abbot emphasized: "Our laws already reflect this attitude in some areas. For example, Jehovah's Witnesses are not required to accept blood transfusions since they believe them to be sinful, but the rest of society is not required to accept their understanding of sin." Even more, said this vice-chairman of the Michigan Clergy Counseling Service, not all Catholic hierarchy are in agreement on this matter. Quoting Cardinal Cushing of Boston, Abbot's position paper to the group said: "We Catholics must recognize the rights of Protestants to their own conscientious beliefs and vice versa. I, as a Catholic, have absolutely no right in my thinking to foist, through legislation or through any other means, any doctrine of my Church upon others." By turning over the pregnancy decision to the woman, a revised abortion law would "respect all the different understandings of the sanctity of life and all religious viewpoints," since there is no inherent sacredness in being born into a situation of "being unwanted, unloved, and inadequately cared for."

As new information and the freedom of choice ideology flowed from reformer groups to non-Catholic church leaders and laity, religious beliefs changed. By 1969 a number of leading religious denominations supported repeal or reform of the criminal abortion laws. The Michigan Organization for Repeal of Abortion Laws listed the following denominations as pro-abortion in their newsletter: American Baptists, American Lutherans, Episcopalian, Jewish, Presbyterian, Quaker, Unitarian, and the Protestant Council of Churches. Others soon followed as the abortion reform issue went to the pulpit, the elders, and church councils. Among the more vocal and liberal clergymen the belief grew that those who view abortion as sinful and morally wrong cannot prohibit the use of such a measure for those who do not affirm such beliefs. Like anti-birth control groups of an earlier period, liberals said, Right-to-Life groups will be "laughed at" for their efforts to legally prescribe their sectarian values.

Fifth, whereas a few physicians could still be heard echoing the "medical responsibility" theme, severely restricting abortion for the woman's—and doctor's good—medical leaders took a more pragmatic approach. Criminal laws controlling abortion were in the process of being changed, either by legislative action or by a decision of the Supreme Court. Physicians will be confronted by a new set of responsibilities, they said, that, admittedly, "few really want" but that most doctors in time will accept. A position paper, this time by the chair of the Department of Obstetrics and Gynecology at the University of Michigan Medical Center, proposed "Abortion: A New Area of Medical Responsibility." As early as 1967, the paper said, the American Medical Association had taken up abortion as a medical issue, rather than relegating it to legislatures and courts. Now, the call was for specifics: safety, type of facility, practitioners, medical protection for the woman, legal protection for the professionals, and medical education in contraception and abortion. Apparently, market decisions played a significant role in this awareness as well. The physician drew on a widely circulated public health report to observe that at least one of five pregnancies, or 31,000 Michigan women, would be seeking abortions once the abortion law was repealed. For physicians to be unprepared, he concluded, would mean to avoid coping with the "multiple problems we will be facing."

Women who die of criminal abortion, a sixth ideological counterattack, are not insane or immoral, but housewives, college girls, working women, and "your daughters and mothers." Reports of the estimates of "back alley" illegitimate operations were circulated, indicating that whereas 1 million illegal abortions had occurred in the United States in 1969, only 8,000 to 10,000 legally approved abortions had been given, despite the liberalization on the law in some states. What reformers could show was that in states where abortion was legal, the maternal death rate showed a "significant reduction."

Wayne State University in Detroit produced the results of a twenty-two-year study of all maternal deaths from septic abortion in Michigan. According to Dr. C. J. Berger, who summarized the findings for the media, from 1950 to 1971 there were 286 maternal deaths from infection—60 percent, or 173, were due to illegal, septic abortion. In 1963, septic abortion was the leading cause of maternal death in Michigan. Another figure, the mean age of women dying of septic abortion in each of the twenty-two years studied, was twenty-seven with an age range of twenty-two to thirty-seven. Most were Protestant, although the ratio of abortion deaths among Catholic women was proportionate to their population. In a dramatic finding, the Wayne State University study showed that deaths among black women from criminal abortion varied between 71 percent and 100 percent of the total, while all of the fatal cases in the past three years of the study were black. This means, said Berger, that more white women in Michigan had gone to New York or other states where abortion was legal, whereas poverty restricted black women's mobility. In a nine-year period (1958–1966) there was actually an epidemic of septic abortion, amounting to 108 deaths. Most women who died were pregnant between nine and fourteen calendar weeks, with a mean of about twelve and a half weeks. And, finally, most deaths occurred among single or divorced women. It is unfortunate, said Berger, but the unmarried woman is usually "more desperate in her need to obtain an abortion."

Death from abortion was depicted in more lurid terms by a member of the Wayne County Medical Society. "What are the risks of a criminal abortion?" he asked:

A recent study of abortion deaths in California over a ten-year period showed that abortion is now responsible for one out of five maternal deaths. Sepsis, or widespread bacterial infection, is by far the most important cause of death, being involved in 55 percent of cases. Embolism and hemorrhage make up most of the rest of the cases. The typical case in this study was as follows: The patient was a twenty-seven-year-old white, married female with five previous pregnancies. She had no pre-natal care during this pregnancy and aborted herself by injecting soap suds into her uterus. The patient was either dead on arrival at the hospital or lived less than two days in septic shock which did not respond to therapy.[2]

Allegations of promiscuity and insanity, labels that once froze illegal abortion clients into silence, diminished and died under the impact of these and other studies. Statistics spoke louder than morality.

Under pressure from reform, the emphasis shifted from a concern over the woman's immorality to the unwanted child's vulnerability and potential criminality. Abortion and child abuse and neglect became linked terms. According to proponents, a law that punishes women who seek to control their own fertility is a law that also produces unwanted children. Society fails on both counts.

A letter from Judge James Lincoln of the Juvenile Division, Wayne County Probate Court, to Michigan legislator and abortion activist Lorraine N. Beebe outlined some of the problems concerning unwanted children that came to his court.

1. Unwanted children become abused children. The rate of increase has skyrocketed (serious abuse has risen from five or six in 1960 to approximately 200 in 1969), and this represents only a fraction of the total. Most cases never appear in court.

2. Emotionally neglected children, most of whom were unwanted children, often become court wards. In this judge's court alone there were 3,000 neglected children in boarding homes and thousands more who were wards of the Court under supervision in their own homes.

3. Unwanted children have weak or criminal characters (Lee Oswald, the killer of President Kennedy, was an unwanted child) and are more likely to be school dropouts and failures.

In a final paragraph, the judge attributed most of the nation's social problems to unwanted children and stressed the impossibility of saving the tens of thousands of these human rejects. "It's like trying to bail out the Detroit River with a bucket. The very structure and fabric of our society is being seriously disrupted by problems that, to no small degree, arise out of unwanted children." No data, however, were presented that supported the relationship between unwantedness and denial of abortion. As pro-life groups offered in rebuttal, many wanted children end up abused or delinquent; many unwanted pregnancies produce beloved children and useful citizens. The judge's implicit claim that it was socially more expedient to prevent these lives from being born in the first place strongly affirmed the legal abortion case. On closer examination, Judge Lincoln's statement bore a racist and classist tinge. When translated into these terms, as black militants did, the "unwanted" often turned out to be the black, the poor, the urban underclass.

Seventh, therapeutic abortion, medically scarce because reserved for what professionals insisted was extraordinary circumstances, increasingly appeared to observers to be merely arbitrary and political. Pro-abortion crusades sponsored by the media in large-city newspapers and prime-time television news broadcast to an entire nation the behind-the-door secrets of hospital abortion committees and how these created barriers to legal abortion. One enterprising woman journalist from a Detroit paper played patient and penetrated both legal and illegal abortion systems. In neither case, she reported, was there much concern for the woman. In her simulated abortion search she said that she confronted delays, high prices, humiliations, professional arrogance, and an absence of medical responsibility.

Once New York State passed its liberal abortion laws, hospitals' machinations, necessary to provide even a modest number of abortions, became increasingly absurd. In one Detroit hospital, months went by without any request for therapeutic abortion. Or doctors refused to play by the old rules anymore. Women were either referred to New York for legal abortion or slipped sideways into the therapeutic system through the emergency room door, where treatment for "miscarriage" or septic abortion would be performed without committee intervention. Sophisticated observers noted that in the first ten months of the new and very permissive New York abortion law (from July 1, 1970 to April 1971), 135,000 legal abortions were done in New York City alone. About 23 percent, or 30,600, were performed in the municipal hospitals, traditional sources of care for low-income women. Forty-six percent of all New York City abortions were from out-of-state, the largest proportion of these from Michigan.[3]

After 1970 the Michigan–New York pipeline was difficult to cover up. Even those physicians who were morally opposed to abortion began to feel that their medical responsibility no longer entitled the prevention of abortion as much as to restrain the patient from having an illegal operation. Catholic physicians often reluctantly referred their patients to local clergy counselors or to Planned Parenthood. Referring to other, non-Catholic physicians might mean losing patients permanently, as well as the strong possibility of consigning women to back-alley practitioners.

Abortion, said a high-ranking member of the Council of the Michigan Society of Obstetricians and Gynecologists, was not an issue of therapeutics or of medical responsibility for regulating traffic. Instead, it was an issue of social class:

The majority of women who get an abortion are not fourteen-year-olds who are raped; they are not eighteen-year-olds who have incest; they are not people with advanced rheumatic heart disease who are going to die if they don't have an abortion—and by the way in my practice they are not poor. In my practice, if you are fairly rich you go to Puerto Rico and get a good abortion. If you are not very rich, you stay around here and get a crummy one, and if you are poor, you have an illegitimate child.

Organized medical opinion began to reverse itself. The Michigan Medical Society issued a statement, dated March 1, 1971, that repudiated the criminal abortion laws. In recommending liberalization, the Medical Society declared that the primary decision for abortion belongs to the woman, and in what appeared to be a radical move, it asserted that consideration of risk entailed the patient's "total environment"—factors such as rape, incest, fetal deformity, parity, contraceptive failure, social economic pressure, and marital or family stress. On fundamentals, though, the Medical Society was conservative. Abortion was to remain "therapeutic" and legalistic. Patients' choice was severely restricted by requirements for in-hospital service, invariably entailing high costs and medical opinions by two other doctors of medicine or osteopathy concurring "in writing" that abortion met the approved conditions. This included informed consent of the husband, if any, or of the parents or legal guardian, if the patient was a minor, and the inclusion of a "conscience clause." This stipulated that no physician or hospital "should be compelled" to perform a therapeutic abortion. Thus buffered, the medical system was to be protected, which eventually opened the door to massive professional withdrawal from abortion service. Medical resistance to patient-initiated service (or "abortion on demand") would eventually evoke a strong counterattack by feminists, who perceived the document as promoting "more of the same"—more abortions, but with the same dehumanized, professional control order.

In a final rebuttal to the pro-natalist contention that criminal abortion laws reflected the will of the people, partisans demonstrated that abortion laws were shaped by historical forces. "What caused a change in the attitude toward abortion in the 1800s?" queried the Michigan Women for Medical Control of Abortion in a 1969 campaign newsletter. Church and state politics, they concluded:

In the 1800's many methods were tried to induce abortions. Poisonous substances were used, in themselves so dangerous as to make abortions more likely to be fatal than pregnancy and childbirth. The subject attracted many quacks. In order to protect women's lives, England prohibited the use of poisons for abortions in 1803. During the 1800's, France was intent on developing a worldwide empire. It was in the interest of both the church and state to have huge numbers of Frenchmen in order to fight the wars, sustain the home economy, and to colonize. There were social pressures: extra pensions for extra children, public ridicule of couples with few children, sermons about one's duty to be fruitful, and so on, to promote larger and larger families. When the discovery of how and when conception takes place was reported in the early 1860's, the ingenious French people who strongly desired to limit family size, developed enough birth controls to cut their birthrate in half within ten years. Outraged at this threat to France's glory and the Church's income, Pope Pius IX in 1869 decreed that any abortion was murder. Thus, abortion which had been practiced for centuries among Roman Catholics and others was suddenly unnatural and ungodly for the simple reasons that abortion was limiting the population growth of France.

Public opinion polls were systematically used; either rejected if they showed unfavorable attitudes toward abortion or widely quoted when demonstrating positive opinions toward liberal abortion. The most persistent use of polls was in highlighting the differences between Catholic Church doctrine and the behavior of individual Catholics. Polls revealed, said advocates, that more than half the Roman Catholics replying were in favor of liberalizing abortion laws. Statistics on women requesting and obtaining abortions indicated that the same percentage of Catholic women obtained abortions as there were Catholic women in the population. The *Detroit Free Press* published national findings in November 1971 showing that among 1,700 adults surveyed, 50 percent said that the decision for abortion should be left to the people involved. Only 6 percent said it should not be allowed under any circumstances. These findings, the newspaper quoted authorities, represented a dramatic change in public attitudes: "As recently as 1968, survey data showed that 85 percent of the public opposed more liberal abortion policies." On the one hand, it was the general loosening of old mores that seemed to be occurring: wide-spread acceptance of birth control and voluntary sterilization. On the other hand, the specter of overpopulation led more than half the respondents to say that government should try to slow population growth. For reformers and their sympathizers, the old ideology had crumbled. Caution and circumspection that once characterized reformers' activities gave way to open attack on the traditional control order.

FEMINIST REACTION

As the abortion movement increasingly became a set of received beliefs, some feminists began to recognize that the compelling lure of legitimacy through law and medicine would offer no alternative to the old mystifications—institutional control over women in society's interest. And paradoxically, they saw that the more the abortion movement succeeded as a one-issue campaign, the more women would lose in terms of acquiring ultimate control over their bodies and their lives.

Already they perceived how the movement had taken a distinct turn: Denial of feminist ideation and images, co-optation of the woman-focused pregnancy counseling into routinized formats of clergy and agency groups, and tokenism of feminist leadership in the abortion movement. These situations stunned and angered feminists. A spirit of resentment arose, fueled by what leaders believed was the feminist movement's capitulation to the original commitment of a woman-centered abortion service.

Since New York's passage of a liberal abortion law, abortion was big business. Entrepreneurs were offering, for a price, referral to fast-turnover abortion clinics, and get-rich schemes were commonplace as out-of-state doctors flew into New York City to perform abortions for a few days a week then returned home to their private practices. Reaction began to build up. Rancor at the social injustice that required women to plead for abortion through medical committees, clergy counseling sessions, and agency referral systems was one expression of their resentment. Another invoked mistrust of established groups altogether, which they felt could not, or more likely would not, put together the necessary innovative abortion service for meeting women's personal needs. Especially among those feminists who had predated the clergy organizers and agencies in counseling and referral work, connecting women through their underground contacts, it was bitter fruit to be shunted to the sidelines. Certainly, there was envy of the superior advantages possessed by affluent professionals who came later but grabbed off the publicity and celebrity status. They begrudged the honor and credit given to reform doctors, lawyers, and clergymen for succeeding in a hostile environment where they had failed. But mainly, they resented their interference and takeover when the issue involved the life and death of women, an oppressed group few had cared about before the abortion issue emerged.

Feminists coveted the autonomy, the freedom from male hierarchies and commands, whether in the abortion movement or out of it. Instead, feminists lamented that they were trapped in secondary positions, lacking the medical, legal, or psychological skills for wresting movement leadership away from male domination. They were sickened at the prospect of Dr. Harvey Karmen, a Los Angeles psychologist and inventor of the Super-Coil, making money off of poor women in experiments with this deadly abortion technology. And they were appalled at the massive contraceptive experiments conducted by U.S.-supported public health or private research groups on Africans and Latin Americans, using suspect or dangerous interventions. They hated the smugness of the temporizers who played the slow negotiator's game; of the indifferent, the women and their daughters who would benefit from repeal but who did nothing to move the cause along; of the remote, those hospital and agency administrators and board members who refused to become involved or speak out against the atrocities of back alley or self-induced abortion. They said "No" to elected officials who displayed little or no social consciousness about abortion as a woman's issue and as a state problem. They were outraged at the media suppression of feminist issues, generally, and abortion events, specifically— marches, lawsuits, legislative and court action. Addressing a radical women's group in Detroit, the irrepressible Flo Kennedy, author of *The Abortion Rap*, protested about media coverage as a whole, which trivialized women and their plight:

Newspapers and nationally broadcast television programs, such as the Today Show, the Tonight Show, and "talk" shows consistently treat women's issues as a joke. For example, the terms "women's lib" were hung on feminists by the male dominated media in an attempt to present them and the ideals they stand for in a derogatory light. Does anyone use the term "black lib" or "Palestine lib?" No, because these are groups with serious problems which must be dealt with. With the women's liberation movement there are serious forces to be dealt with also . . . [but] the Women's Movement is taken lightly on talk shows viewed mainly by women, and the whole abortion issue is generally ignored.

That, along with society's treatment of professionals who attempted to align themselves with victimized women who wish to terminate an unwanted pregnancy, provided evidence of a "heavily aggressive" institutionalized society. Thus, Kennedy concluded, professionals represented the "whorehouse end of prostitute society," where all women are prostitutes—powerless, oppressed, and at the service of men.

Retribution against physicians was a persistent feminist theme. Here is Nancy Hammond, active in Michigan abortion law and medical reform, more moderate than Flo Kennedy but equally angry: "Doctors are conservative, authoritarian, paternalistic, chauvinistic and mostly worry about malpractice suits rather than consumer interests. Doctors simply don't want to be concerned [with abortion laws]."

At a Democratic Women's Caucus in Detroit, the outspoken Bella Abzug linked the issue of abortion with the twin issues of peace and humanity: We can't have one without the others. To the roar and cheering of 1,000, mainly women, participants, Abzug said, "It's because men don't bear children that they can ignore the need for changing the abortion law."

The question was: How to diffuse these radical values of a woman-centered political consciousness and at the same time develop enough momentum for repeal. In their efforts to reach out, feminists soon discovered that black power groups were hostile to their coalition-building efforts. In *Mohammed Speaks*, a male reporter for the Black Muslims found nothing more to say about feminists' efforts to change the law than that feminists "are all sexual deviants working to undermine the family" (quoted in WONAAC Newsletter, 12 January 1972, p. 6).

Another strategy, a feminist-sponsored class action suit, was devised by a group of feminist lawyers active in the National Abortion Action Coalition. This Detroit-based suit, which aimed to demand an injunction to stop prosecutions under the criminal abortion law, argued that criminal abortion laws were unconstitutional, represented an invasion of privacy, violated due process, and produced unequal results: Wealthy women could get an abortion in Michigan and middle-class women could not. The Women's Class Action Suit represented 10,000 complainants, including women who could not receive an abortion in their home state, doctors who were restricted in their practice of medicine because they were denied the right to perform abortions, and social workers who were unable to be fully professional because they had to refuse clients who sought counseling for abortion.

The opposition, calling themselves Friends of the Fetus, were in full force during the hearings, harassing the pro-abortion camp and attacking the credibility of witnesses, including one participating clergyman with the Clergy Counseling Service who had a master's degree in counseling from the University of Chicago. Their presence contributed to giving the hearings some of the atmosphere of a criminal court. Pro-abortion supporters were made to feel that they were on the stand for conspiracy to commit immorality. In some respects, the opposition did less damage than some key witnesses speaking on behalf of the suit. One young woman witness, for instance, embarrassed feminists and reformers alike when the judge elicited evidence of her personal life-style: multiple marriages, divorces, extensive mental health problems, and what appeared as general psychological incompetence. This made the abortion supporters appear to be little more than psychiatric cases, some pro-abortion observers said.

For other feminists, the output of money, energy, and organizational skill for this suit was not worth the trouble. Its immediate effect, though, was to produce a media event, communicating to millions an outcry of injustice against women that was taken seriously enough to earn a respectable legal forum. It took somewhat longer for the presiding judge to assess the evidence and, surprising for most partisans, make a favorable ruling. In the context of the High Court's preparations toward changing the nation's abortion laws, the district judge might have been merely flowing with the trend.

PARADOX AND COUNTERPARADOX

At first, feminists used nihilism to evoke pity, self-abnegation, and a spirit of sacrifice—a turning against the male society among their members. Countermyths were strongly anti-establishment: women against authority, against the nuclear family, against hierarchies, against female subordination. The concept of women as the second sex and as victimized by men accounted for female weakness making them intellectually inferior, physically inadequate, dependent, and overemotional. As a defensive posture, it provided movement cohesion, but it also served to perpetuate the rejected social order. The spirit of denial never really disintegrated but instead was transformed by a positive doctrine. This theory linked abortion and the women's movement into a total revolution in which the body became the overarching symbol for a reconstructed world.

Feminist theorists Shulamith Firestone (1970) and Juliet Mitchell (1966) proposed new frameworks to counteract the traditional male tyranny. Other thinkers emphasized the eternal paradox with which women have had to live. But the paradox is in society, they said, not inherent to women and, as such, part of the structured sex roles within which both men and women live. This is the repetitive and destructive pattern that traps women in a no-win, dependent situation. Biologically rigid sex roles were once necessary for social survival, but now a counterparadox must be developed that makes possible a reshaping of human relationships to transcend the old inequalities. Just as the proletariat must gain control of their production in order to overthrow their oppressors, radical feminist critics insisted, so women must gain control of their reproductive organs in order to overthrow theirs. Casting out sex roles, the cause of the oppression, requires that women must gain total control over their bodies to secure their personal integrity. This includes demands for legal abortion, child-care centers, improved birth control, and humanistic medical care. In the egalitarian age, the new regime offers absolute freedom from the threat of enforced reproduction and childbirth. Writing in a local women's liberation newsletter under the title of "Human Sexuality a la Feminist," a member said:

To make sure that these things are free to all women will come when we decide to make our revolution. Another idea that we can look into can be a modified form of test tube babies. When the egg is fertilized in the woman, it can be removed and allowed to grow in a test tube. Childbirth is simply barbaric, and no woman should be forced to go through with it if they don't have to. This type of growth would allow for both men and women to take on equal responsibilities in the act of child-rearing, and it would make more room for the woman to keep on doing what she wants while the fetus is growing.

Importantly, abortion was not a one-issue movement, but rather the essential stepping-stone to a new harmony of nature and society. The "new age of astrology," reported the Women's Liberation Group of Michigan in April 1971, requires new power alignments:

As Western civilization begins its final phase as the ordered system of life, a new age is being created, partly out of the rubble of the past; but with the emphasis on life in all of its forms. Man, the primary controller of most of the institutions, must begin to realize his false individualism crumble in that he is only partially in charge of his destiny. Women, stepping out of the psychological chaos of her past in which she has too little power, will create her own. The new age will hopefully balance humans with nature in a way harmonious and creative versus the disintegrative and exploitative manner of the past. The connection between all living processes must be integration.

In the final analysis, the abortion movement represented the counterparadox. It was a message that went beyond the good and evil of the current male-dominated order to move society to a "higher plateau." It was a counterparadox inasmuch as involuntary pregnancy symbolized all the injustices and oppressions inflicted on the powerless. This inequality would be overturned once the abortion struggle was victorious. And even if women chose traditional wife-mother roles, the fact of legal abortion meant that such roles require *decision*, not drift or compulsion. Black professionals were particularly prominent during this later phase of the feminist abortion movement and were often featured at rallies, demonstrations, and other public meetings. A black doctor, once jailed for giving illegal (but safe) abortions in Detroit, spoke of the "struggle" as a united effort.

I see this struggle against restrictive abortion laws as an overall struggle for freedom against injustice, against prejudice, against racism, and certainly against sexism, against imperialist war, and a whole broad spectrum of things which we must change, we've got to change in order to make this a decent place to live.

For this physician, mobilizing the medical profession was the essential strategy, making doctors aware of the need for "good comprehensive health care" in keeping with their commitment to their patients. Few feminist leaders believed that this was possible without legal repeal.

"Abortion is a woman's right to choose" ran the banner for what was heralded as the first national women's march in Washington, D.C., on November 20, 1971. The body-focused demands were simple: repeal anti-abortion laws, revoke forced sterilization, and condemn restrictive contraceptive laws. The message was aimed specifically at the Supreme Court, which was scheduled to review the Texas and Georgia abortion cases on December 13 to determine their constitutionality. Hence the emphasis in public statements on "rights." The national emblem, printed on handbills and other advertisements, featured a long-skirted and full-breasted woman posed in a side view with her head thrown back and right arm raised with clenched fist—an image of freedom. The Detroit Women's Abortion Action League, an activist feminist group involved in the November 20 demonstration, also included the women's bill of abortion rights:

Every state in the United States has laws on the books which restrict the right of women to obtain abortions. We believe that all such laws deny us one of our most basic rights—the right to control our own bodies; the right to control our own lives. Restrictive abortion laws provide the basis of legalized murder of thousands of women. Involuntary sterilizations are the price poor women are often forced to pay in order to obtain safe, legal abortions.

Now is the time for all women to come together in a nationally-coordinated effort to win the constitutional and democratic right of women to decide for themselves whether or not they want to bear children, and to control their own lives.

This demonstration brought more than 6,000 persons together across the country in demonstrations in Washington, D.C., and elsewhere. The counterparadox was working. Women were joining together to create the conditions for their own freedom. According to the Women's National Abortion Action Coalition newsletter: "These actions give concrete evidence that women have stepped out of their private agonies and have built a force that is capable of organizing to end the laws which torture and murder women."

In Washington, D.C., the demonstration's focal center, 3,000 persons from twenty-seven states marched on Capitol Hill for the purpose of being counted in the efforts to repeal all abortion laws. The group was given a permit to march past the White House, considered to be an achievement in itself, as most protest groups were denied such permits. The women wore coat hangers to protest the most common form of abortion.

A study of the "typical marcher" by Bobbie Jeanne Deister, then a Ph.D. candidate at American University, revealed that:

1. The overwhelming proportion of marchers were single (74 percent), women (81 percent), between twenty-one and twenty-nine years old (57 percent).
2. Eighty-one percent had participated in demonstrations before, including peace marches (64 percent), women's action groups (12 percent), and abortion demonstrations (7 percent).
3. Nearly everyone (94 percent) knew someone who had had an abortion.
4. Fully 98 percent of the demonstrators said that they supported the women's movement, although most (55 percent) were not members of a women's liberation group.

This demonstration was not solely an American enterprise, nor an issue in numbers. The international women's demonstration had a trial run that same day: 5,000 women in Paris demonstrated for free abortion and contraception and against the position of women in society, chanting, "Work, Family, Country . . . Enough!" In London and in other English cities, New Zealand, Denmark, Austria, and in Vancouver and Ottawa, Canada, women spoke out publicly. A letter from the women's movement organization in Rome, Italy, apologized that they were unable to hold a demonstration on the twentieth but pledged to have one on November 24. "As you probably know," the letter to the New York WOONAAC office read, "our movement is at present mostly concerned with the abortion issue." For feminists leading the Washington, D.C., rally, it was not the number present at the specific demonstrations that counted, but the millions who would benefit from these collective outbursts. One speaker said:

Think of the millions trapped by fear and prejudice who are whispering "Right on Sisters!!" That whisper will become a roar, and these thousands will become hundreds of thousands because this march is proving that women can organize, that we can fight, that we can unite.

To summarize this phase of the abortion movement, feminists were not creating ideology, they were creating truth; it was not error, but a new freedom mythology; it was not illusion, but a revised woman-centered cosmology. In generating their apparatus of truth, feminists were also proposing new forms of power, social formations that were anathema to traditional governing and law groups.

Using abortion as a power wedge, the women's liberation movement took a dramatic leap forward. But in creating this counterparadox, in which woman must be the sole moral agent in choosing her own reproduction with all of its power implications and ramifications, established groups said "No." Instead, reform leaders believed that it was possible to push abortion into the old forms of hegemony. As an integrated, social, economic, legal, and cultural product, abortion would operate solely to reduce unwanted births, especially among the poor and minorities. It could thus reside comfortably in the preexisting medical structure.

Heralding sexuality as the newest civil liberty, a number of liberal Protestant clergymen became actively involved in the abortion movement. In the process their normative theology was brought to bear. Confession, or what clergymen referred to as "problem-pregnancy counseling," brought out a different time-worn truth than that thrown up by feminists. Here the woman's transgressions were featured; her quality of sexual sensibility, her part played in the sexual act, her past, present, and future values, all were on the line. Under clergy control, the feminists' struggle took a distinctly different turn. In their dominion over suffering women, the clergy altered the direction of resentment. Thus, while the organized clergy built bridges between disparate groups—the reformers and the radical feminists—their conception of abortion was eventually limited by the medicalized service delivery model. It was an innovative version, to be sure, yet it precluded and eventually eliminated the world transcendent order proposed by feminists.

NOTES

1. Until the abortion movement, the pro-birth ideology was implicit—part of the commonsense reality of our daily lives. Both social science and the abortion movement directly confronted pro-natalist concepts. But it was feminists who most clearly have articulated the ideological issues. (See, for example, Bolt, et al., 1979, and other selected papers in Freeman, 1979; Bernard, 1972, 1981).

2. Quoted in the Wayne County Medical Society Newsletter, 1971.

3. Quoted from a Michigan director of the Clergy Counseling Service. These data are also available in Pakter and Nelson (1971).

7

Clergy Abortion Brokers

If abortion was to be a genuine choice, a conceptual transformation would be required. This would allow a reorganization of an entirely new sphere of medical knowledge that could possibly revamp the hospital field, offer a new definition of the status of the woman patient, and promote revitalized bonds between medical and community organizations. This is precisely what clergy abortion reformers had in mind.

Before clergy brokers entered the abortion scene, the contrast between an abortion of pathology and an abortion of responsible choice was moot; abortion was a desecration or a crime. Without the clergy movement, any semblance of legitimation of abortion would have been unlikely. For reasons that are bound up with the history of contemporary Protestant Christianity, a selective group of liberal ministers defied traditional church rulings on morality and initiated the institutionalization of abortion.[1]

MORAL ENTREPRENEURS

Whatever its points of theological clarity, the modern Protestant Church is organizationally fragmented and doctrinally disjointed. The multiple denominations and theologies that ride under its banner are, on the whole, local in nature and separated by class, ethnic, regional, and other divisions, although common themes provide some degree of ideological coherence.[2] This structurally loose system, though, is well suited for adaptation, expansion, and change, what the founding father of Methodism, John Wesley, referred to as the concept of "the world is my church." It was no coincidence that the civil rights movement and subsequent protest marches in the South were led and continually fueled by Protestant clergymen and their devotional followers. The "world mission" demanded precisely this entrepreneurial spirit: a willingness to take risks and to organize and manage moral crusades (see Gusfield for analysis of symbolic crusades, 1963).

Early clergy leaders of the abortion movement, although regionally dispersed, tended to be concentrated in highly autonomous situations: university and college health centers, council of churches' social service units, or assistant pastors in affluent suburban parishes. Such locations offered relatively little public surveillance and maximum personal freedom. During the early 1960s some of these same ministers were deeply involved in the protest movements—civil rights, anti-war, women's rights, anti-poverty—as well as in the counseling and teaching of situational ethics and human sexuality. Their involvement later in the abortion movement was thus a logical sequence of commitment to these other ideologies.

What actually induced these religiously trained men to launch a well-organized nucleus of ministers that would eventually expand to fifteen states and two national centers—Washington, D.C., and Canada? How did they rationalize an enterprise that was not only illegal, but, according to the existing religious and secular norms, immoral as well? When the Reverend Howard Moody, pastor of Judson Memorial Church in New York City and the originator of the Clergy Consultation Service, called for a national organization of clergymen for problem-pregnancy counseling and referral, he knew the professional and personal jeopardy involved. Despite these risks, by 1967 many individual clergymen were only waiting for the call.

The first step in creating a clergy consultation service was to place pregnancy termination in the context of some contemporary theological concepts. A crucial concept included the belief that humans have the right, if not necessity, to take life and death questions into their own hands. One university-affiliated minister wrote:

To terminate a pregnancy is not, then, the question of whether or not it is right to terminate a life. Such a question assumes an answer which is itself given *a priori*, or is derived from *a priori* premises. In either case, the question hedges both our freedom and our responsibility. The question is, rather, whether it is more humane to permit that full potential for human life to continue the process of actualization, or whether it is more humane to stop that process.

Assuming that the fruit of sexual behavior bore sin and tragedy, women should not have had to bear the burden alone. But a "male-oriented tradition" forced women to be the sole bearers of responsibility, taking on the "scapegoat" role for the guilt of both the male and herself, and the society as a whole, which was guilty of not facing the whole business responsibly in the first place. A new abortion morality for clergymen was proposed. In the same position paper, the writer said:

It is moral for us to help women seeking termination of an unwanted pregnancy to avoid abusive, unsterile, non- or para-medical services. It is moral to help them avoid the danger of infection, puncture, sterilization, degradation and self-hatred.

It is moral for us to help them in a time of need and crisis to make the most creative and healing decision possible.

The language of moral responsibility now made it mandatory for courageous clergymen to participate in this life-and-death issue.

In Michigan the initial cadre of ten clergymen formed a new covenant involving a second principle, that of mutual support in abortion counseling and reform. Because most of this founding group had been involved with sex and pregnancy counseling for years, the task was not a new one. Rather, the decision to covenant was both spiritual and strategic: It involved a promise to alleviate human suffering and to protect and defend one another in the event of prosecution. Changing attitudes and laws were necessary means to this end. Their covenant read:

We are dedicated to action for modifying and changing attitudes and laws on contraception information and medical procedures, prenatal care and adoptive services for unwed mothers, and all aspects of abortion, including abolition and/ or reform of existing laws.

To accomplish this, Covenant signers agreed, rules and regulations were to specify internal coordination, client confidentiality, shared knowledge, and mutual support in the event that members became involved in civil action or criminal proceedings. No fees or loans were to be exchanged with the counselee, physician, or social agency, although clients could be asked for "gifts" of money in support of the work to help "defer" organizational costs. The reluctance of clients to pay and clergy counselors to demand a gift payment was to become a stumbling block for the entire organization.

Finally, the nature of abortion had to be recast, not as the old personal pathology or as the new women's-centered entitlement, but as a social problem about which society could effect positive change. "Abortion counseling" was a negative term and was systematically abandoned by the clergy consultation group, even if most of the men agreed that this was what they actually did. *Crisis* was the key term to publicize to interested publics and constituencies, including family-planning and other liberal community groups, the nature of the abortion problem as a mental health issue. It was not an abortion service, but a problem-pregnancy counseling and referral service. It was not the women's movement that guided their efforts, but the mandate for religious institutions to mediate in issues of life and death. And it was not individual, or even family, requests for social services that were involved, but the need for spiritual reconciliation.

Ideological contradictions aside, it was primarily a moral issue they wished to articulate more than a legal, political, or medical one. When the clergy spoke with physicians or legislators, they used symbols of life and death, right and wrong, and good and evil, except that such symbols were usually presented in reverse order. Thus, when these reformers identified "life," they meant the woman's life, her options and mental health, not those of the unborn. It was "right" to choose abortion rather than wrongly endure an unwanted pregnancy; and it was "good," indeed a positive outcome, when problem-pregnancy counseling produced a guilt-free abortion. Both the fact of the death of the fetus and the issue of sexual liberation were ignored.

In sum, the clergy entrepreneurs that took up the abortion cause attempted to transform its negative attributes into morally acceptable terms. But the second wave of clergymen who followed the original group were driven less by an ideology of total commitment than by other, more mundane considerations.

CONCEPTIONS OF THE ROLE-MOTIVES, GAINS AND COSTS

Clergy brokers expressed a strong "help" ethic in entering problem-pregnancy counseling. For many, counseling was simply an extension of the pastor's role of professional obligations. For others, it was a new service arising out of social changes, and no other organization was willing or able to grapple with it. For a few, the personal involvement represented the "pioneer" spirit, a breaking of new ground in an area where legal "repression" has stimulated "bootleg" operations. The importance of reducing costs for women, as well as their families, the unwanted child, and the larger society, was supported by the belief that the church must take a position "as advocates for women with problem pregnancies." Almost all involved clergy believed that the service was indispensable. Perception of this "need" entailed a complex set of religious obligations, as these statements of rationale suggest:

I believe that the Church has an obligation to provide the moral and spiritual context in which consideration of an abortion is done. Also, it is essential to provide the best resource if the decision to have an abortion is made.

I'm involved because I want to help girls who have no one else to turn to. Also, I feel the present laws favor the rich and discriminate against those without money and contacts. I think unwanted children are not desirable—to the girl, to society, and probably not even to themselves.

This [counseling] fulfills my need to be a helping person. It helps tragically-trapped women and is a useful way to help my church see themselves supporting a direct ministry to nonmembers.

I believe every child has the right to be wanted. I believe every woman has the right to secure an abortion and should be able to do so where it is legal, medically safe, and as cheaply [sic] as possible.

I continue to see people in terrible turmoil over the problem pregnancy. The length of time I've been involved I haven't yet found other clergymen in the area ready to help.

I want to help those in need. I believe the option [abortion] should be open to all. I do not believe you can legislate morality.

Lack of referral alternatives for women was an overriding consideration. Even when the counselor felt that the work "gets me down," he also recognized that "the job must be done" and that "we seem to be the only ones left to help." The church and local ministries, specifically, had an obligation to move into social problem areas as an extension of their Christian principles and as advocates for women and the unborn.

Professionalism and personal growth were also cited as incentives by many counselors. For example, some counselors emphasized that they moved into this new counseling area to enhance their professional counseling skills, develop new community resources, get needed experience with a range of problem clients, or work more intensively with local community resource groups. Although there was some decline in professional rationales after many months of participation, clergy respondents clearly noted professional and personal benefits.

In one sense, professionalism—expressed as increased skills or greater centrality of the ministerial role in the larger community—became transmuted into another dimension altogether. As counseling began altering traditional views, it opened up new social meanings and opportunities. From the largely closed social world of the parish, the counselor moved into the community, equipped with new insights, an increased awareness of the larger social world, more understanding of conflicting values and deviant life-styles, and greater tolerance for differences. Enhanced sensitivity, in turn, made him more responsive to counselees and more adaptive in his larger ministerial role. Compassion, enlightenment, and increased ability to relate to a larger set of persons and circumstances were definitely primary benefits from participation. Other byproducts included new counseling techniques, increased status with colleagues, and an enlarged network of professional contacts.

Among the first wave of clergy reformers, opportunities were open and ready to be tapped. On every human dimension—moral, physical, economic, psychological, and social—the need was acute, while the available resources for service were few or absent altogether. As the clergy organization grew from its original ten in 1967 to its top membership of 300 clergymen by 1973, the reasons for participation tended to broaden. The protocols returned by sixty active clergy counselors asked the men to indicate their *motives* or "reasons you are now participating" and *gains* or "positive ways the counseling role affected your life." Table 7.1 shows the results of this inquiry.

Table 7.1
Rationale for Participation in Abortion Counseling: Motives and Gains

Rationale for Participation	Motives (n=60)	(% of total)**	Gains (n=60)	(% of total)
Professional	24	40	15	25
Community Service	30	50	9	15
Psychological/ Experiential	10	17	40	67
Political/Legal	7	12	0	0
Concern for Women	18	30	5	8
Concern for Unborn	3	5	2	3
Theological/Church	5	8	5	8
Lack of Organizational Alternatives	10	17	0	0

*Multiple responses
**Percentages are rounded

Four considerations affected clergy participation. First, clergymen drawn into this suspect moral domain were overwhelmingly attracted by pervasive social need, as defined by organizational leaders and their own experiences with local parishioners or counselees. For those who saw the need predominantly in terms of the woman's "problem," two incompatible views emerged: traditional role or liberation ethic. In traditional terms, the woman's problem was believed to be linked to her role as mother, community church member, or "tragically trapped" victim. Here, counseling was an extension of pastoral or professional support and guidance. An opposing ethic viewed the woman's dilemma as the result of repressive laws that prevented medically safe and low-cost abortion. By denying the woman's right to control her body as she morally chooses, the law and medical attitudes created conditions for her exploitation and personal stress.

Second, the more extensive experience a counselor had, the more likely it became that the community service ethic would lose its appeal and be viewed as unrealistic or negative. Although an effective counselor was almost totally dependent on tapping into local community resources for medical and agency assistance, the urgency and repetitiveness of the counseling act undermined the counselor's sense of accomplishment in this "helping" activity, especially when few counselees chose any other option than abortion. Professionalism also declined with a routinized agenda and loss of the earlier pioneer "mystique" attributed to the role.

Third, as increasing agency and law participation in problem-pregnancy counseling no longer made the service a sole community resource for "victimized" women, clergy resentment toward clients increased. This hostility was often open and unguarded at training sessions and other professional forums. The clergy reconciled their work with this needy population by emphasizing that theirs was the only helping resource that offered women in crisis a moral and spiritual context, rather than merely a secular one, in which to consider the decision. As the clergy broker system matured, members also confronted another dilemma: Through counseling and referral in a religious context they were easing the woman's way, thereby helping her to avoid the "hard moral choices." In effect, clergy counselors created a consumers' market for abortion counseling: If they set standards too high, consumers would shop elsewhere.

Fourth, most clergy counselors performed the work for strangers, who may or may not have been believers, and in the process, sometimes violated their own pastoral commitments. Perceived as a one-time encounter, problem-pregnancy counseling depended on a counselor who could quickly appraise the woman and her situation, move her through the decision, and thence into the referral network without moral or emotional difficulty. Negative feedback from physicians, agencies, or abortion facilities about the unsuitability of a client referred for abortion could mean that the clergyman was too hasty, unaware of the client's circumstances, or otherwise ignored signs of ambivalence, conflict, or, less frequently, severe disorientation.

Although an enhanced psychological state benefited many counselors, there were costs of participation, often leading counselors to withdrawal, slowdowns, feelings of anger, impotence, or exasperation. Among the sixty respondents, fully forty-one clergymen experienced personal conflicts ranging from minor irritations to serious moral dilemmas—"feelings of being used"—disruptions in family, professional, or other community commitments; time binds; and anxiety over the ethics of abortion. A few thought their career could be ruined if the "myth" of their "abortion mill" activities were to become known among parishioners or the church board. A persistent question was, Are we promoting irresponsibility among women whose motives for abortion are inappropriate and unjustified? For most clergymen, abortion was supposed to be the outcome of a moral struggle, not merely trafficking in a high-demand medical service. "The easier it [abortion] becomes, the more trouble I have," confessed one counselor.

Yet defections were few; most clergy brokers eventually adapted to the situation, some by reducing the number of counselees, others by cutting the time spent with each counselee (e.g., from one hour to one-half hour). Counselors learned to be nonjudgmental, nondirective, and empathetic, removing the burden of personal responsibility for the decision. A few used group therapy, reducing the amount of time spent. As the movement developed, counselors also "farmed out" routine cases to agency and lay persons, leaving only the difficult assignments for themselves: clients with challenging moral, religious, or sexual problems.

On closer inspection, counseling clergy operated in a four-dimensional world. As problem-pregnancy counselor, the clergyman had two jobs: psychological counselor and social resource person. But as an organizational man in a new health delivery system, his concerns were pragmatic. Questions revolved around routing mechanisms, time scheduling, availability and costs of abortion service, transportation problems, and other financial and logistic arrangements. As minister, he was oriented to community service and the pastoral care of his own congregation, a commitment area that could offer strong competition with service to outsiders, especially if local influentials or church persons took a negative view of abortion. And as a professional, he was concerned with the style, techniques, and organization of the counseling role itself.

But the perceived lack of fit between abortion counseling and the ministerial role was a general problem for many counselors. The scope of the minister's world often lacks a clear definition, inasmuch as spiritual responsibility includes all varieties of social "trouble," without person or place boundaries. Among these clergy brokers, the open structure encouraged movement into new spheres and adoption of nontraditional ideologies (e.g., the feminist ethic) but offered few rules for sorting out priorities or commitments. Being "overburdened," "burned out," or "exhausted." frequent comments from this sample of clergymen, should probably not be interpreted as an individual problem, as much as a structural one. The nearly infinite commitment to "alleviate human suffering in our time" undoubtedly staggered the imagination. This unbounded commitment explains in part why many early organizers devoted as much as sixty to 100 hours a week to abortion-related activities, including counseling, legal reform, referendum activities, teaching, and organizing. The lack of clear boundaries may also be why some clergy organizers abandoned abortion counseling or the ministry altogether for more programmed jobs, including, for a few, the administration of freestanding abortion clinics after abortion was legalized.

ABORTION COUNSELING: THE NEW CONFESSIONAL

Intensive interviews with early clergy organizers and questionnaire returns from rank-and-file counselors emphasized their belief in the primary importance of counseling for the client with a problem pregnancy. Fully 80 percent of the sample believed counseling to be "very important" or "important" for a woman seeking an abortion. No referrals could be given by telephone; all counseling and referral information occurred within the counseling situation, requiring a personal contact with each counselor.

More than half the respondents held to a "crisis client" conception and viewed clients seeking abortion as having "trouble," "guilt," "inability to cope," "extreme moral or sexual problems," and "irrationality." This conception of the client both rationalized the counselors' commitment, especially when other care givers were absent, and psychologized the woman's experience (e.g., "I am concerned with people under stress," or "I want to help those who are struggling with problems created by pregnancy"). Individualizing the woman's problem led to a view of abortion as "traumatic" or one in which guilt, remorse, depression, and negative feelings persisted, sometimes long after the event. And by defining abortion clients as anxious and abortion as traumatic or "like an illness," the moral basis for counseling was established: Counseling was supposed to clarify personal identity and moral values associated with sexuality, contraception, pregnancy, and abortion. Here the counselor "weeds out problems," "picks up faulty attitudes," and "works through consequences of the act" for the future self-concept. In this sense, abortion was believed to have a long-term, even possibly a profoundly disruptive, influence on the personality and the woman's future adjustment. Counseling also promoted catharsis for the ambivalent or confused client, a release from fear and guilt in a confessional-type relationship, enabling the woman to gain insight into herself and her problem.

Finally, counseling permitted exploration of the "reentry" process—a redirecting of "life purpose" and "human potential"—that goes beyond the abortion decision. In this view, abortion was perhaps the most significant choice a woman would ever make. Linking the abortion event to a larger set of existential concerns, some clergymen thought that the woman would be able to establish a new identity and "new roads for the self to travel."

Ideally, the confessional format encouraged openness. It made reconciliation possible by enabling the counselee to work through her loss and trauma. Clergy counselors were conscious of the severe ambivalence they believed beset the problem-pregnancy client.[3] They watched for cues; a woman who spoke of having a "problem" or a "problem-pregnancy" without personalizing it (e.g., as "my baby") was a good candidate for abortion, whereas the woman who asked, "What happens to my baby after the abortion?" suggested a strong contraindication for abortion.

Through counseling, the client was to "discover" the available options—having the baby with marriage, having the baby without marriage, adopting the baby out, abortion, and, sometimes mentioned, suicide—for herself. The counseling process became more difficult, though, as the woman's pregnancy advanced. For example, after twelve weeks of pregnancy, the woman's medical and psychological problems became more acute and counseling tended to be treated either as irrelevant or nonexistent. Counselors often had to rush the woman to appropriate medical care, leaving the counseling to others. Or in other cases, such as in New York City, late abortions by means of saline procedures ("salting out") were provided without the aid of any counseling. Many women were subsequently horrified at the dessicated fetuses they delivered; no one had told them to expect this.

For many counselees going through the broker system, clergy counseling was reported to be one more hurdle before they could secure a name, address, and code number, necessary information for contacting an abortion clinic. While grateful to the individual counselor, most clients felt that it really wasn't the business of these clergymen to ask them personal questions ("after all, he's not my minister"), or that the situation wasn't "right" for the kind of probing that a few counselors insisted on.

As a religiously inspired event, abortion counseling was probably a colossal failure. Too brief for depth and too long for simple information exchange, clergy counseling was modeled, on the whole, after the early psychiatric concept: abortion as a crisis event, requiring extraordinary intervention. Yet many counselors had little more training than that provided by undergraduate ministerial programs; hence their emphasis on "spiritual" and "moral" issues.

The counseling format, with its five options, survived the constitutional changes made by the Supreme Court, and it remains the preferred method in family-planning centers and freestanding abortion clinics. Its primary strength is brevity and adaptability to the range of clients who have already decided on abortion but with the wish to confirm their choice by at least considering other options. Women who experience ambivalence, lack social support for their decision, or suffer from moral or psychological anguish may find the prefabricated format bewildering or even idiotic.

In fairness to the clergy, some counselors did agonize with ambivalent clients on repeat visits, going far beyond the simplistic format. Those counselors most dissatisfied with this new confessional were those who correctly perceived its dangers: an invitation to merely reduce the abortion stigma without moral responsibility for both counselor and counselee and a legitimating device for a medical abortion without medical cause.

The confessional counseling technique was actually a strategic tool, rather than a spiritually based program for clarifying ethics. The counselor-counselee relationship mirrored the forms of male domination that were traditionally found in religion, medicine, law, psychiatry, and the social services. The unspoken agenda: not only will you submit your sexuality to the custody of the clergy, but you will have no sexuality except by subjecting yourself to this regime. This was a regime of sexual freedom with moral strings attached.[4]

ORGANIZING FOR RISK: STRUCTURES OF THE SOCIAL MOVEMENT

The emergence of a clergy problem-pregnancy counseling service was one outcome of what Turner (1957) calls "structural contradictions."[5] These are shifts in public values and morality that give rise to new social demands in a constraining environment. Legal sanctioning is relatively powerless in these circumstances. The clergy abortion broker system, which linked clients to available social and medical services (both legal and illegal), was not a product of a deprivation situation alone. Instead, the social vacuum created by the absence or failure of social agencies and medical-professional organizations to cope with consumer demand for abortion gave free rein to entrepreneurial activity—initially in the illegal or criminal trade and later in the development of a clergy referral network.

Counseling and referral of abortion clients required that the Service act as a social movement, mobilizing resources from legitimate and illegitimate sectors and using them in innovative ways. In turn, mobilization involved a "loose" or fragmented structure that could be adapted to local politics and resources. These were the structural issues: How to diffuse social movement ideology and practice? How to use shifting network alliances to adapt the social movement to new demands?

The *origin* and *growth* to *legitimation* of abortion services represents three organizational phases. These reflect strategies used to deal with the changing elements of risk, including (1) amorphous collectivity—the clandestine operation; (2) segmentary, or decentralized, organization—the visible network; and (3) imperfect bureaucracy—the legitimating structure.

Amorphous Collectivity—The Clandestine Operation

In network analysis the first phase of a social movement organization is often referred to as an "amorphous collectivity." This occurs under conditions of social isolation in which individuals or groups arise to meet special, unmet human needs. These primitive organizational units are unspecialized, perform similar functions, and have no communication with other units or even knowledge of the others' existence.[6]

Prior to the legalization of abortion in, for example, London, California, or New York, individual clergy attempted to cope with the perceived need of "desperate" women with unwanted pregnancy in a totally individualistic manner. The definition was that abortion was illegal, it was "dirty" medicine, and women were harming both themselves and their families by seeking such an operation. For the conscientious clergyman, the options looked grim—early marriage and quick divorce, standard outcomes of a "shotgun" wedding, or delivering the victim to an unknown abortionist. In wrestling with the moral dilemmas, most clergymen confronted with the choice between the woman's need and institutionalized norms took the safer route. Abortion counseling and/or referral was simply too "hot" an item to include in the usual repertoire of clerical duties.

As I indicated earlier, a new breed of socially conscious clergy, generated from a decade of civil rights involvements, community planning, and other citizen action groups, were located in strategic positions where they could exploit resources. With the phasing out of civil rights and the shift to Black Power, along with increased bureaucratization of community planning, some activist clergy found their social niche shrinking.[7] For the "secular" clergy, especially, with no conventional pastoral or sacramental duties to perform, the search for a meaningful role was a significant catalyst for involvement in extra-institutional functions, a feature also noted by Hammond (1966). Sexuality—its uses, abuses, and consequences—became a major preoccupation for some clergy. Counseling women on sexual problems led to a recognition that "talking the situation out" did not resolve the problem of an unwanted pregnancy for a vulnerable or frightened girl or overburdened mother.

Frustrated with the inadequacy of professional services for these women, individual clergy sought more direct measures for linking the girl to medical sources. By 1965, in two Michigan state university religious centers, a series of linkages were forged that tied individual clergy into a network, connecting women to abortionists, abortionists to clergymen, and clergymen to other social or medical agencies. The mode of operation was similar in many respects to the referral system discussed in Chapter 5.

- "Local" or illegal abortionists were located by either direct or indirect contact, such as a "runner system." Women referred for abortions were expected to report back on their experience, providing the necessary feedback on the quality of medical and personal care. One negative report resulted in eliminating that medical "resource" from the list. Assault, seduction, unclean facilities, "hormonal" treatments for "frigidity," and other patient complaints regarding quality of service were common during this clandestine phase.

- Bargaining with abortionists resulted in agreements to send a stipulated number of women in exchange for reduced prices.

- The clients themselves were the primary protection and support for the clergy broker. If apprehended by the police, the woman was told to refuse to give information on any contacts—legitimate or illegitimate.

- University health services and community physicians and hospitals were informally contacted for "repair work" on the post-abortion patient. Because of the primacy of the clergy's sex counseling role, such agencies assumed that this activity was also a routine helping function.

In one university community, three individual brokers—two clergymen and one faculty wife—operated their private lists, "runner-contacts," and

Table 7.2
Abortion Resources Used by Clergy Counseling Service,
September 1969 to December 1970

LOCATION	LEGAL STATUS	TYPE OF SERVICE	PROCEDURE USED	ANESTHETIC	CONDITIONS FOR TREATMENT	ESTIMATED GESTATION AGE	ESTIMATED COSTS FOR MICHIGAN RESIDENTS				EXPRESSED DISADVANTAGES BY CLERGY COUNSELORS
							MED.	AIR	OTHER	TOTAL	
...ltimore, Md.	Legal 1970	In-hospital only	Vacuum Aspiration, D&C Saline, Hysterotomy	General	"Grave physical or mental impairement" of the woman's health, psychiatric evaluation	26 weeks	$700	$100	$50	$850	Cost, psychiatric evaluation, Delays by hospital committee limited number of out-state women accepted.
...thesda	Legal	In-hospital	Vacuum Aspiration, D&C Saline Hysterotomy	General	Consent by husband for married women (notarized letter), Psychiatric eval.	18 weeks	$250-400 $50 (psych)	$100	$50	$450-600	Cost, delays, psychiatric fees
...hicago	Illegal	Office	Vacuum Aspiration, D&C Packing	Local	Clergy counsellor referral only	13-14 weeks	$600 750	$25 car	$25	$650 800	Cost, police surveillance, "dangerous part of town"
...eveland	Illegal				Clergy counsellor	8 weeks	$500	$25 car	$25	$550	Very early termination only mixed reports from on treatment
...y. A		Motel/Hotel	D&C Packing	Local or none		11-12 weeks	$500			$500	Hotel sites unacceptable, reported "botches"
...ys. B		Office	D&C	None	Clergy or physician referral	11-12 weeks	$500			$500	"Harsh treatment", "not cooperative" with counsellees "unsafe" part of town
...ys. C		Office	D&C, Vacuum Aspiration	Local	Black women preferred	8-10 weeks	$500			$500	Police surveillance, limited referral only
...liana-...lis	Illegal	Office	D&C	Local	Clergy referral	14 weeks	$400 500	$15		$415 515	Not indicated
...s Angeles	Legal	In-hospital	Vacuum Aspiration D&C, Saline, Hysterotomy (extra cost)	General	Hospital committee, psychiatric consultation	18 weeks	$400 500	$250	$150	$800 900	Travel expense, psychiatric fees, hospital committee
...n Jose	Legal	In-hospital	Vacuum Aspiration Saline	General	Psychiatric evaluation	20 weeks	$500 600 $50 (psych)	$270	$150	$970 1070	Travel expense, psychiatric fees, hospital committee
...shington	Legal	Office	D&C	Local	2-3 weeks advance appointment	12 weeks	$300	$100	$50	$450	Lack of hospital service, conflicting reports on emotional treatment of patients
...N-USA											
...ndon	Legal	In-patient	Vacuum Aspiration, D&C, Saline, Hysterotomy	General	Routine psychiatric consultation	25 weeks	$500 av.	$500	$100	$1100	Travel outside USA requires relatively elaborate arrangements, cost
...exico ...ty	Illegal	Out-patient clinic	D&C	General	Clergy referral	14 weeks	$400 av.	$300	$100	$800	Out-of-country travel language barriers, reported "exploitation" of women
...erto ...co	Illegal	In-patient clinic	D&C	General	No available information	No information available	$600	$300	$100	$1000	Out-of-country travel, language barriers, refusal to meet competitive price
...kyo	Legal	In-hospital	D&C	No information	None indicated	26 weeks	$800 av.	$1200 (from Detroit)	$100	$1925	Out-of-country travel, language barriers
...ndsor	Illegal	Office	D&C	None	Clergy referral	12 weeks	$500			$500	Surgical pain due to no anesthetic

client feedback system without the others' awareness. Police surveillance, an occasional threat, was controlled by referring to physician-abortionists in other states. Jurisdictional boundaries served to keep the brokers relatively free of legal harassment. Legal risk was also reduced by severely limiting the number of persons informed of the operation. A major task of these early brokers was to establish a list of abortion "resources"—legal and illegal outlets where women could be referred. Although there were vast differences in quality and cost of services, these resources had certain common features: they were expensive, involved additional fees (e.g., referral cost, psychiatrist) and travel out of the state (and sometimes, the country), and were occasionally dangerous and invariably troublesome. Table 7.2 is a partial list of resources used by Michigan clergy counselors in a sixteen-month period, from September 1969 to December 1970.

Legalization of abortion in other states broke the code of silence and generated legislative hearings in Michigan on the abortion law, beginning in 1967. Legislators and reform groups contacted concerned clergy, many of whom became articulate abortion spokespersons. Communication became more open, and referring clergy began to talk of the possibility of duplicating the Clergy Consultation Service in New York—the movement that served as forerunner for state clergy organizations. Individual counseling and referral, while continuing as isolated ventures for almost two years, eventually shifted to a collective effort for more effectively reaching clients and promoting community support.

Segmentary or Decentralized Network—The Visible Organization

The once isolated clergyman became the nucleus for an expanded unit, coordinating local counseling and referral activities. During this organizational phase, the clergy served as moral entrepreneurs, risk takers who broke down traditional barriers to abortion service. They did this by mobilizing community referrals, such as family planning, public and private agencies, university counseling services, and physicians. After securing these social service linkages, early organizers expanded the network by drawing on prestigious professional, university, and community leaders to serve as board members of the Clergy Consultation Service and as general support persons. In a brilliant move, some units neutralized local prosecutors by making "deals," resulting in a policy of "leave well enough alone." In one instance, a clergy broker identified two notorious abortion "rings" for law enforcers on the condition that police would allow the clergy a free hand to deal with reputable physician-abortionists.

Clergy leaders promoted internal cohesion by constructing a moral mandate, the "covenant," in order to reconcile illegal or quasi-legal activity with moral and theological precepts. Later modification of this view presented the woman as victim, with the Service providing necessary moral intervention for what members perceived as inequitable male-dominated arrangements.

Appealing to a transcendent rationale for intervention ("higher laws transcending legal codes"), the clergy promoted a crusader's commitment. Training sessions, a conception of the role as "crisis counseling," and an open-ended counseling schedule that often preempted all other commitments were other mechanisms that contributed to an in-group consciousness. All of these strengthened movement integration.

At the same time, the movement shifted from a disconnected set of activities to a segmental or decentralized network. Connection between units was facilitated by flows of mutual assistance and information. This organizational form used by the broker system had several key features.

Leadership was polycephalous, or "many-headed." Clergy units tended to be regional, autonomous groupings with charismatic leaders who organized a personal following. Survival depended on the leader's ability to secure support from outside groups. By tying local professionals and other members of established groups into independent units operating at the grass-roots level, the movement penetrated the once-formidable barriers of opposition by some resistant health and service organizations. For example, in one university city the leading gynecologists, once unalterably opposed to participation, joined the effort by opening their doors to a limited number of women seeking pre-abortion services (e.g., pelvic examination).

Each segment, or unit, contained but a small number of the range of functions and roles found in the movement as a whole. Specialization of units allowed brokers to influence the local community in terms of specific activities consistent with available niches and opportunity to effect change. This included open counseling and referral activities in a local church, interagency alliances, and legal reform activities. In some areas, brokers pushed hard on agency responsibility for abortion clients; in others, they emphasized legal reform.

Duplication of function and form among a number of groups in any one area was common. Clergy broker units proliferated after the opening of New York clinics and hospitals. As a one-issue movement, participants aimed to cover the state with a duplicative, well-routinized counseling format. This increased reliability of result for the whole movement. Parish clergy who dropped out or moved could be easily replaced by newly trained ministers from other areas.

Variation of cell type existed with varying degrees of permanence and with different and conflicting views of ideology and commitment. Some individual clergymen perceived the problem-pregnancy counseling role as a natural extension of the pastoral function. Alternatively, other clergy participants viewed the activity as the "cutting edge of social change," commitment to victimized women, opportunity for increasing professional expertise, or a way of helping to resolve personal, sexual, or family dilemmas. The duration of participation by clergymen varied by mode of recruitment (whether personal friend or professional associate); strength of personal and professional ties to social agencies, physicians, and other "helping" sources; and personal ability to resolve moral and ethical contradictions. Mobilizing support was related to developing a palatable argument for abortion. In convincing agencies, physicians, and church groups of the "need" for women to have access to a moral-religious source of help, the clergyman convinced himself that the Counseling Service was indispensable.

Leadership was often situation-specific and hence ephemeral. Some clergymen who proved themselves effective organizers during the clandestine or early organizational phase were either "burned out" or unable to continue because of pressure from their church hierarchy, because of financial hardships, or because of leader-follower conflicts. "Secular" ministers, especially, may have found the lure of opportunity in the larger society too strong to resist. Two leaders of large cells abandoned their posts for more lucrative, private employment.

In the absence of a central or unifying force, organizational fission and fusion occurred. Segmental units in the clergy movement split into regional cells, with further cleaving of regions into city, suburbs, and towns. Reproduction of the fissionary structure provided a loose network that spread across the state. Geographical and organizational separation often resulted in each man "doing his own thing." There was neither an overarching organizational mode of control, nor a systematic method for accountability of the individual, or even the unit, to the movement as a whole.

Fusion, or the coming together of autonomous units, was especially pervasive once the right-to-life or other "friends of the fetus" groups erupted into counteraction. This mobilized even clergy-isolates to take action *for* the Service *against* these anti-abortion forces. Clergy groups also coalesced in response to the activities of paid referral groups located in metropolitan areas. Referral-for-profit was big business in Michigan and in other states where abortion was illegal, with an estimated one-half to two-thirds of the market absorbed by these commercial outfits. But despite a unified front by the clergy, the movement was unsuccessful in limiting these profit operations. Decentralization within the movement and loose coalitions between the movement and outside groups may have accounted for the movement's lack of effectiveness in this area.

Network linkages between units formed a loose confederacy. Unit autonomy made for equal status among members during this organizational phase. Leaders represented their units as the "first among equals" but not in a hierarchical sense. The confederacy model was maintained even while the organization adapted to exigencies created by changes in the national and state abortion scene. For instance, a central unit in Detroit organized statewide clergy training sessions and membership recruitment. Coordination of the movement with other non-movement state groups was also handled through this office. By purpose and practice, the central cell limited its influence to a facilitating role.

External movement conditions, however, intervened to transform the central unit to a directing unit. For instance, to facilitate maximum bargaining in negotiating favorable market conditions for out-of-state patients in New York facilities, movement leaders were required to keep in close touch with the National Clergy Consultation Service located in New York. Ties with this group were further reinforced by connections with national and state legal reform groups. The "super-unit" in Detroit, serving originally as a clearinghouse for information, advice, and minor support sources, increasingly assumed the role of movement spokesman and, eventually, movement regulator.

Overall, the segmental system provided an adaptive organizational instrument for penetrating into a variety of social niches. Expanding the referral web involved tying in a variety of individual clergy, church denominations, professionals, and other established groups. In recruiting from a broad cross section of clergy and social agency personnel, training sessions laid the groundwork for institutionalizing the movement's five-option counseling format. While ideology stressed counseling, effective organizational practice was designed for abortion *referral* to out-of-state sources. (One clergyman reported that only two of his 900 clients opted *not* to get an abortion.)

Some clergymen were deeply disturbed over their participation as abortion brokers. Unresolved personal dilemmas in the ethical-theological and psychological areas were one outcome of the segmentalized structure. Infrequent contact between some clergy counselors, with high occupational autonomy among these ministers, created idiosyncratic responses to dilemmas as well as contradictions in practice. Unresolved dilemmas, in turn, undermined organizational goals. Screening out "objectionable" cases (e.g., the teenage girl), cutting back on counseling time, and failing to keep reports or contribute financially to "central office" were counterproductive activities for the movement. Such behavior, though, was an attempt to resolve the contradictions that counselors felt between their attitudes and their actions.

Imperfect Bureaucracy—The Legitimating Structure

The movement's success in invading medical and agency spheres led social service agencies, in time, to rely increasingly on the Service to take over the mass of their problem-pregnancy or "crisis" clients. Reform activities, too, were highly dependent on local counseling clergymen to spread the good word by speaking engagements, person-to-person contact in the community, and organizing lay counseling and referral groups. Arrangements with New York facilities and other out-of-state referral sources required a centralized staff to expedite the interstate business. Activists in the largest funded office gradually began concentrating power through hiring paid staff and introducing such bureaucratic practices as accountability, setting up efficient work loads, and centralizing funding.

The movement organization shifted from units of equal power to a two-level operation. Superimposing this "central" unit on the natural, loosely structured organization entailed transferring a larger number of decisions to this higher level. As yet, no unity of command or strict hierarchy existed. In this "imperfect" bureaucratic structure, the executive board *appointed,* *concurred,* or *consulted* with unit coordinators, with the directing function unobtrusively maintained. In effect, however, most decision making was concentrated in the central office.

Some units resisted bureaucratic centralization, even in this modified form. Individual clergymen reported that, although organizational changes in this direction were undoubtedly essential for efficiency and meeting new organizational demands, the Service had undergone negative changes. Clergymen complained that new recruits were less dedicated; the addition of non-clergy counselors, such as feminists and social agency persons, diluted the moral purpose; political activities interfered with the main thrust of the organization (i.e., counseling); and the tendency grew for many counselors and the public to see the Service as abortion referral rather than as "crisis" counseling.

Bureaucratizing efforts, however, had less to do with internal movement conditions than with changes and pressures from outside the movement. Centralization was probably adaptive at this phase of organizational development for five reasons:

1. The Service had legitimated abortion counseling and referral. The primary, decentralized structure, which initially extended the referral web, succeeded in making this abortion service (or a phase thereof) a necessary part of many social agencies' agendas. Strong personal commitment and flexible adaptation to rapidly changing local conditions, features of the segmental structure, were less significant as legal abortion became more available. Coordinating efforts with the legislature, courts, and state and national reform groups became more important and required unity of leadership for maximum impact.

2. The two-level organization (local unit and central control unit) could maintain the primary function of counseling and referral at the local level and at the same time move into new programs, as in implementing economic and political changes in preparation for the new abortion law. In this way the movement promoted diversity of purpose without abandoning original goals.

3. The once formidable barriers of resisting physicians, reluctant agencies, and hostile law enforcement groups had been largely broken down. Entrepreneurial action moved to new phases, as in a proposed patient-advocacy role, controlling the abortion market after legalization, and making alliances with representatives of powerful established groups—hospitals, legislature, courts. Bureaucratic channels were more useful for activities of this sort.

4. A corporate structure facilitated professional and agency control at a time when many long-term volunteers had exhausted their personal and social resources. In any movement that aims to mobilize citizens at the grass-roots level, there may be a normal phasing out of former leaders as the movement takes hold and becomes part of the mainstream.

5. Finally, organizational visibility, possible in this modified centralized organization, could be more effective in furthering goals after basic ideological themes and citizen awareness of the issue had been widely circulated. The acceleration of the "natural" organization into a bureaucratic structure consolidated gains even as it partially rigidified local efforts. As a basically one-issue movement organization, it had to re-adapt to changing circumstances if its goal of legal

reform were to be realized. The preoccupation of local units with processing clients inhibited extension into new broader spheres of activity. A central unit, relatively free from this dominant counseling function, could move into other spheres of activity and work toward achieving the new goals of the movement.

PROCESSES OF CHANGE IN SOCIAL MOVEMENT STRUCTURE

Moving from an early advocacy role to the later community resource function involved profound changes in the larger environment. How did the clergy broker movement adapt its structure in response to change? We can consider each phase as a separate time unit.

Amorphous Collectivity—The Clandestine Operation (approximately 1963 to September 1969)

Units were single-member and disconnected from one another; that is, there was an absence of communication. Despite the counselor's moderate control of the market, achieved by playing off one medical source against another, counselors carried the primary load. While social or university agencies transferred "problem" clients to clergymen, they operated in a clandestine manner to avoid legal jeopardy. Lack of effective linkages between the counselor and other referral groups made for weak bargaining power with illegal suppliers. High costs of service for patients and counselors were typical in this abortion system. Figure 7.1 plots this network form. Not shown here is a later variation of the isolated unit, in which a "runner" negotiated arrangements between clergyman and abortionist.

Segmentary Network: The Visible Organization (approximately December 1969 to 1973)

In the segmentary network, units were decentralized, split up by regions, cities, and towns.[8] Typically multiperson units, each unit generated its own sources of extra-movement aid or support (e.g., professional, community, or church groups). Interunit linkages were forged by ideological commitment and a consistent counseling format. Reaction to opposition provided the strongest source of movement cohesion. Information, advice, or legal aid flowed from the central unit (in Detroit), which served as a clearinghouse to local units.

Alternating phases of movement cohesion and division occurred and may be clarified by the model of "structural opposition" developed in political anthropology (Epstein, 1958; Mayer, 1962, 576–592). This model shows the shift of movement structure as it operated in different action spheres: social movement, community groups, profession, and denomi-

Figure 7.1
The Isolated Cell Type

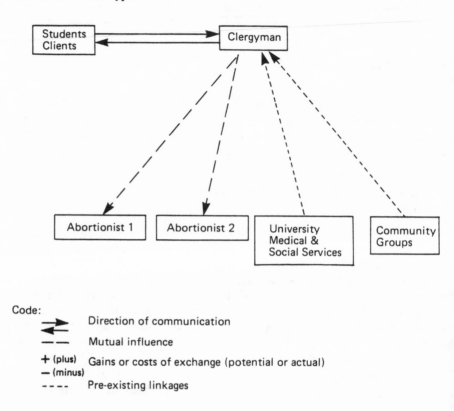

Code:

⇄   Direction of communication

——   Mutual influence

+ (plus)   Gains or costs of exchange (potential or actual)
— (minus)

- - - -   Pre-existing linkages

nations. Processes of fission and fusion imply that segments divide, or split, in competition and relink in alliance. When abortion was defined in terms of an ethic of personal-moral choice or as a mode of family planning, clergy brokers united to form a solidarity group opposed to major opposition groups (anti-abortion organizations, conservative legislators, community resistance, etc.).

Internal movement division, however, was built into this segmentary structure. On one hand, participants had local community memberships tying them to parishioners, church board members, other churches (including Catholic), and professional groups and associations. Among these were groups and persons opposed to both abortion counseling and legal reform. On the other hand, units tended to vary. There were differences in community alliances and law enforcement practices, varying degrees of professionalism and counseling skill, unequal individual commitments, and

Figure 7.2
Social System of the Clergy Counseling Service

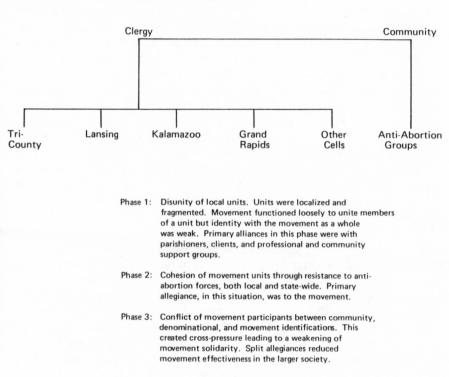

Clergy   Community

Tri-County   Lansing   Kalamazoo   Grand Rapids   Other Cells   Anti-Abortion Groups

Phase 1: Disunity of local units. Units were localized and fragmented. Movement functioned loosely to unite members of a unit but identity with the movement as a whole was weak. Primary alliances in this phase were with parishioners, clients, and professional and community support groups.

Phase 2: Cohesion of movement units through resistance to anti-abortion forces, both local and state-wide. Primary allegiance, in this situation, was to the movement.

Phase 3: Conflict of movement participants between community, denominational, and movement identifications. This created cross-pressure leading to a weakening of movement solidarity. Split allegiances reduced movement effectiveness in the larger society.

a range of counseling styles. In addition, denominational loyalties differentiated one clergyman from another. Resistance to abortion reform by some denominational leaders generated conflicting pressures for participants. These conditions kept units localized and fragmented. In this way the cohesion among units based on movement ideology and practice was offset by opposition between units (or members within the unit) because of differences in local identification and opposed interests. Figure 7.2 plots the "social system" of the Clergy Counseling Service.

For the most part, units were characterized more by variation, especially in the earliest development stages, than by homogeneity. The segmental structure fostered different unit types to fit local circumstances. Three major variants may be noted.

Atomistic cell type. Clergymen, isolated geographically or socially, tended to meet local parish and town demand for counseling services by extending pastoral duties to include this extra counseling load. The personal network, whether few or many linkages, was drawn from local groups who provided professional backup. This limited the clergyman's influence to a few immediate support persons, clientele, and their families. The unit was unconnected to other movement units or to state abortion reform groups. Geographical isolation, especially, limited alignments to local groups.

Mailings and telephone contact with the central unit clearinghouse provided information and minimal assistance. Fear of alienating local support and dependence on local resources made for unbalanced reciprocity in transactions between counselors and outside groups. The result: The atomized units tended to discourage an open-door policy because costs of delivering services were personally and structurally too high.

Unidimensional type. Activity among participants was limited to a single-purpose activity (i.e., counseling and referral). A few individuals within the unit occasionally were involved in speaking engagements to community groups or in other reform activities, but there was no systematic division of labor to increase movement influence. The single-stranded net (i.e., single purpose) was loosely knit, with commitment primarily to clientele; the pastoral mission extended to include non-parishioners. Local loyalties played a more significant role than identification with movement ideology. Each counselor maintained his own list of referral physicians and social service agencies. While this created high redundancy, or duplication of efforts, it also served to widen the total number of community groups contacted for support. In this way the movement ideology spread.

Extra-movement linkages and alliances resulted largely in one-directional flows of energy, assistance, influence, and decision making from the unit to outside groups. This "influence flow" was asymmetrical and favored community groups that shifted the burden of responsibility to individual clergymen. Costs for counselors included overwork, shortcutting other activities, reduction of time spent with family or in leisure activities, and expressed frustration. These problems lowered morale and fostered high turnover or reduction of counselee load.

The loosely knit unit was also more vulnerable to outside attacks. For example, a clergyman prosecuted for ostensibly sending a client to an illegal and nonmedical source for abortion was virtually cut off from member support. In violating the Covenant, or written agreement forbidding in-state illegal sources, he exposed all members to legal jeopardy. The combination of a high-risk situation and relatively fragile bonding between participants required a higher measure of conformity to movement norms if mutual assistance was to be maintained.

Multidimensional cell type. For a few favorably located units established in select niches (e.g., university community or cities with crusading reform groups), movement activities took multiple forms. In these settings, abortion counseling and referral was an added element bonding participants linked by shared religious, professional, ideological, and friendship activities. As autonomous professional persons, each movement participant had his own special area of expertise, yet he could also "fill-in" in a colleague's absence. Non-parish clergy were particularly free to innovate. The personal network was expanded to include contacts with a variety of non-movement professionals, such as in church, school, agency, medical, legal, and reform groups. This permitted maximum influence in key establishment or reform centers with wife, protégé, or new participant also enlisted to assume administrative roles, freeing the organizer for other operations.

This unit type sponsored the highest number of militant, action-oriented, and administrative activities. Typically, leadership was a revolving one, with power largely shared among equals. High autonomy of the unit allowed for rapid changes to meet local conditions. For example, one of the larger units phased out of business altogether because effective coalition building among local service agencies and feminist groups had generated a woman-centered community structure that could stand alone.

A type of balanced reciprocity emerged in exchanges between this unit type and outside groups. Strong support from family-planning projects and other agencies and professional groups allowed for more equitable distribution of the counselee load. In this situation, movement participants were most likely to view the movement as a "progressive" and "legitimating" influence. Members tied into this multistranded (or multipurpose) unit were the most successful in maximizing individual and professional goals, while extending movement ideology and practice into a variety of social spheres. Figure 7.3 summarizes the three identified cell types in the segmentary network.

Imperfect Bureaucracy (approximately September 1970–1973)

Stage 1. Lack of unity because of local autonomy and cell fragmentation persisted, but a super unit assumed some centralizing tasks. Chief among these was coalition building on the state level. The modified hierarchy (board, paid director, and state coordinator) became spokespersons for the movement as a whole. Extra-movement linkages and alliances established viable relations with established and reform groups, enabling the movement to expand influence. During the early phase of centralization, statewide reform efforts concentrated on movement activities. Leaders brought pressure to bear on legislators, physicians, denominational hierarchies, and other professional groups.

Successful penetration of movement norms and standards into the larger abortion movement generated a series of links in a proliferating chain of influence and communication. Boundaries between "believers," supporters, and participants were greatly blurred by introducing lay and professional agency persons into the counseling role. "Fellow-travelers" of both

Figure 7.3
Segmentary, Decentralized Network

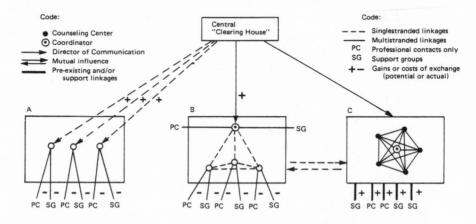

A=Variant 1:   Atomistic unit)(no intra- or inter-unit linkages)

B=Variant 2: | Unidimensional unit singlestranded (or single-purpose)
                linkage between cells and transactions between members
                of the cell and outside groups. [

C=Variant 3:   Multidimensional unit, multistranded (or multi-purpose)
                activities) linked a significant number of members. Pre-
                existing linkages with outside groups by one or more of
                the movement participants generated support for the
                entire unit.

sexes from a variety of occupational groups rallied to the movement's
defense against anti-abortion forces. In this way the extended network may
be said to have been "unbounded," or one that expanded throughout
society. Figure 7.4 maps the structure of interlinkages between the Clergy
Service and other state and national reform groups at the high point of
this organizational phase.

Stage 2. A citizen drive to bypass the stalemated legislature by putting
abortion reform on a proposed referendum upstaged the clergy movement.
Impetus for reform shifted to political action groups dominated by physicians, legislators, and volunteer women. Eventually, there was a slow-
down and gradual contraction of the clergy/counselor phase of the
movement. For instance, during the last few months of operation before
the Supreme Court's 1973 decision (November-December 1972), clientele
contributions steadily decreased, a perpetual deficit existed in the state

Figure 7.4
**Types of Interlinkages Between the Clergy Counseling Service
and Other State and National Reform Groups**

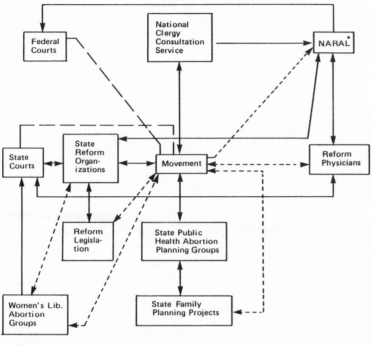

*National Association for Repeal of Abortion Laws (N.Y.C.)

Code:

———— Mutual Membership Groups
———— Mutual Aid
- - - - - Direction of Communication
— — — Indirect Linkages Only

board's budget, and movement leaders talked of "phasing out" after legalization. In triggering abortion reform, the movement served an essential stopgap function in providing partial abortion services and alerting citizens to this social need. Final discharging of the mission was carried through by other state and national political forces.

The abortion network created by clergy brokers formed an innovative structure that was based on medical guidelines but without the medical structure. It was intended as a means of transforming medical care and social services to reflect new demands and public perceptions of inequality. The movement grouped all abortion experience into the category of mental health problems—the better to legitimate it. In doing so, it performed a paternalistic role, shaping the way abortion was defined and addressed in male terms: as a female crisis, a woman problem, a deviant act. Thus women negotiating the broker system ran the risk, according to the play of clergy-manipulated chance or skill, of winning or losing in illegal and medical markets.

As a legitimating umbrella for eventual medical control over legal abortion, the broker structure silenced dissident clergy and feminist voices. Originally relegated to the sidelines where neither morality nor personal experience counted, the medical field eventually imposed a language and practice that was to identify abortion with marginal medicine, a half-legitimated place.

NOTES

1. Sources for this chapter are taken, in part, from eighteen months' fieldwork in six Michigan communities (January 1971 to June 1972). To study the counseling clergymen's role in legitimating abortion service, I interviewed twenty-nine clergy participants involved in counseling abortion clients and/or in leadership positions, with the average interview time between one and a half and four hours. Four of the informants provided two or more interviews. Informal contact included participants' observation in clergy-related activities (e.g., board meetings, training sessions, counselor-client interactions). A mailed questionnaire, randomly distributed to 105 members of the Clergy Service (with 57 percent returns), asked for changing network affiliations over the problem-pregnancy counseling career. I also collected documents, newsletters, and personal memoranda that were useful for analysis of the organization.

2. Protestant history, church structure, and doctrine are examined by Marty, 1972; Miller, 1971; and Leonard, 1961. The phenomenon of the secularization of history and its impact on a "nonreligious Christianity" (e.g., the "death of God") is offered by Shiner, 1966, and Berger, 1967. Much of the ferment of modern Christianity, including commitments to human existence as a subjective reality, not objective law, is supported in the work of the influential spokesperson of the "new theology," Paul Tillich (see Adams, 1965). The focus of this secular theology is not only in debunking traditional doctrine, but also in a positive concern for the pluralization of culture and theology. This orientation helps to explain the "nonreligious" calling of certain of the earlier leaders of the Clergy Consultation Service. In this analysis, abortion is a spiritual crisis, not a matter of doctrinal right and wrong.

3. Mental health centers from 1969 to 1972, critical years for abortion counseling and referral, saw few patients with abortion "crisis." That term was largely seen by mental health professionals as an artifact of the movement, rather than as an accurate description of a patient type.

4. Rokeach (1970) argues, on the basis of a national study using the Rokeach Value Survey, that a negative relationship was found between religious values and social compassion, a relationship strongest for Protestant groups. The general picture that emerges from Rokeach's study is that those who place a high value on salvation are anxious to maintain the status quo and are unsympathetic to underdogs, nor do they want the church to become involved with social and political issues. Churches use their value systems to rationalize individual self-preoccupation and withdrawal from worldly concerns, Rokeach concludes. Do the clergymen in

my sample run counter to this general charge? I believe the Service was severely divided, both ideologically and structurally, but that the overall impact was meant to be a compassionate soul-saving operation. The effect, however, was to impose male conceptual models and hierarchies on the emerging legal abortion field, thereby crowding out the possibility of a genuine woman-centered procedure.

5. This section is adapted from Davis, 1975.

6. In one sense, this phase of activity, that of meeting local demand conditions, provides the preconditions for the emergence of a social movement. In Blumer's (1951, 167–222) conception, these changes are part of "cultural drifts" or the groping, discoordinated efforts that provide the background out of which the movement develops. Blumer holds that, at this stage, the movement is unorganized, with neither established leadership nor recognized membership. Individual lines of action based on individual decisions and selections are characteristic of this period. See also Ash, 1972; Zald and Ash, 1966; and Smelser, 1963, for discussion of social movement development.

7. The concept of "*niche*" and transactional behavior used in this section is taken from Barth (1963). A niche is the position occupied by an individual or group in relation to resources, competitors, and clients.

8. This segmentary type of network formation characterizes a variety of social movements (Gerlach and Hines, 1968, 23–40).

8

The Crisis Client Network

In a matter of only a few years, clergy counselors became the link between the woman and abortionists, licensed physicians supplanted illicit or quack practitioners, and public health analysts documented the decline in maternal and infant health, replacing police reporters and coroners. But separating the old and new modes of operation proved more problematic than anticipated. Because a moral justification for intervention, especially among family-planning and organized clergy reformers, was required, the woman came to be viewed as a victim. "Crisis client" became the unifying code that tied clergy and agency advocates and their supporters together. After all, the reasoning went, if women have "problem" pregnancies, then they must be in crisis—an unwanted and abnormal state of affairs. Implicit in this view was the notion that women were incapable of controlling their own reproductive functions; hence their private pathologies necessarily became converted to public problems. Women seeking abortions in this context became "patients," or "counselees," rather than unencumbered information seekers.

Confession, a feature of the traditional morality, was used as a consensus technique. By telling all—how they became pregnant, with whom, with what degree of sexual involvement or love, their sexual dreams, and mismanaged plans—women could be relieved of their unwanted burden. The confession format, outlined in Chapter 7, offered an apparently liberated discourse. It absolved the abortion seeker of the sexual sin, without repentence or sorrow, and it exonerated the willful rejection of the fetus in advance of the deed. Penance came later—after the abortion, after the disappearance of the network supports. Because there was little or no psychological follow-up and an almost total absence of discussion among women who had experienced abortions, many women were forced to mourn alone for what only later they came to recognize as a significant loss. For some women, it was not always or only the loss of the baby, sometimes manifestly grieved over on a monthly or yearly basis ("today the baby would be four months," or "three years," or "twelve years"), but the protracted loss of belief, the injury to innocence, the privation of moral isolation, the bereavement of a way of life. Neither protected by the patriarchal buffers nor free to self-determine her own existence, the crisis client was a transitional figure created out of political necessity by a naive and cynical movement leadership.

What did the movement network offer to the hundreds of thousands of women who made it through the complex routing? In what way was the experience transitional, incorporating features of the new and old system? And how did the women respond to what some human service advocates preferred to call the "enlightened service delivery" system? Before turning to the women's self-reported experiences, we need to know how this evolving system integrated both repressive and liberating features.

First, it took abortion out of the kinship and family group matrix and turned it over to the individual. Here for the first time on a vast scale, women were treated as responsible agents, both for their own sexuality and the resulting products, whether venereal disease, raising the child (alone or in marriage), or rejecting the child through abortion, adoption, and, less publicized but increasingly visible, child abuse or murder. The role of the family as the anchor of control and support receded, sometimes disappearing altogether. Women sought their abortions alone or negotiated with clergymen, agencies, professionals, friends, small loan companies, and other non-family persons, often concealing the facts of the abortion search and event from parents and other intimates, which occasionally included the putative father. Moral, social, and psychological isolation were built-in features of the new order.

Second, the network normalized sexuality by making distinctions between sex and procreation. Sex was good; unplanned or untimely pregnancy was not so good; or worse, it was dreadful. Because an unplanned pregnancy disrupted the woman's life, it prevented the full realization of her potential and deprived her of basic rights: the right to life, to control of her body, to health, to happiness, to satisfaction of needs, and, especially, the right to discover her personal goals and aspirations. Once a woman found her way into the abortion network, caretakers presumed that she needed an abortion, rather than considering the possibility that she sought to understand the pregnancy as an integral part of her life project.

In a third move, the network dispersed the old legal and medical power centers and created an entirely new web of relations. Here lawyers and physicians played the minor roles of consultant, technician, part-time advocate, and, invariably, opponent. New occupations arose in the power vacuum—abortion counselors, freestanding clinic administrators, and operating room nurse advocates. The deference order was eliminated. In a

management style befitting a conception of the doctor as medical technician, attending doctors were reduced to a first-name basis and were openly
criticized for sexist and hierarchical manners. In some abortion clinics, the
counselor-advocate, herself an ex-abortion patient functioning in a low-
paid, high-energy, demanding role, dominated the scene. By hiring and
firing doctors, threatening strikes when physicians and administrators failed
to fall into line, taking the woman's side in disputes, treating the service
as strictly a market product (physicians as providers, women as consumers),
and denouncing cost-benefit considerations, these feminist advocates designed a reversal of the traditional order. This annexed medical power
served as the foundation for the feminist health collectives that rapidly
sprouted in the urban environment after 1971.

The next and fourth change—the loss of secrecy—had a volatile outcome.
On the one hand, the open sex and abortion talk by clergy and agency
staff aimed to remove the fears and anxieties associated with criminal
abortion. Abortion was declared a medical event within this new regime,
and providers could thus offer a rational solution to a problem pregnancy.
Secrecy, anonymity, and privacy, all features of the illegal system, were
abandoned. The new system demanded openness, discussion of options,
and a conscious evaluation of decisions among the concerned parties (viz.,
the woman, husband, lover, parents, intimate friends). The abortion event
was altered from a clandestine, dirty act to a "maturing," "sobering," and
"emancipating" experience within the rhetoric of respectable medicine or
mental health care. On the other hand, loss of secrecy induced fears about
how to control what abortion seekers believed was contaminating information; yet failure to play by the new open rules prompted guilty reactions.
Not telling parents represented a retrograde act, yet many women believed
that the telling could be disastrous: loss of college tuition and other financial
supports, forced abandonment of the often cherished good-girl image, and
a disquieting sense that parents would be unforgiving and unloving when
they discovered their daughter to be, after all and fundamentally, a
transgressor.

The demographic situation, a fifth transformation, had undergone change
after 1970, once the abortion laws were substantially revised in New York
State and elsewhere. A larger proportion of pregnancies were terminated
by abortion, rather than resolved by marriage or adoption. Most abortions
were performed on single rather than married women, and both the younger
and older women were most likely to end a pregnancy than to carry the
child to term.

This public health data, quickly released to a confused public and resistant medical groups, helped to generate a new, opposing abortion mythology. According to this anti-abortion myth, the kind of women getting
abortions, while not "whores," were undoubtedly promiscuous women
basically undeserving of social protection. Certainly, they were careless

and disruptive, making a mockery of appropriate sexual conduct: "She who plays must pay." Instead of rewarding mature women who conscientiously practiced family planning, this new abortion scheme rewarded contraceptive failures—those who used abortion after the fact as an irrational solution to a rejected conception. In a final denunciatory statement, opponents disclaimed what they perceived as an overly permissive state of affairs. It encouraged recidivism—abortion repeaters who had no shame in publicly announcing their sexuality and their indifference to traditional norms and life-styles—and it severely reduced the moral significance of marriage and family. In this contentious and tumultuous environment, women sought, and often successfully resolved, their unwanted pregnancy with varying degrees of difficulty.

THE SEARCH FOR AN ABORTION

Multiple routes had been opened for abortion seekers, yet personal and social dislocations persisted. Trouble for clients included concern for traditional values, fear of discovery, loss of a love relationship, agency backlogs and stalls necessitating delays, high costs, out-of-state travel, and medical and psychological complications. Together, these made abortion a fearful and anxious experience for many women.

Using a "natural history" approach, which traced the woman's search for an abortion, the perspectives and strategies of forty-two Michigan women were used to describe entrance into the network, the abortion experience, and the aftermath. Retrospective data elicited from interviews provided information *after* the abortion experience. This focused on essential features of the crisis client network.[1]

Defining the Problem

How do women themselves define the situation—being involved in sex, missing a period, and confronting a possible pregnancy? Sociologists emphasize that premarital or unwanted pregnancies are probably the result of "primary deviation" or behavior that is polygenetic in origin, diverse in meaning, widely distributed in a given population, and with little significance for the self and role of those involved.[2] They also point out that we have little reason to assume that women who have unplanned pregnancies differ in any way from other females of similar age, class, ethnicity, or social circumstances. While married pregnancy may be a normal and natural event that needs no accounting because it is an expected result of sexuality, abortion, especially for the single woman, is neither normal nor natural and continues to be defined as problematic. For the woman who finds herself with an unwanted pregnancy, there is a period of crucial assessment revolving around three questions: (1) Physically, what is happening to me? (2) Psychologically, how did this happen to me? (3) Socially, what are the consequences of this now and for my future? Although these body-mind-social questions may never be openly articulated, they provide a starting point for sorting out the meanings of the pregnancy and constructing solutions to the "problem."

For most women, a missed menstrual period triggers the first phase of the assessing process. A few women reported that they knew they were pregnant, although only two or three days "late." Others drifted for days or weeks until a second "missed" period forced them to recognize that this was an "abnormal" situation, or a situation in which they had to take positive action of some sort. Fear, anxiety, and expressed feelings of confusion dated from the awareness that a missed period was the first significant sign of pregnancy. For some women, nausea, fatigue, and a bodily state defined as "generally sick all over" were other signs of a likely pregnancy. For a few women with irregular periods, there was the additional apprehension of "how far along am I?" Confirming the suspected pregnancy by a urine test (if an early pregnancy) or a pelvic examination (if at a later stage) was the first action taken. If the findings were positive (that is, if the woman was medically defined as pregnant), the next action was to construct alternatives.

In the process of recognizing and dealing with the signs of a probable pregnancy, the woman also reconstructed *how* the event occurred, the *meaning* of the sexual relationship(s) she was involved in, and the *consequences* of the pregnancy. These assessments preceded the construction of alternatives.

"How it happened" may be sorted into five patterns:[3] (1) the "Snow White syndrome," (2) "everywoman's problem," (3) unplanned sexuality, (4) rationalized sexuality, and (5) contraceptive failures. These suggest the degree to which the woman was aware of or recognized the possible outcome of routinizing a sexual relationship.

Snow White syndrome. Although termed as such by a physician-informant, the young, naive woman who failed or refused to perceive the implications of intercourse was a common clinical phenomenon. Clergy-counselors and physicians alike reported that the women most likely to get pregnant were those who apparently had little awareness that sexuality carried cartain risks. The "syndrome" included a perception of the self as innocent, as a "good" girl, denial of wrongdoing, and expressed love for the male she was currently dating. Planning sex, as in the use of birth control, entailed a recognition of a deviant act. Unplanned, spontaneous sex, by contrast, legitimated the love relationship. After confirmation of the pregnancy, the girl reported, "It can't happen to me, I don't believe it," or "I never could accept the fact that I was pregnant."

Everywoman's problem. For many women, married or unmarried, and who were regularly engaged in sex relations, there was routine recognition that pregnancy could be a likely outcome. A pragmatic definition of the situation included the notion that "if you're doing it, you're liable to get caught." These women may or may not have used contraceptives, but once pregnant, there was a move to contact someone else who had also had the experience. Pregnancy was perceived as noncatastrophic and perhaps even expected. As one woman interviewed said, "I'm Joe average. If it happened to me, it could happen to anyone."

Unplanned sexuality. While unplanned sexuality is the most common reason given by most women for the pregnancy,[4] the significance for the self varies, depending on whether she is married or not. The first pregnancy, whether planned or unplanned, is rarely a "disaster" for the married woman. Instead, economics or life-style was the primary consideration influencing whether the married woman viewed the pregnancy as "untimely" or not. For the single woman, aware of chance taking, a definitional gap often existed—between sex and pregnancy and between pregnancy and having a child. Unplanned sex simply involved short-term affairs, postponing an appointment with a physician for contraceptives, or the belief that "if anything happens, we'll get married anyway."

Rationalizing the sexual relationship. A few single girls expressed the sex act as a rational expression of love, experimentation, or emancipation. An assertion of "this is something I wanted to do, and I thought a great deal about it" implied that the girl had considered not only what the sex act meant, but also what to do if she became pregnant. One now-married woman, in reporting her first love affair and subsequent pregnancy, said, "We had discussed the possibility of my getting pregnant, and decided that if anything happened, I'd just get an abortion." These women were most apt to refer to their abortion experience as "emancipating."

Contraceptive failure. Gynecologic problems, illness related to the use of pills or the I.U.D. requiring discontinuance of these techniques, or becoming pregnant while on physician-prescribed contraception was a problem for twelve women in this group. Some reported that physicians advised going off "the Pill" because of adverse effects but suggested no alternative birth control. These women were least likely to impute self-blame regarding the unwanted pregnancy. Because they had taken pre-cautions, they felt justified in following through with their intention to avoid having a child.

Reconstructing the meaning of the sexual relationship(s) occurred at all phases—defining the problem, constructing alternatives, seeking contacts, and post-abortion evaluations. Considerations generating mild to extreme anxiety for many women included uncertainty about the love relationship, fear that it would end if the lover discovered the pregnancy, indecision about feelings for the lover, recognition that marriage was probably im-possible because of youthfulness or financial incapacity of the parties, and awareness, after the fact, that the relationship was only a casual dating one.

Thus, while the woman almost always considered the preferences of the involved man, if he was still in the picture at all, her primary concern in constructing alternatives revolved around consequences of the pregnancy for *her* future. Fear of discovery by parents, expressed by six women, strongly contributed to a narrowing of options and a definition that abortion may be the only choice. Other reasons stated for the decision to have an abortion were reluctance to jeopardize school or career plans or an already tenuous love relationship and perceived inability to carry an unwanted child to term only to have it adopted out.

Constructing Alternatives

For most women retrospectively reporting an abortion, there was an ambivalent period before making contacts and arrangements in which the woman found herself unable to cope. "Panic," "alienation," "worry," "frustration," "nervousness," or even "suicidal" feelings characterized the experience for seventeen women. During the brief period of a few days or weeks, she "tried out" solutions in her mind before consulting with the involved man, her friends, or professional contacts. Although most women who eventually got the abortion very early struck on that option as the *only* possible alternative in the circumstances, others contemplated the possibility of marriage or adoption or fantasized about having the baby alone. Rejection of these solutions by friends, lover, or parents proved shocking but relieved the woman of the burden of responsibility.

Contacting Help

Before the emergence of legitimate brokers, abortion alternatives and decisions were largely resolved *before* the search. Under abortion movement direction, the abortion decision was complicated by a proliferation of professional contacts. Regardless of whom the woman initially turned to for assistance—friends, the lover, or professional workers—she often redefined the situation. This replay of options was particularly acute for the largest proportion of women routed through the reform network by established groups (clergy, physicians, agencies). Women reported that clergy and physicians, especially, spent "too much time" discussing "unsuitable" options (for example, marriage or adoption) and not enough time providing information about problems of out-of-state travel, expenses, and medical complications. Unplanned contingencies, such as the boyfriend's rejection of marriage or, for some, his opposition to abortion, may have created confusion and indecision. For a few women, options shifted depending on the time and who they consulted with, as in this sequence[5]:

Time 1: Girlfriend urges illegal abortion.
Time 2: Boyfriend decides marriage after physician confirms pregnancy.
Time 3: Clergy advises against marriage, suggests adoption.
Time 4: Boyfriend and woman decide abortion best option.

Ambivalence and guilt, even after the final decision had been made, were frequent outcomes of these shifts. Indeed, it was the rare woman who did not express some confusion at one or another contact point regarding the appropriate course of action. Only four women (of thirty-eight reporting) expressed no fear or anxiety at any time regarding the decision. Of these four, three were experienced abortion users (one woman had two previous abortions).

For many women, of course, there was primarily the "trouble" of getting "through it all"—making contacts requiring telephone calls to and appointments with clergy, agency, or physician; eliminating false leads; getting funds; informing parents and/or the biological father; and traveling to a strange city (New York), often alone, only to be served in a typically large, impersonal setting by unknown physicians. Twenty-four (of thirty-eight reporting) women characterized the pre-abortion experience as "worrisome," "fearful," or "traumatic," with excessive concern expressed by more than half these women, as in fear of sterility, a panic state, continuous weeping, generalized guilt, or suicidal ideas.

Whether professional contacts reduced or exacerbated this general anxiety state was not completely clear. For some women, encounters with two or more professionals actually heightened awareness that abortion was an extraordinary event. For many single women, the "normal" physical and psychological symptoms associated with pregnancy tended subjectively to increase as time delays and number of contacts multiplied. Fifteen women linked pre-abortion stress to difficulty in establishing helping sources.

Two essential features in securing a safe abortion included availability of medical care and time. Yet the structure of abortion referral services, at least from the experience of these women, was one often perceived as time-consuming, repetitive, disconnected, and expensive. In one sense, the former *sub-rosa*, or illegal, system, wherein abortion information was "private," "personal," "unshared," and of "little use to moral friends," was still operative.[6] But imposed on this "shadow world" of private knowledge learned from friends or personal sources was the new structure of counseling and referral services. Clergymen, physicians, referral businesses, feminist counselors, and other professional contacts complicated the search activity. The abortion search extended contacts into spheres formerly unavailable or unknown under the "old" system. This had three consequences in terms of number of resources contacted and time spent by women in contacting them.

1. *The number of intermediaries, or contacts, to secure an abortion increased.* Lee found in 1967 that half the women found an abortion within a chain having less than two intermediaries (mean, 2.82; median, 2.0). In my data, under conditions of a "mixed" system, private information among friends and public information among brokers, among thirty-six women reporting, they located an abortion with a chain typically having four intermediaries (mean, 4.14; median, 4.0), with a range of from one to eight persons contacted *before* locating an abortion source. Thirty-one percent of this group had five contacts or more, and only 17 percent had two contacts or less. Table 8.1 summarizes the number of contacts used by this group before an abortion was located.

Social chains may be reduced, as in this one-step process used by a woman seeking her second abortion:

Paid referral business—New York source

More characteristic is the chain that involves contacting two friends and two professionals:

Girlfriend—boyfriend—clergy—physician—New York source

This chain actually involves an additional step, although I have not "counted" it accordingly. After clergy counseling, the woman has the pregnancy confirmed by the physician. The woman then *returns* to the clergy for specific information and referral to New York.

In still another pattern, the woman's search involved contacting friends, who then connected her to a local feminist counselor. Physicians tended to reject the feminist groups as legitimate referral persons (unless operating under the clergy umbrella). Instead, they sent the woman to a clergy counselor for a repeat session. Then the process included as many as six links before a final New York referral:

Girlfriend (1)—girlfriend (2)—boyfriend—feminist counselor—physician—clergy—New York source

For two women, the initial effort to locate a "local" (or illegal) abortionist resulted in two chains in two time periods involving six persons:

Girlfriend (1)—girlfriend (2)—"Dr. X." (rejected—four weeks' delay) girlfriend (3)—clergy—physician—New York source

Table 8.1
Number of Persons Contacted Before Abortion Source Was Located

Number of Contacts[a] (x)	n	Number of Persons Involved in Search (x.n)	Cumulative Percentage Who Secured Abortion by x Contacts or Less
1	1	1	3
2	4	8	14
3	5	15	28
4	15	60	69
5	4	20	80
6	5	30	94
7	1	7	97
8	1	8	100
Total	36	149	

Mean=4.14
Median=4.0

a. Contacts: Persons used for information, service, or routing

Or, the chain may have been a temporally continuous one in time, with links from one route connecting to an illegal abortion and links from another route leading to a legal source:

(Route 1) male friend (1)—male friend (2)—bartender—midwife—(Route 2) male friend (3)—clergy—feminist counselor—physician—New York source

Despite the extensive length of this double chain, the woman succeeded in getting an early termination (nine weeks) because she resumed her search almost immediately after the initial illegal lead was rejected.

Undoubtedly, it was not the length of the chain (or number of contacts), or even the time involved, that alone determined the woman's subjective experience in the abortion search. Sometimes the woman's ambivalence or fear *magnified* as a result of frequent contacts. At other times, multiple contacts really expressed the woman's ambivalence or reluctance to make a decision. "Being in love," planning marriage, using pregnancy as "revenge" against a former lover, and moral objections to abortion all constrained the woman from taking the decisive step. Counseling clergymen, recognizing this ambivalence, sometimes requested that the client return for further counseling or moved such difficult cases to a woman counselor with more patience or who was more adept at handling group contacts: parents and/or the biological father. Extended counseling often resolved such problems, but in a few cases, this actually created greater confusion for the woman, particularly if the involved man deserted during this time.

Table 8.2
Type of Contact Secured in Search for an Abortion

Type of Contact	n	Percentage of Total Number of Contacts
Friend		
Male	25	
Female	28	
Total	53	35.6
Family		
Father (or older male relative)	5	
Mother (or older female relative)	6	
Total	11	7.4
Professional (or business contacts)		
Clergy	24	
Physician	31	
Feminist Counsellor	13	
Social Service Agency	6	
Paid Referral	3	
Other	9	
Total	85	57.0
Total	149	

2. *The number of professional, or paraprofessional, persons contacted greatly exceeded helping family members and was somewhat greater than contacts with friends.* In Lee's data, connections into the criminal abortion network occurred through the woman's close female friends, with the father often an important helping source. My data, in contrast, showed that women had few family support sources, with male and female peers almost equally involved in the search. The greatest *single* structural change of course, was the number of professionals involved. Table 8.2 shows the number and percentage of types of persons contacted.

In large part, this network was created and defined by the variety of professional persons who processed the woman at various phases of service. Unlike the illegal "system," which was re-created with each individual search, this structure existed independently of individuals processed through it. But professional control of services, because of legal restriction of access, assured that information was available primarily only to those women who either had passed previously through the system or were ideologically or politically committed to the abortion movement.

Contacts typically followed a two-step process. First, the attempt to get information from friends led the woman to confide in intimates, her boy-friend, girfriend, or a mutual friend known to her intimates. Second, mov-ing through the legitimate network required phases of service, such as urine test for pregnancy here, clergy counseling there, physician's pelvic examination at still another point. Lack of unity between phases of service was the single greatest complaint about the organization of services. Some women felt that the situation exposed them to a variety of possible cen-suring agents they would have preferred not to face.

Figure 8.1 describes the "typical" movement of women through the abortion network.[7] Charting clients' decisions at different points suggests a *modal* network and its alternatives. Not included here were the "deviant" cases for this group, as in use of one intermediary only or six to eight contacts used by a few. No woman in this group connected directly (that is, without intermediaries) with clinics or hospitals. After four contacts, the boyfriend of one woman secured a telephone number of a New York clinic from *Playboy* magazine. Even when direct contact was made without counselor mediation, the woman still had to rely on local medical diagnosis and appropriate papers from a medical office stating period of gestation and general health condition. Freestanding clinics and hospitals refused an out-of-state woman who lacked documentation because they did not want to confront unanticipated medical or psychiatric conditions that contrain-dicated abortion (for example, diabetes, overweight, cardiac problems, and mental disorder).

From discussions with New York clinic counselors and college students (both women and men), it appeared that it was the rare woman who did not first negotiate the options with friends or the involved man. Abortion, while not necessarily a crisis decision for some women, was certainly not among the standard encounters of everyday life. The event, surrounded by myth, medical rituals, and, for some, identity transgressions, appeared to demand strong social reinforcement.

3. *The amount of time involved to secure a legal abortion was actually as great, or even greater, than under the illegal order.* With the demise of the "friendly neighborhood abortionist" or the metropolitan physician who provided abortions "for a price," most women had to go through the clergy referral system. This involved time delays because of client backlogs on the part of professionals or agencies, a two-step process in procuring pre-abortion medical services, different personnel and/or agency processing for counseling and medical services, repetitive services, and so on.

Compared with the "therapeutic" hospital abortion route, however, which often took months to negotiate and required a more complicated proce-dure, this structure was medically efficient. Almost all of these women had abortions before the ten- or eleven-week deadline, allowing for the vacuum aspiration or D & C (dilatation and curettage) procedure. Only one woman

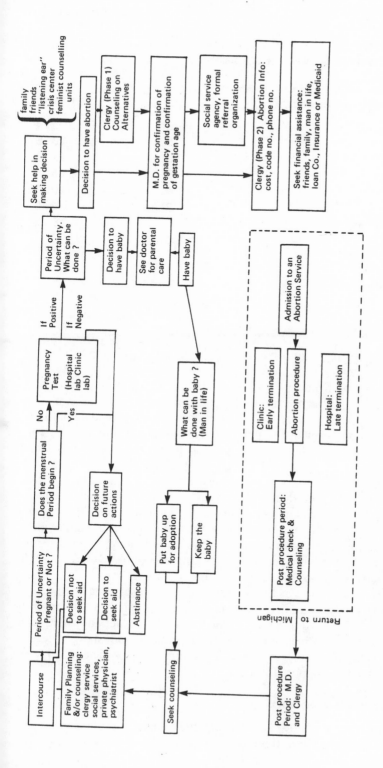

Figure 8.1
A Modal Abortion Referral Network and Its Alternatives

Table 8.3
Period from First Contact to Time of Abortion

Time Period (approximate)	n	Percentage
Under 1 week	2	5.4
1-2 weeks	5	13.5
2-3 weeks	12	32.4
3-4 weeks	5	13.5
4-5 weeks	4	10.8
5-6 weeks	3	8.2
6 weeks or more	6	16.2
Total	37	100.0

Mean Time = 3.0

Median = 2.5

(out of forty-two reporting) had a "late" abortion (eighteen weeks), necessitating a complex procedure, such as saline injection.

The time period from first contact to date of abortion underscores the relative efficiency of the referral routing system (mean, 3.0 weeks; median, 2.5 weeks). The range varied from one day (or no time delay) for the woman who went through the paid referral system to four months for a fourteen-year-old girl who received an illegal abortion. Thirteen women, or approximately 35 percent of the group, had a delay of four weeks or more. Table 8.3 summarizes the time period required to seek an abortion.

While inordinate time delays (five weeks or more) may have reflected indecision for a few women, lack of funds was the major hurdle for almost all latecomers. Credit denials because of student status or unemployment, fear of informing parents who could have provided money, and desertion or nonsupport by the biological father (twenty-one of forty-two) made the abortion enterprise a hazardous undertaking. Fourteen women cited money "hassles" or indebtedness as the primary difficulty in securing an abortion. Money difficulties required extending the search, this time in order to secure a loan. Three women found it necessary to contact anywhere from eight to twelve persons before funds were available. Feminist organizations or related campus radical groups (for example, Peace Coalition) were sources of financial support for some.

Terminating the Pregnancy

After completing the movement through the friendship-professional chain, the woman connected with the abortion source. For most women (thirty-

Table 8.4
Type of Abortion Received by Year and Location

Type of Abortion	Year		Location
Illegal (6)	1964	(1)	Detroit
	1967	(1)	Detroit
	1969	(3)	Chicago
	1969	(1)	Windsor
Legal (36)	1970	(5)	New York[a]
	1971	(19)	New York
	1972	(12)	New York

a. New York includes primarily clinics in New York
City, although suburban and upper state facilities
were used by some.

six of forty-two), this was a New York clinic or hospital. Abortion sites
varied, depending on *time* of abortion and *location* of helping sources.
Before 1970 the abortion was likely to be illegal, carried out in Detroit,
Chicago, or other out-of-state locations. A characteristic pattern reported
by some Michigan clergy groups was dependence on a Chicago source,
even after abortion was legalized in New York. Proximity, familiarity with
the physician, and favorable feedback from former patients were some
features that kept the old routing going.

Agencies, clergy, and feminist groups, while sharing information on New
York abortion sources, often had strong preferences. By far the largest
number of out-of-state women were served in a clergy-sponsored, nonprofit clinic, performing an estimated 26,000 abortions in a two-year period,
92 percent of women from outside the state, according to its chief clinician.
Clergy clients were most likely to have the abortion performed in this
setting. Feminist groups also referred here but gradually turned to their
own source in New York City. Depending on the type of agency-clergy
alliance, agency professionals either relied on the clergy source or developed alternatives recommended or sponsored by Planned Parenthood or
other groups. Invariably, physicians preferred *not* to refer directly because
of presumed legal or professional jeopardy, but used clergy or agency
brokers. Table 8.4 summarizes type of abortion (legal or illegal) by year
and location as reported by this Michigan sample.

Costs, too, were contingent on time, place, and type of abortion. Certainly, the most expensive abortion was the illegal one that occurred in the
days before New York abortions were legalized; but this, too, varied from

Table 8.5
Average Costs for New York Clinical Abortion and Travel Expenses

	Abortion	Travel Expenses	Average Total
1970 (n= 5)	$173.00	$61.00	$234.00
1971 (n=19)	158.65	75.00	233.65
1972 (n=12)	143.00	70.00	210.00

a low of $25, for an office D & C, to a high of $575 in a Chicago "clinic" (pre-1970 prices).

New York abortion prices began a decline with increased competition after legalization. Table 8.5 shows the change in costs for a clinical abortion over a three-year period documented by these users.

Late terminations (including saline procedure, hysterotomy, or hysterectomy), requiring hospitalization remained expensive procedures ($350 to $450 in New York City) but were still less costly than inpatient abortion care in metropolitan Michigan ($500 to $800). Even clinical abortions could be expensive for many women. The relatively low travel expenses reported by this group (averaging $61 to $75) reflect the large number of women who traveled to New York by car (averaging $50 to $60) rather than by air ($98). The clergy-sponsored or women's liberation clinics offered the lowest-cost abortions ($125 and $110, respectively), but medication ran as high as an additional $50 before the woman returned to Michigan.

In response to the question, "Did you experience any economic hardships because of the cost of your abortion?" fourteen women replied that either they or their boyfriends were "very much in debt" or "having trouble" repaying loans borrowed for the operation. Abortion-related money "troubles," while not an enduring problem, forced occupational changes, including dropping out of school for three women. One woman, who postponed the abortion beyond the "safe" period because of inadequate funds, emphasized the inequity of high abortion costs. Her expenses included $350 for saline injection plus $132 for travel, totaling $482 for the abortion. She found these costs exorbitant. In her words, "I think the cost of this abortion was out of reason. There are very few women, myself included, who can afford it. Abortions should not be a luxury item for the rich."

Abortion clinic staff defined the termination procedure as a relatively simple matter for most women receiving a vacuum aspiration. The woman entered the clinic on an appointment basis. Because there was usually an hour or so wait, with women processed by groups of six to eight for contraceptive information, counseling, and medical work, conversation soon developed among each time-cohort of clients. Having the same counselor and undergoing the same four-stage process—counseling, pre-abortion examination, termination procedure, and recovery—at approximately the same time, the women shared with one another the preoperation apprehensions and later the relief, following the abortion.

Clinic counseling was usually conducted by young paraprofessional women who themselves had had an abortion and was aimed at ventilating feelings regarding sex, pregnancy, contraception, and abortion. The counselor urged the women in these group sessions to accept the pregnancy and to recognize the meanings of the experience. Abortion in this context became a viable option, rather than a "mistake" for wrongdoing. The counseling repertoire excluded the language of morality, pain, suffering, or guilt. In fact, the counselor looked aggrieved if a woman mentioned these "objectionable" topics. Abortion was articulated, not as atonement for sins, but as a rational medical procedure, somewhat safer than a tonsillectomy and with far less complications than childbirth. Because a local anesthetic was given, the counselor required the full cooperation of the woman.[8] Fearful, tense, or hysterical patients not only were unable to take the "local," these counselors said, but they could also greatly disrupt the smooth flow of events in a typically crowded and tightly scheduled setting.

Counselors, then, performed a dual role. They oriented the woman to the setting and provided her with a vocabulary of motives—how to feel, how to think, how to express the experience. And the counselor acted as the chief support person throughout the various phases of service. Physicians, nurses, secretaries, and administrators were all transient functionaries who played only specialized roles. The counselor, by contrast, acted as a relatively permanent feature of the four- to six-hour experience. She often held the woman's hand or head during and after the operation and gave strength by her compassionate attention.[9] Patients' reports from New York clinics emphasized the strategic role of the counselor in making the abortion experience a "good," or even "memorable," event.

Post-abortion evaluations among the group studied showed the extent to which a standardized rhetoric had developed. Asking respondents to describe the feelings they had immediately *after* the abortion, thirty (of thirty-eight reporting) women used the term "relief" (or a related term) associated with "thankful," "happy," "good feelings," "extreme high," "never felt better," "felt fine," or "relaxed." It is interesting to speculate why the women almost uniformly used the term "relief," which suggests deliverance, alleviation, or ease through the removal of pain, distress, or oppression. In view of the official avoidance of the concepts of pain, sin, burden, or wrong, the word "relief" could summarize many of these taboo subjective feelings, while providing a neutral cover term in keeping with the controlled milieu of respectable medicine and mental health.

Again, "relief" could also express the before-after contrast. Before the abortion most women (thirty of thirty-six reporting) expressed a moderate to highly anxious state, as in "worried," "scared," "guilty," "mental anguish," "alienated," and so on, much of which expressed situational stress. Once the procedure was over, and the woman found herself still physically intact, conscious, and sharing the experience with others who had undergone a similar ordeal, the feeling of freedom from former fears and concerns brought the expressed relief.

Finally, after a two- to three-hour recovery period spent in either a large room filled with cots or a reception-type room with easy chairs and sofas, the clinic released the woman with antibiotics or other standard medication. Most women returned immediately to their homes by car or air. A few reported that they made a "weekend of it" with their boyfriends, either visiting New York nightspots or friends.

Evaluating the Experience

Sociologists analyzing the criminal abortion experience in the framework of labeling theory emphasize that while the abortion decision and search may be a negative experience, the overall impact of abortion has few, if any, long-term consequences for the woman's perception of her role or identity. This normalization is attributed to neutralizing techniques or justifications for the act, which are said to render social controls inoperative and shield the self-concept from blame. According to this logic, neutralizing rhetorics, as in rationales of "the lesser evil" or "the only solution," eliminate or reduce guilt for persons who have internalized conventional norms.

Turning to the psychiatric literature, we can discern two contradictory positions regarding the abortion experience during this period. On the one hand, the earliest clinical data suggested that abortion is tantamount to denial of the woman's role and indicates underlying personality problems. Long-range consequences for adjustment were presumed to follow the abortion experience. On the other hand, more recent data released during the early 1970s showed that most women had few or no psychological problems, either before or after abortion, except insofar as these may have been situationally induced. A straddling position was also apparent in some findings. Women were said to experience a sense of *loss* associated with medical abortion, a condition absent among women who sought nonmedical abortion. Expressed deprivation was reported to be related to preexisting stressful life situations, with the unwanted pregnancy an attempt to resolve the crisis. Fear of the abortion procedure further exacerbated the psychiatric problem.[10]

How did these Michigan women in our study define the experience? Was there a single set of perceptions that could be said to characterize this relatively socially homogeneous group? What conclusions can be drawn regarding psychological consequences of a "mixed-game" abortion, or one that was quasi-legal and medically still suspect? And what role, if any, did the broker structure play in facilitating a normal versus deviant identity?

First, women's perceptions varied by previous social experience, contingencies encountered in the search, and point of time in the abortion process (before, during, and after the operation).

Second, no single set of perceptions was consistent among this group. Except for the official rhetoric developed at the abortion site itself, most women who reported abortion did *not* share this experience with other aborted women and thus lacked a common neutralizing rhetoric. This means that, in the absence of continuity in medical and supportive services after the abortion, the woman was left to "work it out" herself unless she had maintained the relationship with the biological father or had other strong support figures. The frequency of male desertion or lack of effective support by the involved man for almost half of this group implied that the follow-up period was often difficult. For a few, translating the experience into an ideological or political event linked them to radical or reform groups that could be highly supportive of abortion. For eight women, only one of whom was previously ideologically committed, involvement in abortion reform, the feminist movement, or counseling activities transformed the event into a positive act.[11]

Third, although abortion had been officially redefined from a deviant to a medical, or even ideological, matter, a few women continued to define the act as deviant, with negative implications for the self. Almost 29 percent of this group experienced some psychological difficulties after either illegally induced (n = 1) or legally induced (n = 11) abortion, with approximately 12 percent (n = 5) having serious physical or psychological impairment and 5 percent (n = 2) incapacitated for some months or years (for example, severe uterine infections, psychiatric disorder).[12]

For most of the twelve women who failed immediately to neutralize labels of deviance, the return to "normalcy" was a slower, more agonizing process than for those who could early normalize the effects of the act. For most women, experiential or cognitive mechanisms operated to reduce strain, as in finding a new love, marriage, a subsequent pregnancy, reintegration into school or work, blaming the economic order for personal suffering, and "learning to live with it."

The final and fourth question was raised earlier: How did the broker arrangements contribute to, or reduce, labeling and subsequent self-recrimination? Developing protective mechanisms could be related, in part, to the type of abortion network itself. In other words, the ease or difficulty of making it through the network may account for later reactions to abortion.

The abortion network studied here was a morally "mixed" order—traditional prescriptions against abortion combined with availability of resources, if the woman was willing to take the necessary "trouble." Whereas the illegal route to abortion promoted secrecy and anonymity, the broker

route required openness and exposure to established representatives—
clergy, social workers, physicians. The greater proliferation of these professional contacts subjected the woman to possible reinterpretations of her
conduct. Shielding the self-esteem from moralistic implications became
difficult with bureaucratic forms to be filled out, questions raised about
marital status, and the woman asked to reconstruct the past to discover
"why she became pregnant" or what kind of social and sexual relationships
she had experienced.

The lack of continuity in medical and supportive services, still pervasive
for abortion services in the 1980s, provoked problems, especially for clients
who lacked local medical and agency care and had to travel out of their
city and state for an abortion. Clergy informants estimate client "loss" in
the context of these arrangements to run as high as 25 percent of all abortion
seekers. Some of these women, fearful of discovery, may have attempted
an illegal abortion, believing it to be easier than negotiating a complex
routing system. Four women of this group actually tried the illegal route
but found that "good" abortionists were impossible to locate or, if located,
the women were rejected because of "emotional" or "physical" problems.
The market had altered drastically but not necessarily progressively.

First, client routing through the legitimate network was somewhat *more*
complex, both *logistically* and *psychologically*, than movement through the
illegal structure, a comparison based on Lee's (1969) data. But while the
number of contacts had apparently increased, leading to greater public
exposure of the woman's "problem," the time required to negotiate service
was probably similar (average, two to three weeks) for both abortion routes.

Surgical costs for clinical abortions were significantly lower than for
illegal abortions or for hospital abortions, whether in New York or Michigan. If total costs for the service are compared, however (that is, pre-
abortion lab tests, pelvic examination, car or plane fare, limousine and
taxi costs, motel, restaurant, and postoperative physician fees), the cost
of a legally induced clinical termination began to approximate, but still did
not equal, illegal or hospital abortions. The "high" cost of abortion continued to be the emotional experience itself, which was compounded by
delays, "trouble" with the involved man, and reluctance to travel out-of-
state for the procedure.

Gaps and redundancies in the referral network, noted by Cumming
(1968), for social services generally were most acute in the follow-up period.
Discontinuity between phases of service implies that social support before
the abortion received at point A (for example, clergy counselor) may be
unavailable or lacking at point B (for example, social service agency or
physician). Client postponements or evasions in contacting professionals
after the abortion were commonly reported. Physical or psychological dis-
abilities, relatively easy to modify after initial onset of the disturbance,
may have developed into more serious problems when left unattended. A

chief factor in client reluctance to seek postoperative treatment was lack of a local, central referral system, incorporating pre- and post-abortion counseling and medical services in a single setting.

The persistence of normative constraints on abortion, leading women to define themselves as deviants, either temporarily or for an extended period, was probably facilitated by the relatively elaborate rituals of counseling, physician advice, or agency processing. The term "counseling" itself, developed within the therapeutic ethic, implies "opinion," or "instruction" in "directing" the judgment or conduct of another. Most persons seek professional counseling when they experience an impasse in their everyday lives perceived as too overwhelming or problematic for self-correction.

For these women, the transformation from a self-perception of normal to an "object" for professional concern and official labeling appeared to have had little to do with their past biographies or current goals. The construction of their experience seemed obscure, defined by others in unfamiliar settings. In this way abortion, as a medical and mental health service, ostensibly a woman-centered service, became mystified in the interests of preserving an archaic stigma. But the nonerasability and reappearance of the abortion stigma continued to be resisted by feminists and some clergy brokers. The advance to fully legitimate abortion by law was on.

NOTES

1. Forty-two interviews, with thirty-six completed protocols, were conducted by three college students and myself on three college campuses in Michigan and were limited almost exclusively to present or former college students or their friends. Women were predominantly college age or older, although the women's ages at the time of the abortion range from fourteen to thirty. Most of the women had never been married (83%) and were students when aborted (82%). Only two were not white, with one black woman and one Chicano. Almost all respondents were Protestants, except three Catholics. All but three lived in a college community. The three lived in a metropolitan area when involved in the abortion search. Overall, the group interviewed were previously known, either by the interviewers or by their immediate helping contacts. Our collective interviewing experience in seeking women who had previously had an abortion clarified a number of issues regarding research in this area. Until the Supreme Court decision (1973), abortion was legal in Michigan only under the most narrowly construed definition of "therapeutic" conditions ("to save the life of the mother"). This required almost all abortion seekers to travel out-of-state to "liberal" abortion states (e.g., New York, Washington, D.C., and California). For Michigan residents, the process of obtaining an abortion was complicated by the lack of verifiable public information regarding out-of-state abortion clinics.

2. See Lemert, 1951; Vincent, 1961; Lee, 1969; Manning, 1971; Rains, 1971; and Zimmerman, 1977 for an analysis of the relationship between sex and pregnancy as status-attaining or status-demoting phenomena.

3. These categories are constructed by the observer rather than by the actors, although the aim was to develop the meanings in terms of the expressed experiences of the women.

4. Clergy data showed that for approximately 69 percent of women counselled, there was *no* or irregular use of contraceptives.

5. My data on social chains is presented in a somewhat different manner than that of Lee or Manning, who first proposed this tracking method. Whereas they "count" each unit (person) as a link in the social chain only when the chain was successfully completed (that is, an abortionist was located), I include all contacts made as inclusive of a linear movement through the quasi-private, quasi-public structure of abortion communication. My approach, while not strictly comparable, seems warranted by the particular arrangements. My aim is to show that, despite the relatively high incidence of abortion among college women, the number of persons required to reach an abortion in this quasi-legal system remains approximately the same, or even greater, than under the illegal structure.

6. Manning (1971, 147) holds that under conditions of an illegal abortion "system," the infrastructure is both "unknown" and "invisible" until a search begins.

7. I am indebted to Joan Mulligan, R.N., Public Health professor, University of Michigan, for the original flowchart. I have added, primarily, the abortion social services network to her scheme of "alternatives and decisions in the pregnancy cycle."

8. In an unpublished paper reported by the *New York Times*, 8 June 1972, Tietze shows that a higher incidence of complications follows from the use of local rather than general anesthetic. The reason for this apparent anomaly is that doctors may "operate in a hurry," when the patient is under local anesthetic.

9. Freestanding-clinic counselors report that after eight months or so on the job as a counselor-circulating nurse, the pressure is frequently unendurable. Absenteeism or high turnover is said to be one way to resolve the strain.

10. Medical and psychiatric information changed rapidly as a result of movement activity. For some representative interpretations, see Dunbar, 1945, 179–210; Ekblad, 1955; Osofsky and Osofsky, 1971; Potts, 1971, 651–653; Downs and Clayson, 1972; and Nathanson, 1972.

11. Significantly, I found only one difference between my cases and Henslin's (1971, 113–135) in this regard. My cases included clients routed by feminists' groups. Such persons were likely to eschew personal guilt and to assign "blame" to outside agents—the law, culture, political order, and so on.

12. Gebhard et al. (1958, 208–210) found 9 percent of abortionees with psychological difficulties after illegal abortion. Swedish data show that 26 percent experienced self-reproach after *legal* abortion (where therapeutic hospital committees were involved); 14 percent in mild form, 11 percent seriously so, and 1 percent to the point of impaired capacities (Ekblad, 1955). By comparison, more than 50 percent of the group analyzed by Lee (1969, 105) report either moderate or severe depression and/or nightmares after their abortion experience.

9

Medicalization

Social control through medical institutions offered a metaphysical and cultural solution to the unacceptability of unregulated abortion. This solution was based on medical experience and the traditional supervision of health structures by doctors. It was related to the pathology of pregnancy, to the administrative requirements for medical abortion, to a medical consciousness whose constant task was to provide information, supervision, and constraint, all of which related as much to the police function as to the field of medicine proper.

But abortion by choice is opposed at every point to the traditional medicine of therapeutics. Abortion as choice is a collective enterprise; it is an outgrowth of the freedom movements involving the leveling of professional hierarchies, the search for an essential woman-centered experience, the integration of the helping professions, and the subtle perception of a complex historical transformation of gender roles. Choice implies medicine as the method for achieving a chosen result. The abortion procedure is thus a technical activity without metaphysical or cultural meanings. It is applied science, and hence it can be used by any individual or group and be adapted to market demands or individual need.

By contrast, medicalization represents the penetration of a medicine of therapeutics into all aspects of the organization and distribution of abortion. Such an arrangement is a professional monopoly run by and for medical and administrative experts in the purported interests of society (Freidson, 1970). It is a development of the professionalizing society, of the complex division of labor resulting from high levels of specialization and hierarchy that characterizes modern bureaucratic organizations. Medicine thus becomes a master ideology for defining not only the technological method for performing abortions, but the social reality of abortion as well, excluding social considerations that had been established by women involved in the abortion movement (Conrad and Schneider, 1980; Davis and Anderson, 1983).

As state by state gradually shifted from the defunct criminal abortion code to a more permissive abortion policy—whether *de jure* or *de facto*—these opposing models of therapeutic and elective abortion moved into a collision course. Through a series of adroit political moves, professional medicine regained its monopoly over pregnancy care, delivery, and late terminations, while considerably loosening its grip on early abortion. This chapter deals with problems and outcomes of this conflicting regime.

MOBILIZING FOR CONTROL

When choice advocates demanded the abolition of the hospital for medical abortion and proposed, instead, the use of doctors' offices and free-standing clinics (or clinics not attached to larger hospital structures), state public health and hospital associations began mobilizing against this threat to hospital rule. Their task was threefold: draining power out of the competing illegal or nonmedical systems; assessing the state of the abortion field to determine availability and safety features of different abortion techniques and sites; and, finally, exploring various models of abortion and coming up with a model that would satisfy the conservative hospital group as well as meet the demands of abortion reformers.

The first concern was criminal abortion. The illegal market remained a viable competitor in all states until well after the Supreme Court decision of 1973, being directly related to availability and cost of legal abortion. Generally, in nations or states where a repressive policy is pursued, illegal abortion continues to be the major cause of maternal deaths. For most reformers, the battle with the "back-alley" abortionist would not be won until there was a total legal repudiation of all criminal abortion laws. To hasten favorable court or legislative action, medical reformers in states with a permissive law set up model low- or no-cost abortion clinics. Here women, who were formerly denied medical abortion could have contraceptive information and pregnancy termination services. Such demonstration projects were political entities. Their presence alerted national medical and community elites that alternative abortion programs were geared up and ready to go once the legal order gave the go-ahead sign. Hospitals were increasingly rejected as inappropriate, if not punitive, sites for early abortion. Reformers continued to identify the hospital as the source of the problem: They said it denied the largest proportion of women access to abortion because of red tape and costs, and it only dealt with the woman's need in the emergency room after the botched abortion.

Hospital advocates also had to eliminate other nonmedical systems in order to maintain medical control over abortion. One such innovative nonmedical program, described by sociologist Pauline Bart,[1] was run by a feminist group in Hyde Park, Chicago, with a code name of "Jane." Growing out of the protest movements of the 1960s, this organization gave 11,000 illegal abortions over a four-year period for an average fee of $50 for a first-trimester abortion. "Jane" had many features later associated with the Women's Health Movement, such as politicizing health care, demystifying medicine, spiritualizing health, eliminating hierarchy and specialization, and emphasizing an explicit doctrine of women's control over their bodies. "Seizing the means of reproduction" was the theme, combining the tenets of the radical health movement and the feminist movement. As one proponent asserted, self-help was both a philosophy and a practice through which "women became active creators of our own destinies." Antiprofessionals played a crucial role by creating *esprit de corps* among members. This sentiment was expressed in rage and, occasionally, in humor. The spirit of the group is exemplified by pro-abortion activist Patricia McGinnis in a cartoon of a sobbing woman holding a $500 check in front of "Mercy Hospital" on her knees saying: "Please may I have a state-approved, politician-sanctioned, clergy-counseled, psychiatrist-rubber-stamped, residency-investigated, abortion committee-inspected, therapuked, public health department statistized, contraceptive failure, accredited-hospital abortion?"

Abortion skills could be taught; there was no monopoly over knowledge or technique. All members shared tasks in a revolving fashion; an administrator this week could act as an abortionist next week with additional training. Despite the often casual division of labor, the "Jane" organization claimed high morale among members and low complication rates (although no written records were kept for security reasons). Counseling was personal—a woman-to-woman exchange—and aimed to provide maximum information about the procedure as well as to allow the woman an opportunity for expressing misgivings or doubts. In fact, one-fourth of the women did not return after counseling. There were no consent requirements, few hierarchical relationships, and an absence of other features of traditional "delivery" of medical services.

Like many other alternative institutions that grew out of the social movement turmoil of the 1960s, "Jane" was a self-dissolving entity. After 1973 the organization underwent a transformation into a licensed women's health collective, with abortion service limited to counseling and referrals.

If "Jane" was a self-destruct organization, other nonmedical systems were more resistant. Abortion referral for profit emerged as a result of the tens of thousands of women who sought legal abortion but who lived in states where abortion was illegal. One New York–Michigan system worked as follows: A Detroit businessman who had connections with three or four New York doctors advertised legal abortion referral and medical services in Michigan papers. Subsequent telephone contacts resulted in a daily (or every other day) small plane load of from six to ten women who were flown by the same businessman from Detroit to New York City or Buffalo for the doctor-performed abortion. To reduce police suspicion, the owner-pilot picked up a load of fruit or other light cargo for the return trip, which also brought back the aborted women. Patient's cost: $450 for round-trip air transportation and the vacuum aspiration abortion. Physicians were usually paid $100 per abortion, so the businessman realized a healthy profit.

Organized medicine, appalled at this questionable arrangement, took their case to a New York court. Approximately one year after New York passed its permissive abortion law, medical referral services for profit were declared "invalid and unlawful," along with their now-illegal practices of discounts and fee splitting. Such arrangements led to "patient exploitation" and other "practices inimical to the public interest," declared the court (*S.P.S. Consultants v. Lefkowitz* and *Mitchell v. Lefkowitz*). Although physician interest was not spelled out, a law approved a few weeks later by the same court determined that any person who finds performing abortion contrary to his or her conscience or religious beliefs may refuse to perform or assist in such abortion without risk of incurring civil action for negligence or malpractice (*Laws of New York*, 1971). This conscience clause was significant because it laid the groundwork for the massive withdrawal of hospital and medical personnel from abortion, with no civil or professional penalties.

Even with the proposed defeat of illegal and nonmedical operators, professional power over abortion could not be fully legitimated unless abortion facilities were completely regulated. What kind of facilities these would be, who would serve in such settings, and what kind of procedures would be offered once the law changed were murky and disputed issues.

PLANNING FACILITIES

Moving from therapeutic to elective abortion required a journey that was akin to crossing a boundary from one nation to another, including attendant customs officials, surveillance by patrol guards, search and seizure threats, and unknown, but potentially hazardous, penalties. In developing new public health rules, reformers confronted the specter of the old system at every turn. Challenging tradition created a series of either-or situations. In effect, planning efforts provided alternative scenarios. One scenario offered maximum rules and norms that severely limited access but enhanced professional control. The other scenario, a minimalist statement, offered a permissive delivery system, relying on the free market to sort out clients, providers, quality, and cost of services. In both scenarios, the therapeutic ideology took stage center, either supported by traditionalists, who were primarily hospital administrators, or resisted by reformers—physicians, public health groups, and clergy counseling members.

What were the crucial questions that reformers debated and agonized over?

1. How could professional control and surveillance be instituted in an area of dubious therapeutic value for doctors and patients? In other words, abortion on "request" or "demand" placed the physician at the disposal of the patient and thereby weakened professional control without providing long-term help for the patient, thus the belief that doctors became the contraceptive tool for "disorganized" and "immoral" women.

2. How could organized medicine encourage necessary innovation—the reorganization of hospitals and staffing—in a field where financial exploitation of patients was traditional? Providing the necessary freedom to improvise could open the door to unscrupulous profit-oriented operators within even the most security-minded hospital. In other words, how could the medical system control its own?

3. How could safe, legal, low-cost abortion alter the stigmatizing features long associated with abortion, such as dehumanized treatment, lack of privacy, mandatory sterilization, unnecessary psychiatric intervention, and pain? This stigma pertains to patients as well as providers—facilities, physicians, nurses, and technical staff.

4. A related question—How could a noncoercive, patient-centered atmosphere be created that rejected the abortion stigma by normalizing the medical procedure and treating it as an everyday, normal occurrence? And among a few planners, would this altered situation encourage "promiscuous" or repeat abortion?

5. How could the emotional trauma and patient's sense of loss long associated with abortion be eliminated or reduced? Should doctors take on the responsibility, or delegate this sensitive area to specially trained counselors? And what would the counselors' role be?

6. How could the proposed system attract highly qualified physicians and facilities willing to specialize in and, in some cases, to limit practice exclusively to abortion? What would be the effects of such repetitive medical work on professional staff?

7. What kind of surgical procedures would be offered and in what kind of facilities? What should treatment rooms, waiting rooms, recovery rooms, and other areas look like; size, decor, relation to other rooms? What happens to emergency cases in non-hospital settings?

8. What kind of record keeping should be required of abortion facilities that would both protect the patient's privacy and provide necessary information about patients? How would such records be used—for or against women?

Although many of these questions appeared highly technical and outside the expertise of nonmedical participants, each item was politically charged. Six months' observation of a Michigan facility planning committee shows how the medicalization process evolved.[2]

At the outset the Abortion Planning Committee, which was mandated to set medical standards and which comprised hospital administrators, physicians, clergy reformers, and university public health professors, assumed that theirs was a "rubber-stamping" function. The task, as it turned out, was far more politically demanding, as they discovered in attempting to define this "brand-new field." A series of working drafts served as a catalyst for evaluating, differentiating, and interpreting the problem: What is abortion, and what does it mean for different occupational groups involved in this service? The immediate issue was the nomenclature. How abortion was defined would be important for determining the shape and outcome of legal abortion services.

In the view of some, "abortion" evoked a set of meanings that were medically and publicly objectionable. The term "abortion" continued to be equated with "abortion mill," "charletans," "butchers," "back alley," "medically hazardous," "shoddy medicine," "criminal," "medically uncontrolled," and others. In most contexts the use of any one of these terms (e.g., catheter, charletan, septic) became identical with every other negatively related abortion term. The prevailing myth of the "evils" of the old order was juxtaposed against the new medically approved terminology, as in the following contrast set:

criminal order/legal order
abortion mill/hospital
charletan (or butcher)/physician
catheter/surgery
sepsis/antibiotic control
sterilization/planned pregnancies

For some members, inability to distinguish which discourse speakers were referring to led to repeated misunderstandings and tension. For a few participants "abortion" invariably implied "abortion mill," with additional negative implications, as Figure 9.1 indicates.

If the term "abortion" was presumably identical to the nomenclature of the illegal structure, this required changing the term to fit the new conception of a procedure associated with licensed facilities and medically controlled surgery. "Abortion" was duly replaced with "termination of pregnancy" or "termination procedure." By draft 3 of these constructed guidelines, the terminological shift was complete, but the document continued to retain the "old" language, "abortion mill." This conceptual holdover provoked a dialogue between some members.

Physician A: What is an abortion mill?

Public Health Professor: The "abortion mill" is a loaded word. It means cranking out illegal operations in mass numbers. In time, the word came to mean any facility giving large numbers of abortions. I would hate to see the term metamorphasized to mean any facility that provides large numbers of abortions.

Figure 9.1
Connotations of the Term "Abortion Mill"

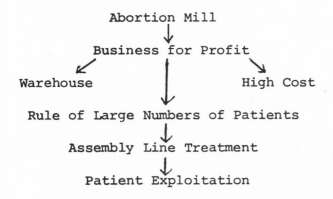

It's important that we give safe, low-cost procedures. This is the most important thing.

Committee Chairman: I want to avoid the word "abortion." I used "miscarriage" to mean abortion in the document. But what we're talking about is termination of pre-viable fetuses. We could call it "removal of the products of conception." That's the definition given by the College of Obstetrics and Gynecology.

Physician A: ACOG [American College of Obstetrics and Gynecology] uses the word "abortion." The opposition will say that this whole guideline says nothing about abortion, and that's what we're talking about.

Public Health Professor: We're concerned about language. We want to make sure action is not being directed against contraceptives. . . . This whole issue may be a spook. That is, the opposition may use this factor. Many of these contraceptives interfere *after* fertilization [emphasis by speaker].

Defining the object, then, required additional clarification. Abortion and contraception were to be separated, even if, in medical terms, abortion and some types of contraceptives (e.g., intrauterine devices and chemical abortifacients) performed similar functions: removal of the products of conception. Separating terms into distinct spheres avoided lay and professional recognition that abortion was *also* a form of birth control. Political considerations, the group agreed, demanded that potential impact of the terminology be taken into account in constructing guidelines and evaluations for proposed facilities.

Shifting categories from a "lay" classification (or "what everyone knows about abortion") to a "medical" one, members identified deficiencies between deviant and nondeviant abortion (see Figure 9.2).

Figure 9.2
Deviant and Non-Deviant Definitions of Abortion

		Two Dimensions of Abortion	
Features	Contrast Set	Deviant	Non-Deviant
Operation	Hazardous	X	
	Safe		X
Operator	Disreputable, Incompetent	X	
	Respectable, competent (Board certified OB-GYN)		X
Rationale for Treatment	"Mental" reason	X	
	Illegitimacy	X	
	Social reason		X
	Preventive health		X
Treatment	Catheter	X	
	Sterilization	X	
	Procedure		X
	Vacuum aspiration		X
Consequences for Patient	Psychological reaction	X	
	Sterility	X	
	Illness	X	
	Health		X
	Contraceptive use		X
Consequences for Institution	Legal liability	X	
	Malpractice	X	
	Loss of licensure	X	
	Legally controlled		X

SOCIAL ORGANIZATION OF SERVICES

What abortion "means" also became associated with the site or location of the operation. Where abortion took place related to another set of issues: the stage of pregnancy, type of procedure to be used, setting, mode of care (inpatient or outpatient), organization of staff and services, and cost. After repeated discussions over the kind of facilities that public health guidelines were supposed to regulate, the group focused on freestanding clinics. Hospitals, hospital outpatient units, and hospital-based clinics were, in large part, covered by hospital licensing acts. Freestanding clinics, though, represented a new concept imported from New York that threatened many hospital administrators and a few public health officials. For more than two-thirds of the sessions, the Committee reviewed some phase or other of this new conception of abortion service. Conflict centered on innovative features but especially on the discontinuities between standard hospital procedures and "free-swinging," or presumably loosely structured, clinics. Figure 9.3 shows contrasting features of the two facilities.

Misunderstandings and disagreements over the setting generated con-

Figure 9.3
Contrast Sets of Two Abortion Facilities

Features	Termination Procedure in Two Settings	
Referent	New York City Freestanding Clinic	Michigan OB-GYN Hospital Unit
Location	Clinic	Hospital
Time of Gestation	↓ Early Pregnancy	↓ Late Pregnancy
Type of Procedure	↓ Vacuum Aspiration	↓ Saline, Hysterotomy, Hysterectomy ↓ Tubal Ligation
Type of Patient Care	Ambulatory patient	↓ Resident, patient
Length of Treatment	↓ Short-term (4-6 hours)	↓ Long-term (24-48 hours)
Type of Setting	↓ "Mental-health" type	↓ Surgical type
Organization of Staff	↓ Team Unit: Physician-counsellor-nurse	↓ Hierarchical Unit: physician ↓ nurse ↓ counsellor (if any) ↓ ancillary personnel
Organization of Staff	↓ Team Unit	↓ Hierarchical Unit:
Key Staff Person	↓ Counsellor	↓ Physician
Organization of Supplementary Services	↓ Minimal	↓ Maximum
Record-Keeping	↓ Simple	↓ Complex

troversy about which set of rules were to be applied to which medical situations. On the one hand, hospital administrators demanded that the integrity of the hospital be maintained with restricted rules of access and tight hospital "standards," whereas reform elements insisted on open access and low cost. Between these two camps there seemed little hope of resolution. Only after the Committee determined meaningful differences between the two facilities—"early" abortion in clinics, "late" abortion in hospitals—was this issue temporarily resolved. In effect, almost all debate, once nomenclature itself was decided, centered on various aspects of the setting.

Key issues revolved around four areas. Although these issues appeared to have little in common, they were actually symptomatic of a continuous need to create careful behavioral boundaries between hospitals and free-standing clinics: problems of blood supply, referral, identification and disposal of fetal remains, and the regulatory scope of the guidelines. Demystifying abortion also required connecting it to more familiar medical concepts, while disconnecting it from its therapeutic context. Some questions raised were: What is abortion similar to? What is it different from? Is it a *special* type of medical service? Is it the *same* as a standard surgical service? Or is it *similar* to something else—for example, oral surgery in a dentist's office or outpatient mental health therapy? These debates about scenarios were crucial, for they had direct implications for organizing services and staff. The Committee proposed three scenarios: (1) exceptionalistic medical service, (2) standard medical service, and (3) nonstandard medical service. On these three dimensions, abortion was viewed, respectively, as medically special, medically nonspecial, and medically unlike other services known. Figure 9.4 charts these alternative models.

SOCIAL CONTROL OF ABORTION SERVICE

On four issues—blood supply, patient referral, fetal residue, and regulatory control—the clash between diverse occupational viewpoints became apparent. The clash related to the issue of who controls and, conversely, who benefits from institutionalizing abortion. Disputes about organizing and controlling service had profound ramifications for public health management.

Blood Supply

As a surgical procedure, abortion required that facilities maintain a blood bank in the event of an emergency. Ostensibly a purely technical consideration, the organization of blood relates in complex ways to political and economic concerns.[3] Increasingly, storing and using blood has become a commercialized venture, requiring elaborate bureaucratic and medical con-

Figure 9.4
Three Medical Interpretations of Abortion and Implications for Organization

Organizational Dimensions	Medical Interpretations		
	Exceptionalistic Medical Service	Standard Medical Service	Non-Standard Medical Service
Setting (or facility)	Hospital Only	Hospital, or hospital satellite, or freestanding clinic*	Freestanding clinic,* doctor's office,.or mental health-type setting
Description of Procedure	Hazardous (e.g. "hemorrhage", "infection", "anesthetic and drug misadventures", "emotional reaction")	"normal" outcomes of surgery; statistically computed complications	Low or no complications
Type of Procedure Appropriate	Dilatation and Curretage, hysterotomy, hysterectomy, butal ligation (sterilization)	D&C; vacuum aspiration	Vacuum aspiration only
Procedure Analogous to:	Major gynecological surgery	Minor gynecological surgery	Vasectomy in doctor's office; out-patient mental health therapy
Administration of Anesthetic	General anesthetic (temporary loss of consciousness) administered by certified board anesthesiologist	Local anesthetic (action limited to area of application of injection;) administered by performing physician	Local anesthetic; administered by office nurse or LPN

Figure 9.4 *continued*

Organizational Dimensions	Medical Interpretations		
	Exceptionalistic Medical Service	Standard Medical Service	Non-Standard Medical Service
Minimal Equipment for Procedure	ECG machine; suction equipment; gas and oxygen machines; airways, laryngoscopes, cardiac defibrilator.	Gas and Oxygen machines, suction equipment, resusitator	Suction equipment
Director of Program	Hospital Chief of OB-GYN staff	Physician or Physician-Administrative Team	Physician or Physician-Counsellor-Administrative Team or Administrator-Counsellor Team
Counseling Staff	Psychiatrist or Psychiatric social worker	Social Worker	Para-professional or attending physician
Administration of Pathological Examination of Fetal Tissue	Hospital Tissue Committee	Hospital pathologist	Physician performing operation
Required Tests	Blood counts, hematocrit determination, blood typing and crossmatching, serology, pregnancy tests, urinalysis rhogam injections, sickle cell, and gonorrheal examinations	Blood counts, typing and matching, pregnancy tests, rhogam and sickle cell	Blood counts, pregnancy test, rhogam injections

Figure 9.4 *continued*

Organizational Dimensions	Medical Interpretations		
	Exceptionalistic Medical Service	Standard Medical Service	Non-Standard Medical Service
Recommended Tests	Papanicolau smears, rubella, hepatitis screening	Pathological examination of tissue for gynecological irregularities	None
Blood Storage	Ample supply to meet any transfusions needs (all blood types inc.)	Minimum supply to meet immediate projected transfusion needs (refer patient to hospital)	None
Physical Arrangements	Separate Procedure, examination, and recovery rooms	Operating room as procedure/examination room; dormitory style recovery room	Office examination rooms as procedure rooms; reception room as recovery room (no beds)
Patient Referral	Physician-physician	Physician-agency	Open-physician, agency, clergy, self, other
Projected Costs	High (est.$500+)	Moderate (est.$300+)	Low (est.under $150)

*Freestanding Clinics were conceived as either "standard medical service", or alternatively, as "non-standard medical service", depending on the speaker and/or the context.

trol to prevent the spread of hepatitis through the blood and to ensure an adequate, safe supply for recipients. In this Committee, public health officials and clergy, especially, voiced concern over the practice of private laboratories selling placentas and other blood residue, implicating health organizations in what they considered questionable market transactions. Hospital administrators agreed but said that policing this activity could be an overwhelming administrative task. Moreover, facilities primarily devoted to abortion service lacked built-in controls available in more elaborate hospital bureaucracies. Profit seeking in blood thus became a real possibility in these new systems. And since most terminations would take place in freestanding clinics, questions of both administrative costs and supply had to be confronted.

Countering the traditionalists, who believed that abortion was inevitably a bloody, if not deadly, business, reform physicians and public health professors rejected the idea that abortion was identified with enormous blood loss. If clinics were limited to first-trimester abortions, with their low complication rates, they probably did not need to store blood in the first place.

Once it became apparent that all facilities would *not* be performing the same type of abortion procedures, blood supply could remain a specialized service for facilities with the technical capacity to manage it. In separating domains—clinic abortion for early (safe) abortions and hospital abortion for late (risky) terminations—members considered the blood issue, first as analogous to the blood bank, where blood loss is socially acceptable, and, then as a problem of bureaucratic management.

Hospital Administrator A: Where did you get the idea of two persons to a room?

Chairman: I'm thinking of the mental and physical trauma associated with this procedure—hemorrhaging, and so forth.

Hospital Administrator A: I'm with you here.

Public Health Professor B: I think we are considering two different things here. One is the freestanding clinics where you don't have serious complicated procedures; and the other is the hospital situation. That's a different matter.

* * * * * * * *

Public Health Professor B: There's a good analogy with the blood bank. They've lost a great deal more blood in the blood bank situation than in this procedure. The patient must be on the table for ten or fifteen minutes. This is a critical point right after the procedure. This is where equilibrium, that is, body homeostatis, is occurring. If patients will follow directions, there are going to be very few who are going to have any kind of repercussions.

Public Health Professor C: We simply have to orient ourselves here to a different concept.

(But traditionalists persisted.)

Hospital Administrator D: How practical is the storing of blood? Blood can be a very severe problem in terms of the amount of actual supplies you have to keep on hand. The typing and matching of ladies in the pregnancy-age class are very complicated. You have to be aware of type and cross-match reference. You need a great deal of supply here. You also need an alarm system, and you're probably going to have to consult a pharmacist. The storing of blood by modern technological requirements is very complex. If you're going to have an effective blood service, you need a more involved business than a free-standing clinic would be able to provide. A medical dictum is that if a person needs blood, he probably needs more than one unit. The transfusion requires full-scale equipment and technology. Why have this done in a second-rate facility?

Public Health Professor B: I agree.

Once planners identified blood loss with the former therapeutic procedure and thus the hospital setting, freestanding clinic opponents (primarily hospital administrators) could then get down to the business of preserving the hospital order from possible infringements from the new upstart facilities.

Patient Referral

Issues of patient referral, examination of fetal tissue, and types of facilities to be covered by the guidelines raised three unsettled matters: (1) What was the legal responsibility of the facility for providing treatment programs? (2) What was the physician's responsibility to patients? and (3) What were the problems of medical control posed by a still-indeterminate clinic organization?

Controversy over professional prerogatives versus patients' referral rights took the following line: If physicians have *no* responsibility for interagency referral and yet are legally and morally responsible for controlling patient care, who, then, is responsible for referral? Is it professional control without responsibility? Or is it professional responsibility without power to control the situation? Further, if providing abortion depends on first organizing an interagency referral system, both the costs of the referral system and the administrative complexity of network building could prevent any service from starting up. Broker arrangements—clergy counselor, social agency, and physician linkages—some members asserted, must be integrated into the new structure. Such a model of health care as a community enterprise was contrasted with a professional control model. The dispute took the following line:

Public Health Professor A: Dr. W. [president of OB-GYN Assn.] believes that any patient not given complete information on protection or family planning at the time of abortion is not receiving good medical care.

Physician B: For the freestanding clinic, the main function is to provide abortion and to take care of all the rehabilitation [i.e., postoperative] cases.

Public Health Professor C: But the clinic must have the means to hook the patient up for health care. The clinic is not responsible for being saddled with all the health care, however. Liaison with referral agencies must be maintained for follow-up of abortion patients. Yet I'm scared to death that the rules and regulations for licensing are getting to be too much. If we have to prove by document that we have established liaisons, we never will open up the free-standing clinics.

Clergyman: The issue here is whether we are going to give abortions or give social services as well.

Public Health Professor C: I would like the social services concept built into the clinic service.

(Discussion of language of "should" ([i.e., recommended] or "shall" [i.e., mandatory] for organizational referral.)

Physician D: I don't have to refer [patients] if I'm busy. I just say, "I can't take you."

Public Health Professor C: But there's a time limit here. And how are we going to handle this? For instance, women [in need of abortion] are running around New York now. They can't be taken in by one facility, and they may be wandering around trying to get a termination.

(Reading from the document relating to referral and preoperative and postoperative care, one physician said:)

Physician S: What do all these things have to do with abortions—referral, physicals, and so on? What does checking the woman's ear have to do with sucking out her uterus? *It's not a question of what I do, but what we're going to require by law* [speaker's emphasis].

(Discussion of physical examination.)

Physician B: Who's going to make the referral out of the clinic—not the counselor?

Committee Chairman: The physician is captain of the ship, and he has to know the counselor's evaluation. The physician properly makes the appropriate referral.

Public Health Professor C: Who should make the appropriate referral? The counselor may know more about the patient than the physician.

Committee Chairman: Doctors are legally and morally responsible for patients throughout their contact in the facility.

Public Health Professor C: We're talking about a larger set of issues—marital counseling, sex counseling, and other social needs.

Physician B: The natural childbirth people try to take over the physician function. But I want to know what's happening to that patient when I'm responsible for an institution [facility or medical staff direction]. My name and reputation are involved in this. I want to know what's happening in this referral business. . . . The doctor has to have the word on everything. After all, he may be sued.

Public Health Professor C: The physician, in controlling the referral, is taking on a domain outside his control. The physician's awareness of the community resources is involved here. We're concerned with patients who can't get care because the doctor does not grant permission.

Patients' rights, from subsequent discussion, hinged on the autonomy of the counselor or, at least, the counselor in a viable team relationship with the physician.

Physician S: The counselor-circulating nurse role is most important. This is the support person for the patient. A model that we have is the counselor as the doctor's helper.

Social Work Professor: The counselors in New York are unionized. They are not only doctors' helpers, but doctors' critics. The doctor can be fired if they don't like his style.

Physician A: This is the doctor as technician?

Social Work Professor: Yes.

Physician S: We have a model in our minds of New York, and that's the one we want!

Chairman: I don't question what's going on in New York, but I question if Michigan should initiate this.

This Committee eventually resolved referral and control issues in *favor* of physicians. They declared referral to be nonmandatory and counselors to be dependent on physicians.

Fetal Residue

Committee physicians, whether private practitioners or public health officers and doctors, recognized that physician autonomy and control had to be well defined and regulated. "Profiteering" in the lucrative abortion trade was seen as a temptation to doctors, just as it had been to practitioners in the criminal abortion system. "Charlatans" could ruin it for everyone, especially if they moved into this potentially open market and set up unregulated clinics and abortion programs. How to keep physicians "in line" without encroaching on their occupational rights was the crucial problem. Discussing tissue examination of fetal residue brought into focus the dilemma of professional control versus public health regulation. The reasoning took this course:

Physician A: We shouldn't put too many controls on the private physician. The hospital licensing law covers the inspection of all pathological tissue which is removed. Nathanson's [New York clinic director] experience was that it's a good idea to have pathological examinations. But he hasn't come up with anything in 26,000 cases. The reason for this is really monitoring the cases and this is done, actually, to control the physician. Under _____[former director], all the physician had to do was lay out the tissue and put it in a bottle to show pregnancy. It was a concern that unscrupulous men would be cutting up the tissue and putting it in different bottles.

Physician B: I was trained to do my own pathological examinations. You don't need to have a licensed pathologist to do this. But there should be some way to report the pathological finding.

Committee Chairman: There are medical, legal reasons why there would be pathological examinations. In a licensed institution, there is a need to have responsibility fixed. This is built in for protection of the institution.

Public Health Professor C: The purpose of the pathological examination in terms of the abortion is to make sure that the products of conception are cleaned out.

The issue of tissue examination was unresolved at this time. The question was reopened at a later meeting dealing with physical plant requirements. Members' observations played a critical role here.

Committee Chairman: We need to build these regulations [for the physical plant] into the document because, although this is an obvious thing for us, we need to have this as a protection against those facilities that may not take these basic physical plants into consideration.

Public Health Professor D: How would you dispose of the fetal remains? Would this plug up the drainage system, that is, the fetal materials? If you do not plan on disposing of them, would you save them as placentas are often now saved?

Public Health Engineer: This is not a problem. We'll just chop it up, and it can be disposed of in the toilet.

Public Health Official: From my observation in eastern Europe, the fetus can be readily chopped up, head in one piece, thorax in another, and these will be the only pieces that will be identified. I've seen where they collect these materials for a day in a jar, and then dump them into the john.

Public Health Professor C: But what about identification of fetal tissue? What happens here?

Public Health Official: We determine in the clinical field what the fetal residue looks like.

Public Health Professor C: I believe that the individual examination of fetal material falls within my comfort level. . . . There's a film out from San Francisco put out by _____, in which they used a beaker to identify the placenta and materials after they were out. This was a procedure simply of straining it on the cheesecloth.

Public Health Official: There was only one place [in eastern Europe] where I've actually seen a nurse spread out the materials on cheesecloth so the doctor could identify at least two-thirds of the fetus.

Hospital Administrator E: This must be the first operative procedure where the doctor is not subject to peer review.

Committee Chairman: With relation to this problem, it's very easy to cheat. You can put the materials in two different jars.

Hospital Administrator F: It seems that there is a lack of equity in this situation. Hospital administrators are going to have to require pathological examination, but this doesn't hold for freestanding clinics [said with passion].

Public Health Professor N: This is for hospital-legal protection.

Hospital Administrator F: But there's no protection in the clinics. We'll do it anyway. But I don't like the idea that we are controlled. The freestanding clinic can do anything it wants to. If the doctor is going to put the fetal material in a jar and then throw it down the hatch, then we'll never see it. I think there's inequity here!

Regulatory Control

Some committee members were incensed by the discussion. Absence of peer review, inequity in the control situation among types of abortion facilities and procedures that, for some members, appeared to be little more than technicalities (plant arrangement, fetal remains, blood drainage, and numbers served) violated traditional expectations of medical order. For these members, the entire business of "regulating" versus "recommending" implied that for hospitals, control was maximum; for clinics, control was minimum or absent. These members interpreted "Let the facility decide" as a code for introducing a professionally suspect program, less related to a medical order than to a factory system. Although members conceded that availability of resources, low cost, and a simplified bureaucratic structure were essentials for abortion service, they resisted the technical drift of the proceedings that threatened to turn treatment into an assembly-line process.

Committee Chairman: My whole emphasis here is to avoid the warehousing concept in that you wheel the patient in through an assembly line, and the doctor is just a technician. It's just like a Ford assembly line with five-minute treatment. I want to avoid this kind of situation, if I can. The woman runs through a conveyor belt. It's very dehumanizing. The doctor becomes a technician . . . someone who just scrapes the woman.

(General agreement.)
Public Health Professor B: [Name of New York City facility] is running 250 a day.
It's just like an assembly line. It's really a warehouse.

Freestanding clinic proponents pushed hard to get members to recognize
that, with women making the choice, abortion became a simple medical
procedure, and as such, the new concept was legitimate. Hospital supporters rejected this view. The hospital team could "buy" the clinic idea,
with its nonmedical orientation of "facility as a recreational center." But
somehow loss of "peer review" continued to concern some members. When
physicians moved to consider doctors' offices as possible "termination"
sites, the hospital supporters reacted negatively. In their view, it was serious
enough that "hackers" would be getting into the "business," but to allow
"incompetents" to hold forth in doctors' offices, where they could not be
touched by public health regulations and where the physician license was
practically nonrevokable under existing rules, was unthinkable.

Physicians argued, in turn, that the most "logical" place for cheap,
unrestricted patient service was still the office practice; after all, most clinics
began as doctors' offices. Despite pleas, warnings, and even threats by
proponents of physician office abortion, the hospital group held firm. Even
public health advocates, though recognizing the appeal of low cost and
ready accessibility of office sites, resisted association with what members
unanimously believed was an unregulated situation.

After more extensive negotiations, the Committee arrived at a settle-
ment. By reducing physical plant requirements and by eliminating a suggestion for franchise-type facilities supervised by the Department of Public
Health, it was agreed that doctors' offices could be licensed *if they met the
criteria established by the guidelines*. Quasi-clinic, quasi-office arrangements
offered a compromise between the extremes of elaborate, expensive special
plant arrangements and standard, smaller, local office settings.

The facilities compromise, then, resulted from a "mix" between conceptions of abortion. Abortion as an exceptionalistic health service? Yes.
But not solely hospital-based, as originally conceived. Regulations were
designed to accommodate local practitioners—those who were willing to
expand office space to "fit" requirements but who were unable to afford
building an "abortion mill."

Abortion as a standard medical service? Yes. By linking the clinic concept to hospital practice and back-up support, maximum utilization of
special services was possible without disrupting normal hospital routines.
Equipment, testing, and supplementary services would be minimum. The
clinic would be restricted to early abortion, counseling, and a limited referral system, the latter depending on the whim of the director. These
standards were not satisfying to all but were adequate for consensus building.

Abortion as a nonmedical service? Yes. Successful patient outcome would be, in large part, a consequence of the support role played by counselors. As paraprofessional staff, counselors were expected to work *through* the physician in much the same way that the social worker operates within the diagnostic directives of the psychiatrist in traditional mental health settings. Consensus upheld hierarchy but preserved a large area of autonomy for the counselor.

ALTERNATIVE SCENARIOS

What kinds of legal abortion services were actually available in this emerging medical model? On the one hand, the freestanding abortion clinic flourished in urban centers where anonymity and segmental services kept costs down and patient volume high. On the other hand, hospitals were the only legitimate facility providing second-trimester abortion, a far more medically risky intervention. Inevitably, there were abuses in both systems, especially in the early stages: unnecessarily high complication rates; poor or no counseling; excessive costs, especially for hospitalization; inadequately trained or punitive medical and nursing staff; and lack of follow-up care. To assure a good track record for abortion service, public health advocates monitored facilities carefully, hoping to correct deficiencies and enhance the quality of service.

Two years of experience with liberalized abortion law in New York City, with the highest abortion volume in the United States, showed significant social and medical trends (Pakter, et al., 1973, 524–535; see also Harting and Hunter, 1971):

- There were a total of 334,865 abortions between July 1, 1970, and June 30, 1972; of this number, 63.4 percent of the patients wre nonresidents and 36.6 percent were residents. New Jersey, Illinois, Michigan, and Ohio, respectively, led in the number of women coming to the city for abortions. Only 5 percent of non–New York City residents lived in New York State.

- Resident patients tended to be mothers, with 60 percent having had one to three previous pregnancies. Nonresidents, by contrast, were typically experiencing a first pregnancy.

- Among residents receiving abortion in this period, 44.9 percent were nonwhite, 44.2 percent were white, and 10.9 percent were Puerto Rican. Among nonresidents, 87.2 percent were white; only 12.1 percent were nonwhite. Out-of-state travel costs prevented most poor minorities from using the new abortion broker arrangements.

- The saline instillation method, associated with the highest complication rate, actually increased in the second year of reporting. The complication rate was more than ten times greater for saline instillation than it was for suction or D & C methods.

- For every 1,000 abortions, there were thirty-four women with various complications, including hemorrhage, infection, perforated uterus, anesthesia-related problems, retained tissue, lacerated cervix, and failure to abort. Many complications were related to inexperienced medical staff or "hurry," the rushing through a procedure or anesthesia because of case backlogs.

- Abortion facilities accounted for twenty-nine deaths in New York City. Of these deaths, sixteen resulted from abortions performed in legal facilities, and thirteen fatalities occurred as the result of illegal abortions. Eight of the sixteen deaths after legal abortion were associated with the saline instillation method.

- The number of abortions rose by 40 percent in the second year of reporting, with most of the increase accounted for by nonresidents. Almost two-thirds of all abortions performed during this two-year period were for nonresidents.

- The legal abortion program was associated with noticeable declines in maternal and infant mortality and a reduction in births. But one report concluded that the system remained highly imperfect. Inadequate family planning kept the abortion rate high and contributed to "repeaters." Also, too many women were delaying the abortion beyond the safe period (i.e., the first twelve weeks). Continuous surveillance was necessary to prevent further increases in complication rates. And there was a necessity to have the abortion law liberalized across the nation, so that terminations could be handled locally, avoiding strain, expense, and increased risk because of insufficient follow-up.

Despite public health and clergy surveillance, the legal abortion service remained inconsistent and was sometimes as dangerous as the illegal service it was designed to replace. The following two case studies—one a demonstration model of a freestanding clinic and the other an abortion hospital service—reflect the polarities characterizing this early period.[4]

A CLIENT-CENTERED ABORTION FACILITY

The Washington, D.C., clinic that opened its doors to abortion patients on March 15, 1971, was a self-consciously bureaucratic health organization. It was a product of the new legal definitions handed down by one state after another. In 1969 a U.S. District Court had ruled that the city's abortion law was unconstitutionally vague because it set no guidelines for doctors. The clinic thus opened its doors with the assurance that the medical licensure board and legal system of Washington, D.C., would support this new venture. And they were right.

The clinic managers were astute and knowledgeable. The director had previously worked for Population Council, an organization long associated with interests in national and international population planning, and the associate director had held a professional position in the Peace Corps.

Clinic organizers began with an idealized blueprint because there was little actual national experience that could be used as the basis for the planning, policy, and research model they had in mind. Beginning with the setting, and continuing throughout all phases of the program, there was an effort to avoid any throwbacks to "back alley" abortionists. Gentility was the sign of a new era in abortion practice, and organizational reports stressed that managers should create a "carefully modulated environment of refined elegance."

The privately operated, nonprofit clinic occupied about 4,000 square feet, or almost the entire second floor, of an eight-story structure that was filled mainly with doctors' and dentists' offices. An elaborate hospital back-up system was available for any medical emergency.

The ideology, articulated by its director, was that the facility would serve as a "model for the rest of the country and maybe the world." The organization collected data on patient numbers, rate of increase, statistical computations of complication rates, and geographical tracking, as well as social data of patients. It was a tight schedule: Directors kept careful track of patient flows, physicians' hours, counseling sessions and other staff activity with a steady stream of written instructions. In order to meet their goal of treating 300 women a week, organizational bottlenecks had to be eliminated. For example, the intake referral system was analyzed as inefficient. Records showed that, of 142 appointments in one week, only eighty-two procedures had been completed. Thirteen cancellations and other patient dropouts (mainly because of the advanced stage of pregnancy and a few women who turned out not to be pregnant at all) reduced patient load considerably. Educating the public about the new abortion concept through a favorable media helped to reduce the intake snags.

A major problem in all of the early freestanding clinics was securing medically licensed and, preferably, obstetrically trained board-certified physicians. Doctors typically resisted becoming involved with what many believed was "bad" medicine in poorly equipped facilities. The clinic circumvented established medicine by drawing on local or out-of-state physicians who were attracted to this type of medicine, who lacked full practices, or who were newly minted medical school graduates. By breaking the practice down into three-and-a-half-hour sessions, the clinic reduced the tedium associated with performing a repetitive procedure. And since almost all of the revolving staff of sixteen doctors had practices elsewhere, the stigma of being the "abortionist" could be avoided.

In this facility the greatest impediment to patient access was the strict clinic criteria. Abortions cost $200; payments were in cash only, with no deferred-payment plan. Pregnancy termination was limited to ten weeks' gestation. Women over thirty-five years of age and patients with three or more previous pregnancies were excluded. The patient under eighteen years of age required parental consent. Although regulations were later eased and abortion costs reduced, the directors believed that only the most cautious approach could guarantee a good track record. Such a cautious approach by clinics, however, resulted in overall higher complication rates of hospital abortions because hospitals handled the high-risk patients rejected by the clinics. A few cynics complained that if hospital abortion services could get rid of the "minority mother of five with chronic health problems," their complication rates would compare favorably with those of the clinics.

Clinic treatment included a well-rehearsed routine. Women were organized into time-cohorts of six to eight patients, who moved through the intake, laboratory tests, counseling, vacuum suction procedure, and recovery room in a smooth, predictable flow. The abortion itself was handled like an office procedure, with the physician serving as anesthesiologist and surgeon and the counselor providing nursing and social support.

Counseling played a crucial role in treatment: It provided standard medical information on the pre- and post-abortion procedure; it dealt with guilt as both a constructive and a destructive emotion; it offered support during the procedure; it reviewed health care after the abortion. The counselor also attempted to discuss birth control issues frankly as problems in regularity, unconscious failure, and future choices. The clinic asserted that without counseling, "we would be just another medical facility." Counseling was on an individual basis, with the counselee referred to as a "woman" or by her name, never as a "client" or a "patient."

The clinic collected comments of women who had received abortions and reprinted these in their newsletters. One patient said: "My counselor was really nice. She was two years older than me so that we really got along well. We talked about everything, and she held my hand through the whole procedure. I really needed that." Another patient, who was initially hesitant, came to see the experience in a new light after the counseling:

There I was, me, doing something that I had always frowned on. I really couldn't believe it. I went through the usual steps and my apprehension increased with each completed phase, until I met my counselor, Liz. Liz was my strength. She pulled me through. I couldn't have made it alone. I had no idea there were still people in the world like her... thank you and thank all the wonderful people at _____ who helped make my day more comfortable. I lost but I gained.

In effect, the counselor humanized the proceedings in the context of a highly bureaucratized service. In this and other abortion clinics a new health worker emerged—less educated, more specialized, and more person-centered than social workers, psychologists, and other highly trained therapists. Later studies, however, show that counseling is not a uniform experience (see Bracken, et al., 1973). Younger, single, never-previously-pregnant women prefer group counseling. The relatively older, married women with children express a preference for individual counseling, finding the group discussion superficial and uninformative and unconsoling for problems of guilt and loss.

Directors conceded that in 1971 the clinic was ahead of its time. Experimental programs such as medical and counseling follow-up, sex education, full-scale research, and in-service training of medical and counseling staff were expensive drains on these new facilities. But the view of the problem-pregnant woman as one in crisis, whose normality hinged on the availability of a nontraumatic termination, made this demonstration project a huge success.

The rush to build clinics that followed the Supreme Court decision to strike down states' abortion laws gave birth to dozens of small, poorly equipped facilities that competed for patients within the same city. Lacking both professionalism and humanistic treatment, these medically irregular facilities continue to plague public health and lay advocates. Model facilities were evidently not exportable in a market long geared for profit and rapid client turnover.

DEGRADATION CEREMONY: HOSPITAL SALINE ABORTION

The road to a hospital abortion contrasted sharply with the model clinic routing and included seemingly endless delays, clerical errors, complicated procedures, high costs, and unnecessary emotional trauma. In New York City the hospital system became the bane of abortion reformers, who wanted to liberate abortion from what they perceived to be the antithesis of good abortion care; the hospital was invariably equated with the punitive, profiteering, and red tape of the pre-legal era.

As New York City health codes piled further regulations on hospitals, the saline, or "salting out," procedures—the method of choice for second-trimester abortion—were increasingly restricted to fewer and fewer facilities. With increased shortages and heavier out-of-state traffic, the hospital system became overloaded. For example, in the first 111 days after abortion was legalized, there were more than 30,000 reported terminations. Yet the number of women admitted to city hospital emergency rooms after botched, presumably illegal abortions was as high as ever.

"The system isn't working," an obstetrician at Mount Sinai Hospital remarked to a public hearing. "The hospital waiting lists are getting longer, not shorter, the hospitals are unable and unwilling to provide compassionate service for the abortion patient and the profiteering is unbelievable." (quoted in the New York Times, 20 October 1970). New York City clergy and lay advocates, working under the Reverend Howard Moody, set up a complaint service. Jane E. Brody (May 9, 1970), medical reporter for the New York Times, printed these typical statements out of a total of 1,000 patient complaints.

A 20–year-old Brooklyn woman was sent to a city hospital three days in a row and each time was told to come back the next day. On her fourth visit, she was told that the hospital was filled, and she couldn't be given an appointment.

A woman who was 10 weeks pregnant when examined at Kings County Hospital on September 22 was scheduled for an abortion on December 4, her 21st week, although the hospital was not doing abortions beyond the 16th week of pregnancy.

A 17–year-old Brooklyn girl who applied at a municipal hospital when she was nine weeks pregnant and still able to get a simple one-day $160 abortion was given an appointment for an examination six weeks later. She was then told she would have to pay $325 in advance for the more complicated abortion she then required.

A low-income mother of three was given this oversimplified explanation of the abortion she was about to receive: "We stick a needle in your belly to kill the baby."

A mother of two was emotionally shattered when, upon admission to a voluntary hospital, she was asked to sign a fetal death certificate as "maternal parent of the deceased."

Hospital abortions were unbelievably costly. In one case a private for-profit hospital turned over fifty of its 118 beds to abortion, charging $575 for a simple, early abortion on an outpatient basis. The fee for a saline procedure ran $300 to $400 higher. Another hospital, a voluntary, nonprofit facility, charged $450 for a "salting-out" abortion; the doctor's fee was an additional $400.

In the clergy-referred New York City hospital for second-trimester abortion that I observed, women and their family and friends stood or milled about in a tiny, sparsely furnished, waiting room that lacked adequate chairs. The entire organization appeared primitive: Patients were over-booked; long lines of shuffling, silent women wound around halls waiting for various stages of services; and no counseling or other patient-professional interaction could be observed. All patients were examined by a physician to determine the number of weeks of pregnancy. Although the law had declared twenty-four weeks as the upper limit for a legal abortion, even the most experienced obstetrician could misdiagnose by a few weeks. And because a large proportion of late abortions were among teenagers, who were often vague about their last menstrual period, very late abortions producing fetuses well over six months' gestation were not uncommon.

Physician examinations were often casual, even lacking a female attendant or any semblance of privacy. Patients were given pelvic examinations in rooms with doors left open and sometimes without a cloth or paper drapery to cover themselves. In one instance, a professional group was discussing the health records of women who had received saline abortions in one corner of a fairly large treatment room. A young girl was pushed into the room by a staff person who complained that there was no other space available, and while the group continued their discussion, one of the doctors removed himself from the group, walked over to the treatment table, told the young woman to pull down her jeans, and proceeded to do the internal pelvic examination. The teenager, who had a very late pregnancy, appeared too glazed to react to what I and the other two women found to be a traumatizing event.

This same hospital had initiated its abortion service by consulting feminists, who introduced a full-scale counseling service. After the facility was purchased by a group of foreign businessmen, the innovative system was scrapped in favor of higher patient loads.

Treatment entailed two parts. First, an empty syringe was inserted into the wall of the abdomen to withdraw amniotic fluid. Another needle was then inserted with a saline solution. Other injections also were added, such as antibiotics and medications for speeding up the labor. In the second phase, approximately twenty-four hours later, the patient delivered a mummified-like fetus in the hospital bed. With two patients assigned to each room, roommates were usually at different stages of labor. Hence a woman might have witnessed or assisted at the delivery of her roommate's fetus. Chronic shortages of nursing personnel was the reason cited for this practice.

After delivery the woman was usually wheeled to a treatment room for removal of the placenta and other corrective surgery. Because patients were not provided information about what to expect of the procedure, delivery, or appearance of the fetus, some women were reported by clergy advocates to be in shock after delivery. Nursing personnel also admitted that screaming, crying, moaning, and severe depression were common (and expected) responses of patients after saline delivery.

After the 1973 *Roe v. Wade* decision, hospital abortions in New York City were more competitively priced, although abortion service continued to remain medically marginal except in the city-funded Metropolitan Hospital System, where the largest proportion of abortion patients were drawn from minority and poor residents. Long associated with sterilization, high costs, and punitive treatment, New York City hospitals paradoxically served abortion reform by offering a countermodel of abortion care. Advocates continued to push hard to move all early abortions into the clinics. For the 20 percent of women who received late abortions and who were likely to be either younger or older than the average abortion patient, there was little human service and no advocacy.

IMPLICATIONS OF MEDICALIZING ABORTION

Joseph Gusfield (1980, vii) observes that "solutions to human problems often create new problems in solving the initial ones." The transformation of abortion from a therapeutic, or highly complex, hospital regime to elective surgery was initiated by medical and clergy reformers who were convinced that women's mental health depended on humanitarian, professional medicine. They drew on studies of complication rates that showed the vast superiority of an early-diagnosed pregnancy followed by a suction abortion for an unwanted birth compared with a delayed termination or full-term delivery. They believed that counseling and an upbeat medical setting would change the nature of abortion from its illegal polluted state to a normal, life-enhancing event.

But there is a moral connotation to medical control that underlies the humanitarian perception of the abortion seeker as a crisis patient. This focuses on what Gusfield calls a "politics of reality." Here institutions and agents are assigned the power of categorizing and defining what is "real" and thus determine the cognitive, moral, and institutional dimensions of the issue. And whether the issue is hyperactivity in children or homosexuality in adults, the power to categorize and define displaces or wipes out competing definitions.

Medicalizing abortion has been no exception.[5] The medical model, as opposed to religious, legal, feminist, or even psychiatric models, is positivist and correctional. It takes the sickness perspective as natural and unquestioning, and it offers treatment and other technical interventions under professional control. Illness puts abortion under a different moral light than does "sin," "crime," or "preference." But it also introduces an element of compulsive behavior (doctor knows best), suggesting the woman's helplessness and loss of control. Doctors and hospitals determine rules of practice and techniques; women remain ignorant and excluded from these important institutional processes.

Proponents of medical abortion aimed to depoliticize the procedure, a policy that failed. If it had succeeded, the medicalization of abortion would have diminished or possibly obliterated altogether recognition of differences in moral preferences, presenting abortion as a mere technical issue. This could facilitate state control over population planning, since a "rationalized" policy would center on technical hardware and outputs, not individual choice.

Medicalization has the result of reducing social condemnation, but at the same time it arouses ambivalence about what can meaningfully be construed as evil. In such morally ambivalent contexts, there is "the banality of evil," as Hannah Arendt (1963) warned.

In the new abortion concept, exemplified in the model clinic, pain, violence, oppression, exploitation, and loss are muted or denied; there is no evil. In the old abortion concept, illustrated in the New York City hospital case, evil is manifest and punishment is deserved. All participants in this punitive structure—doctors, nurses, technical staff, and patients—are locked into it. Is it any wonder that recruiting medical staff into these systems has been so difficult? Hospital regimes were almost universally perceived as places of death. But clinics are not exempt from the stigma of abortion; they are reported to experience chronic staff turnover, a burn-out phenomenon.

The polarization in abortion services continued, with unattached clinics turning out as high as 95 percent of the abortions in a given area, while hospitals provided the scant remainder. Medical and lay abortion reformers confronting a hostile or inadequate care environment looked to the courts for remedy. But implementing a permissive policy after *Roe v. Wade* was stymied by what the Supreme Court *failed* to do. The Constitution only prohibits states from limiting the provision of abortion service by physicians, clinics, and hospitals; it does *not* require states or the medical community to provide such services (Bond and Johnson, 1982, 1–24). Without mandated implementation, a controversial policy, whether school desegregation or abortion, remains vulnerable to attack from disenchanted supporters and opponents alike.

NOTES

1. Bart's (1977) analysis of a feminist abortion system, drawn on for this section, may have been a one-of-a-kind operation. While many of the health collectives had referrals to illegal abortionists, both in the United States and abroad, most collectives actually gave few or no abortions. Where abortions were part of the program, they were handled by professional medical or nursing staff (fieldwork notes). (See Peterson, 1976 for another view.)

2. Sample and method for this section include: Attendance at a Michigan State Public Health–sponsored Abortion Facilities Planning Committee meeting over a six-month period (October 15, 1971 to March 18, 1972) provided the major source of data. Nineteen representatives from medical or health-related occupations and organizations were included as permanent members of the working committee, including physicians, public health officials, professors, nurses, hospital administrators, one social worker, and one official representative from the Clergy Counseling Service, who had permanent membership. Two other "visitors," including myself, attended almost all meetings. There was *no* consumer representative. I conducted formal interviews with eleven of nineteen full-time members and had extensive outside committee contact with eight of the eleven persons. Almost all members knew one another *before* the Committee formed. This promoted friendly interaction on a first-name basis. It also contributed to verbal moderation (for the most part), despite strong philosophical differences, and toward efforts to resolve apparent disputes or "table" them until the group felt they had adequate information to move ahead. The practice of tabling or evading issues made it difficult, if not impossible, to segment the "natural" speech flow. Discourse took a zigzag pattern, with issues appearing, disappearing, and reappearing weeks later. I had to reconstruct meanings out of what often seemed to be irrational and inexplicable utterances, a task that was simplified once I discovered the *logical* connections between disputed issues, opposing beliefs, and contending authority claims. Undoubtedly, I neglected issues considered strategic by some Committee members. I touch only briefly, for example, on plant requirements and room space, despite whole meetings dedicated to these issues. I try to convey some of the substantive content that was exchanged, although I cannot capture the various mood shifts of humor, seriousness, pettiness, altruism, anger, and, by a few opposed to change, genuine anguish. To discern salience of issues, I used *repetition* and *time spent* on each issue as indicators of problem areas. Dispute required little investigative

subtlety. After a few meetings it was comparatively easy to read cues and detect significant ideological differences. Key informants, also present at these sessions, helped to bridge the gaps in my understanding of the proceedings. In sum, the methods of analysis for this section include (1) nearly verbatim transcription of most meetings, (2) analysis of documents (seven drafts of the Guidelines and minutes of meetings), (3) follow-up interviews clarifying meanings, and (4) linguistic techniques used in anthropology for mapping semantic domains (see Tyler, 1969).

3. The issue of blood and social policy is richly analyzed in Titmuss (1971).

4. Whereas it was extraordinarily difficult to gain access to illegal abortion clinics, much less observe procedures and interview staff and patients, "model" clinics welcomed academic observers. The Washington, D.C., clinic, discussed here, was one of the most successful efforts in that city and in New York State to reverse the professional and public image of abortion as "dirty medicine." The New York hospital situation was off limits to almost all observers. I was aided in my efforts to gain access through the help of Dr. Raymond C. Lerner, an abortion researcher, then working at Albert Einstein Hospital in New York City.

5. Conrad and Schneider (1980) argue that the medicalization of abortion resulted largely because middle-class women were among the largest recipients of abortion in the 1960s. As public perception of abortion moved from a lower-class to a middle-class problem, deviance designations tended to change from "badness" to "sickness."

10

Strategic Legitimations

For more than a century, legal policies in abortion were arenas of repression. Proscribed in all the states' criminal codes, the law excluded, repressed, censored, and concealed women's reproduction under the guise that bearing and delivering infants was "natural" and "normal," a woman's place. During the decriminalization phase (circa 1969 to 1973), which involved legal change in more than thirty states, a general loosening of restrictions occurred. Nontherapeutic abortion became a legal possibility but with various strings attached: husband's or parents' consent, residency requirements, inhospital procedures, abortion committees or additional physicians' concurrence, highly limited access, and often excessive costs.

In *Roe v. Wade*, decided January 22, 1973, the Supreme Court held unconstitutional Texas's (and virtually every other states') criminal abortion statutes.[1] From the point of view of civil libertarians and pro-abortion groups, such judicial activism was an instrument of mercy. Women were formally given the right to make a legal abortion choice without state interference. Indeed, for many observers, the law appeared to have withdrawn altogether from its formal sources located in the text or court structure and traditions. Now it appeared that the law was primarily responsive to social trends and public opinion. "The court has no business getting into that business," said one critic (Ely, 1973). When the court supplants the legislature with its own view of "wise social policy," Ely (1973) said, judicial interference in state operations signals the rise of an "imperial judiciary." In the *Roe* case, the Court clearly went beyond its traditional mandate: application of established law to a relatively narrow factual situation, said another critic (Cramton, 1976, 522).

Courts of law are increasingly called on to derive acceptable solutions to difficult problems involving the legal profession, the criminally accused, family matters, moral issues, environmental pollution, consumer rights, fundamental liberties, sex discrimination, and political matters (Webb,

1976, vii). For many court watchers, though, abortion was perceived as the most problematic from a legal point of view. Pregnancy by consent totally ignored social and medical care for the unborn, produced an unregulated abortion market (especially in the first trimester), and granted liberty exclusively to the pregnant woman. This untenable situation, said detractors, undermined constitutional integrity and weakened social control.[2]

Was this law an exclusively pro-woman ruling, as some legal scholars contended? Or were there other, more germane agendas that the Court had in mind? In this chapter I examine how the declaration of constitutional guarantees allegedly protecting women's reproductive choice offered technical freedom only. The Court's strategy, which some observers believed was basically aimed for more effective population control, especially among minorities (Francome, 1984, ch. 8), was designed to end the chaotic enforcement situation by giving a positive signal to the medical community that the woman's choice would be contingent on the doctor's professional authority. Inasmuch as the right to an abortion was hedged with qualifiers and modifiers, legal intervention opened the way to legitimate medical control under state auspices, while maintaining a panoply of legal impartiality. After *Roe*, the medicalization of women's reproductive power has perhaps never been stronger (Conrad and Schneider, 1980).

ALTERNATIVE LEGAL POLICIES FOR CONTROLLING ABORTION

At this juncture it may be useful to review the various social factors involved in changing legal policies in abortion. Here we identify law as a power instrument, not as a neutral or impartial party to a social dispute. The law as a consensus tool has served as a convenient ideological fiction in liberal democratic theory. The decline of moral consensus and of social institutions, such as the family and church, places more pressure on the law to serve as an instrument of conflict resolution and social control.[3] And as the Supreme Court increasingly exercises its special decisional procedures for policymaking, especially in areas of strong moral dilemmas, the courts become the arena of political controversy.

In legalizing abortion, the Court offered the promise of equality to women, an affirmation of fundamental rights of choice without stigma. But medicalization of abortion in the absence of legally mandated access and public funding for poor women merely reinforces the professional authority model. This entails social distance between doctor and patient. It also subordinates the woman and "treats" her unwanted pregnancy as a deviant event. Figure 10.1 shows the comparison between four distinct state doctrines of legal control.

Criminalization

Over the last century, abortion policy moved through four distinct stages—criminalization, decriminalization, legalization and medicalization—demonstrating the changing character of social control over women's reproduction.

Abortion has not always been a crime in the United States. Abortion was never illegal in the colonial period and was a relatively common practice in the United States between 1840 and the late 1870s. Estimates indicate that there was one abortion for every twenty-five to thirty births during the first three decades of the nineteenth century and leaped as high as one abortion for every five to six live births for the period from 1840 to 1870. As a competitive medical activity, abortion was both a highly visible and commercialized practice (Mohr, 1978).

While Comstock and the anti-vice movement are often credited with the successful passing of criminal abortion laws (Pivar, 1973), there were other, more significant factors giving rise to legal change. According to Mohr (1978), there were five social elements that played into the criminalizing of abortion. One was the death of patients, usually married women with children, and notorious court cases that condemned both the woman and the practitioner. The view held by legalists and physicians was that women had to be saved from themselves through outlawing abortion.

A second condition was general distress over falling birth rates. Legislation in New York State, for example, was expressly opposed to "checks on population," as native white Protestants were allegedly underproducing children relative to immigrant Catholics. Large profits in abortion, a third factor, upset doctors especially. But in addition, public disgust over "immoral and corrupting" advertising led to legislation against the advertising of abortion services. Until 1860, outlawing abortion itself was viewed as unenforceable, a fourth consideration. Instead, by forbidding public advertising, crusaders hoped to eliminate the thriving abortion market. And, finally, a physicians' crusade aimed to control professional medicine and eliminate the *laissez-faire* market—a missionary-like effort that convinced legislators that the "great and growing evil" (Mohr, 1978, 153) of abortion must be eradicated. The American Medical Association, which campaigned for anti-abortion statutes in every state, used the rhetoric of professionalism but sought state help to enforce their largely unenforceable codes of medical conduct. According to Mohr, the "anti-abortion crusade was nearly perfect" as a method of establishing the regular physician against competitors (Mohr, 1978, 164).

Cyril Means, who was quoted a total of seven times in the *Roe v. Wade* Court transcript, proposed, contrariwise, that sound medical reasons existed for making abortion illegal. Means (1971, 385) argues that, in the early part of the nineteenth century, abortion was a dangerous procedure.

Figure 10.1

Alternative Legal Policies for Controlling Deviance—Criminalization, Decriminalization, Legalization, and Medicalization—and Implications for Social Conflict and Change

Legal Factors	Criminalization	Decriminalization	Legalization (Equality Model)	Medicalization (Professional Model)
State Doctrine	Crime—mala es se	Moral problem official state disengagement; retention of formal or informal control	Equal protection due process	Social problems rehabilitation/ treatment
Sanction	Punitive	Mixed: punitive/ rehabilitative	None—freechoice	Deviant label
Nature of Rule	Prescriptive: criminal liability	Unspecified; less criminal sanction	Prescriptive: rights stipulated for clients	Prescriptive: rights stipulated for medical system
Market Conditions				
Access	Severely limited for legal services (e.g. therapeutic abortion)	Relatively selective; legal market competes with illegal market	Affirmative	Varies by client status and ability-to-pay
Technology	Primitive; high risk	Adaptive; reduced risk	Highly advanced	Highly advanced low risk for preferred clientele
Social Costs	High; stigmatizing act; prison, fine, reputational loss	Moderate; retention of stigma	Low or none; little or no stigma	Varies by client status
Economic Costs	Very high: scarcity situation	Moderate: limited supply relative to demand	Low: supply/demand in equilibrium	Price discrimination
Beneficiaries	Criminal justice system	Social agencies; psychia- trists; middle class	Clients	Middle class women and restricted sectors of the medical system
Implications for Social Conflict & Change	Consensus among elites; resistance among alienated groups; collective apathy shifts to collective reaction	Conflict amont elites; collective action among partisans	Relative consensus among elites; collect- ive reaction among some partisans	Dissenus among elites; organizational regula- tion of deviant behavior

He provides figures to suggest that the death rate from sepsis from abortion surgery, even when performed in a hospital, was more than 30 percent in 1828, when New York's first abortion law was passed. The danger of this operation, as well as all other surgical procedures, was the key factor behind legal restrictions.

From another perspective, Douglas (1977) argues that the strict division of labor that arose in the last quarter of the nineteenth century—men in the factories and offices and women confined to the home—was a general reaction to the oppression and powerlessness experienced by men in their narrow industrial work roles. A restrictive abortion code helped to facilitate the separatist ideology and promote homemaking as a full-time commitment among the middle class. By 1900 it was the unwed lower-class and immigrant wives who used abortion, not married, Protestant women (Mohr, 1978, 24).

The criminalization policy represented, then, a sharp break from previous tolerance norms. As a response to changed social conditions, the criminal sanction was certainly reactive. But as a change-generating policy—reinforcing the cult of domesticity, increasing the birth rate among the middle class and decreasing it among the lower class, and supporting a medical monopoly in health care, especially for women (Scully, 1980)—the criminal abortion laws performed highly directive state functions.

Decriminalization

Technological changes in medicine in the twentieth century resulted in advanced knowledge and use of fertility control methods. First-trimester abortion became *safer* than a full-term delivery and, among some women, less medically risky than some standard contraceptives (e.g., "the Pill" and the I.U.D.) (Potts, et al., 1977). These conditions along with other secular trends, supported the widespread movement of women into the labor force and initiated fairly dramatic life-style and sex-role changes (Hymowitz and Weissman, 1978). In the last quarter of this century, increased social and economic participation by women has undermined the patriarchal family and made possible a commitment to nonfamilial roles for many women. Urban life-styles have also contributed to demographic change, as delayed marriage and a preference for few or no children tipped the birth rate down. In this context the absence of a safe and effective contraceptive may have actually increased women's dependence on abortion as an alternative method of fertility control (Bumpass and Presser, 1973:33, 46).

Despite the high medical risk and economic costs of illegal abortion, it is estimated that nearly 1 million criminal abortions were performed in the United States during the 1960s (Sarvis and Rodman, 1973). Among educated and professional groups, this was viewed as clearly an anachronistic approach to both population control and individual reproductive choice (Francome, 1984; Jaffe, 1981). By the late 1960s it was clear to advocates and medical groups alike that the policy of criminalizing abortion had failed (Bates and Zawadski, 1964; Packer, 1968; Schur, 1968).

1. Illegal abortions were readily available, either self-induced or performed secretly by physicians or lay persons, and, while costly, were sought by women of all social classes. In New York City, for example, Health Department officials estimated that more than 6,000 women resorted to illegal abortion every year before the abortion law was repealed (Westoff and Westoff, 1971, 123). National estimates of the total number of illegal abortions up to 1973 run from 200,000 to 1 million annually (Mohr, 1978).

2. Infections, ruptures, hemorrhage, and blood clot were frequent sequelae of illegal abortion. Primitive methods of induced abortion and lack of hospital care made abortion the major cause of maternal death until recently. Public health groups had relatively little success in reducing morbidity and increasing access to hospital abortion until the combined efforts of the thalidomide scare and diffusion of medical knowledge about the effects of German measles and other maternal diseases on fetal development mobilized middle-class and professional groups into action.

3. Enforcement officials lacked a clear mandate for controlling the illegal abortion market. Legal intervention was stymied by collusion between officials and practitioners, lack of substantive evidence, and unwillingness of women to serve as court witnesses.

4. Collective opposition by medical and legal reformers to criminal abortion laws also undermined law enforcement. The American Law Institute proposed a model abortion code as early as 1957, followed by similar reform activity among organized medicine, women's groups, and population control partisans in the 1960s. Prosecutors were reluctant to bring abortion cases to court unless the woman's death resulted.

5. From 1969 to 1973, the abortion cause witnessed an explosive development at the court level (Goldstein, 1979, 272). In 1969 and 1970 the abortion laws of California, Texas, Wisconsin, Georgia, and the District of Columbia were declared unconstitutional in lower courts. In 1970 four states (Alaska, Hawaii, New York, and Washington) legalized abortion. In the same year, pro-legalization forces attained a number of "near misses" in Arizona, Maryland, and Vermont. In addition, by 1972, abortion laws had been successfully challenged in Florida, New Jersey, and Connecticut. After 1970, in many other states, a tacit state policy of decriminalization foreshadowed the 1973 Supreme Court decision to outlaw abortion in all states.

The decriminalization policy, initiated by a number of states in the late 1960s and early 1970s, formally revoked the criminal sanction but retained informal restrictions: husband's or parent's consent, hospital quotas, high costs, rejection of indigent patients, psychiatric screening, and involuntary sterilization. Such barriers produced extensive negative effects for both society and individuals, for example, high rates of infant mortality, of pregnancy-related deaths, of teenage pregnancy, of child abuse and others (Caine, et al., 1978).

Tacit sanctions, which persist today, have been mainly directed at powerless groups—the young, poor, uneducated, minority, unmarried, or those women otherwise lacking officially approved statuses and life-styles. Among states having permissive laws, the out-of-state abortion traffic frequently exceeded local demand. Costs plummeted as competition grew and outpatient clinics, sometimes initiated and regulated by feminists, replaced traditional hospital abortion services.

The Supreme Court's decision to legalize abortion in 1973, based on the Texas (*Roe v. Wade*) and Georgia (*Doe v. Bolton*) cases (in Babcock, et al., 1975:943, 958), attempted to equalize access and to turn the abortion problem over to medical and community groups by prohibiting state intervention in the first trimester of abortion, based on the privacy clause. The Court further stipulated, however, that in the second and third trimesters, other interests exceeded the woman's privacy needs, specifically the state's interest in maternal health and protection of the fetus. As the following sections clarify, medical implementation of the abortion law has subsequently resulted in differential impact: pronounced social benefits for middle and upper strata and unresolved social problems for marginal and under-class groups.

Legalization

In *Roe v. Wade*, Justice Blackmun, speaking for the majority, presented the Court's arguments (from *Roe v. Wade*, see also Goldstein, 1979; 1981: 5–28).

1. The right to privacy, though not explicitly mentioned in the Constitution, is protected by the Due Process Clause of the Fourteenth Amendment. In turn, this protection is based on the traditional concern of the Court for protection of the family and motherhood.

2. The Fourteenth Amendment, while not specifically stipulating abortion rights, is broad enough to encompass a woman's decision whether or not to terminate her pregnancy.

3. This right to an abortion is "fundamental" and can therefore be regulated only on the basis of a "compelling state interest."

4. The state does have two "important and legitimate" interests here, the first in protecting maternal health, the second in protecting the life (or potential life) of the fetus. But neither of these interests can be counted as "compelling" throughout the entire pregnancy: each matures with the unborn child.

5. During the first trimester of pregnancy, neither interest is sufficiently compelling to justify state interference with the decision between the woman and her phy-

sician. Citing medical data, the Court indicated that mortality for women undergoing early, legal abortions "appear to be as low as or lower than the rates for normal childbirth." Thus the states' interest in promoting maternal health is not compelling during the first trimester, and it cannot prohibit an abortion nor regulate the conditions under which one is performed (excluding the requirement that abortion must be performed by a licensed physician).

6. As we move into the second trimester, the interest in protecting the fetus remains less compelling. However, because the health risks of abortion begin to exceed those of childbirth, "it follows that, from and after this point a state may regulate the abortion procedure to the extent that the regulation reasonably relates to the preservation and protection of maternal health." Although abortion can be regulated for the second trimester, it cannot be prohibited.

7. At the point at which the fetus becomes "viable" (capable of living outside the mother's uterus), the state's interest in protecting it becomes compelling. Therefore, from the third trimester, the state can prohibit all abortion except when necessary to protect maternal life and health.

In *Doe v. Bolton* (Georgia), the companion case to *Roe v. Wade*, the Court rejected both the hospital committee's and additional physicians' concurrence for an abortion. In both cases the Court attempted to place limits on excessive entanglement in legal processes around abortion. In the language of the Court, privacy meant "the right to be let alone."

But other legal principles intervened to diminish and sometimes wipe out the declared constitutional guarantees. Whether explicit or implicit, the Court enunciated only vaguely the "zone of privacy" doctrine for women, while clearly articulating the principle of "moral paternalism" (Hart, 1963) and judicial omniscience. By dividing pregnancy into early, middle, and late stages, the Court strategically applied a sliding scale of multivariable approach to the equal protection problem. And by placing the abortion decision as a relational matter between a woman and her doctor on the presumption that their interests were identical, legal equality succumbed to the hierarchy of professional medicine.

For example, in *Roe v. Wade* the Court often spoke of the abortion decision in terms of the rights of the physicians, as in the language that follows: "The decision vindicates the right of the physician to administer medical treatment according to his professional judgment to the points where important state interests provide compelling justifications for intervention. Up to those points, the abortion decision in all its respects is inherently and *primarily a medical decision and basic responsibility for it must rest with the physician*" [italics added].

THE PRIVACY PRINCIPLE

The constitutional argument in *Roe v. Wade* theoretically hinged on the Ninth Amendment, which in the then recently established case of *Griswold v. Connecticut* determined that the law against the use of contraceptives by a married couple would entail excessive state interference were the law to be enforced. This decision for married people was later extended to single persons in *Eisenstadt v. Baird*. The theory of the Ninth Amendment provided that the "repository" of all rights "possessed" by the people at the time the Constitution was enacted were retained by the people, unless they were explicitly given up in the Constitution itself. Therefore, any common law rights enjoyed under Anglo-American law in 1776 were themselves preserved and "guaranteed" by the Ninth Amendment. Extensive historical research clearly demonstrated that abortion, at least in the first trimester (pre-"quickening"), was not criminal at the time the Constitution was adopted (Means, 1971, 335; Glen, 1978, 7). In Griswold, the privacy doctrine was extended to prevent the state from intrusions in intimate relations, especially as this affects family affairs, sexuality, contraception, pregnancy, and rearing children. In both *Griswold* and *Roe*, privacy was treated as self-explanatory: a unitary concept, instead of its various legal and social meanings.

"Does privacy have a principle?" asks Tyler Baker in the *Stanford Law Review* (1974, 1161–1189). Instead of various related legal and social meanings, there were at least two opposing legal principles, Baker proposed. According to Baker, the most common legal rendering of privacy is the concept of "selective disclosure," which refers to the right of individuals to determine when, how, and to what extent information about them is communicated to others. The second and more complex meaning of privacy refers to the broader aspect of autonomy. This entails the generalized ability of individuals to determine for themselves whether to perform certain acts or undergo certain experiences. Third, the most significant, although not mentioned in the Baker article, is that privacy is essentially a culturally determined reality, so that a situation profoundly offensive to one society might be a matter of indifference in another (Shils, 1966).

The *Griswold* case involving use of contraceptives aimed to eliminate certain types of "government snooping," not necessarily protect married couples' autonomy to use contraceptives. While somewhat ambiguous, *Griswold* stands as a privacy right of the first type, that of selective disclosure, rather than the second, that of freedom of choice.

Roe signaled a change in the privacy doctrine, away from the legally clearer (if disputed) case of selective disclosure to the constitutionally murkier issue of "privacy" as a "fundamental" right (see Baker, 1974, 1161–1189). The constitutional grounds, however, were highly suspect, as Glen (1978, 9) emphasizes:

But what was this "right to privacy" and where did it come from? Not from the Ninth Amendment, but from the Fourteenth Amendment's guarantee of substantive due process. Because the Court used the Fourteenth rather than the Ninth

Amendment in its ruling, this seemingly progressive decision in fact had a reactionary basis. Unlike procedural due process, which is concerned with the way in which legal decisions are made, substantive due process decrees that there are areas in which legislative bodies have no power to make laws. . . . Although [this] might seem a "liberal" proscription against undue governmental involvement in people's lives, it has been used by American courts almost entirely in the service of vested property interests and not in support of meaningful individual rights. . . . Substantive due process was last used by a reactionary Supreme Court to strike down progressive labor legislation in the early part of the century.

Even using this principle, the Court did not revoke the right of states to regulate the morality of abortion or other legally contested cases. Rather, it determined that there was greater harm in state interference in personal autonomy during the first three months of pregnancy than in the morally problematic abortion choice. Overall, Court articulation of the law severely limited the woman's scope for making the abortion decision, while at the same time it protected the physician's right to refuse treatment.

"Moral paternalism," a concept proposed by the distinguished legal scholar H.L.A. Hart (1963) regarding all legislation that substitutes society's view of morality for the individual's, was only too apparent in the *Roe v. Wade* decision. In the first place, the Court offered "modified rights"—an adjustable choice structure contingent on medical and state judgments. As the Court said:

> "Privacy is not an absolute. The pregnant woman cannot be isolated in her privacy. She carries an embryo and later, a fetus. . . . The situation, therefore, is inherently different from marital intimacy, or bedroom possession of obscene material, or marriage or procreation or education."

It was also clear that the state's conception of maternal health and fetal care preceded the woman's privacy needs, however "fundamental" such rights were supposed to be.

In effect, the question before the Court was something very different than simply a choice between abortion and continued pregnancy. According to Tribe (1973), the Court was actually "choosing among alternative allocations of decision-making authority": the woman and doctor versus a government agency. Who should make judgments of that sort?—that was the real question, said Tribe. The answer, however, revealed a severely diluted conception of the woman's power to make the abortion decision.

The Court's case hinged on the relationship between the woman and her doctor (not the woman and her unborn child or the woman and her husband or lover). Physicians were expected to exercise professional judgment and medical "rights and responsibilities," which had a major claim over state interference. This, of course, left great room for the play of doctors' "best clinical judgment." In effect, the Court gave physicians almost total immunity from outside interference, while also granting the medical system final discretion over who received abortion, the conditions for abortion, and costs of services.

Thus the abortion choice was constrained at three distinct points. In the first three months of pregnancy, the woman could have an abortion if she could locate a physician and medical facility that was located within convenient traveling distance and had affordable services. In the second trimester, the situation was at once more medically risky and legally suspect, particularly after the initial indictment of a Boston physician in 1975. After this incident many hospitals withdrew from provision of abortion services. In the last trimester, the fetus took clear precedence over the woman's legal and social interests.

What was at stake was the right of the judiciary to intervene when moral consensus was in flux (Tribe, 1973). But intervene in whose favor? In the final analysis, the rights of women to abortion hinged on a number of legal fictions: that rights are automatically translatable into medical and social programs; that public, legislative, and judicial support would be forthcoming for widening the arena of women's freedom (e.g., day-care centers, federally funded abortion for poor women); that physicians would respond to women's reproductive choices in the face of relentless political pressure by anti-abortion factions; and that the individual woman could demand rights in the absence of legal and medical support.

LEGAL BATTLES AFTER *ROE V. WADE*

Although the Court decision of 1973 had legalized abortion under a wide variety of circumstances, it left a number of issues open for opponents of abortion to use to try to restrict rights. Francome (1984, 200–201) indicates some of the areas not ruled on in the decision.

1. To what extent could the states regulate abortion in the second trimester?

2. What regulations could be forced on abortion clinics?

3. What restrictions could be placed on the distribution of information and advertisements?

4. How far could the woman be forced to find the consent of other parties, such as her husband or parents?

5. Could the states prohibit abortions by non-physicians?

6. May public hospitals refuse to perform abortions?

7. Must Medicaid payments be made to women who want abortions?

8. May the states require records to be kept?

9. Can the woman be forced to take note of certain information before she makes her decision?
10. Should a doctor try to save the life of a viable fetus?

With all these areas of uncertainty, there was obviously wide scope for court cases. The Court subsequently supported some restrictions wanted by the anti-abortionists. More immediately, it placed the medical system on alert, resulting in reduction of services.

The privacy doctrine, articulated in the abortion case, worked in two opposing ways: It protected the woman from state regulation in early pregnancy, and it shielded hospitals and medical personnel who desisted from abortion service on morality grounds (i.e., "conscience clause"). The doctrine offered no support, though, to a beleaguered medical system that sought to serve women's needs under the impact of an ever-watchful pro-fetus faction. The right to privacy had to be fought on a case-by-case basis, leaving many states' pro-abortion forces scattered and demoralized.

In 1975 the manslaughter conviction of Dr. Kenneth C. Edelin, a black physician in Boston who had performed a second-trimester abortion by hysterotomy (small cesarean section), focused attention on the second- or mid-trimester period of pregnancy. Dr. Edelin's patient, a seventeen-year-old who had previously had two unsuccessful saline procedures, was estimated to be twenty weeks pregnant, giving her ample time to meet the legal deadline of twenty-four weeks. Edelin's mistake was to assume that there was no risk that the fetus was viable, given the degree of chemical onslaught from the previous abortion attempts. The doctor miscalculated. A pro-life sympathizer had observed Edelin's surgical procedure and in court testified that the physician had waited out the clock, allowing the fetus to die in utero.[4] Edelin's conviction was eventually overturned by a higher court. But the implications of the Boston case were profound and raised a number of questions. Would doctors severely cut back interruptions in the mid-trimester in order to avoid the viability problem altogether? Should doctors ask a state supreme court justice for clarification of murky areas of the law before doctors carry out an abortion or other procedure that might become the subject of court action? Was the physician's responsibility primarily to the mother, or did the doctor owe a separate obligation to the fetus (in effect, going against the wishes of the patient who does not want the child)? Should the medical community cease performing amniocentesis, a procedure widely used in the mid-trimester for genetic counseling, especially for people who have had a previous child with Down's syndrome (mongolism)? Would this verdict push the obstetric profession to come up with a generally accepted definition of viability, or the point at which the fetus can sustain life on its own outside the mother? Doctors interviewed across the country, the *New York Times* reported, believed that it would be the "rare, audacious obstetrician" who would go ahead with abortion in the second trimester, and then only if life-support equipment were in the delivery room to salvage the fetus if it were born alive. But this, too, raised other serious questions:

What about the mother, who thinking she was having an abortion was later handed a child—one with a substantial risk of being born brain-damaged or cerebral palsied? Who would pay the bills that can reach $500 per day in the limited number of intensive care units available to keep premature infants alive. The mother? The hospital? The State? (*New York Times*, 17 February 1975, 41)

Reflecting on Edelin's earlier manslaughter conviction, editor Harry Schwartz took a pro-medicine stance: "Will medicine be strangled in the law?" (*New York Times*, 25 February 1975, 35). What was proved in the abortion area, Schwartz said, was that it was possible to get public, legislative, and judicial support for widening the area of freedom and discretion in doctor-patient relations. Yet what actually happened was just the reverse: a flood of laws, bureaucratic ordinances, and judicial decisions tending to restrict ever more greatly the freedom in this area. Medicine itself under pressure from increasing stringency of state control over all branches of medical care was totally unprepared for the new freedom of abortion on convenience. Add to this the outpouring of legislation to curb abortion, and it was not surprising that medicine failed to assume leadership in the abortion choice controversy.

Shifting to legislative activity in 1973, nearly 200 abortion bills were introduced by state legislatures within the first four months after the Supreme Court decision (*Abortion Law Reporter*, 1976). The largest category of bills related to the regulations by states of the overall conditions under which abortion could be obtained legally. They specified who was qualified to perform abortions, at what stage of pregnancy, in what types of facilities, and on what grounds. Many bills detailed requirements to enhance the safety of abortion procedures.[5]

Others used "health" and "safety" clauses to restrict access to abortion with burdensome regulations or protective measures for doctors and hospitals, including elaborate preoperative instruction and counseling; requiring information on fetal development, as in describing the fetus in "anatomical detail"; the provision of parent or husband consent forms; twenty-four-hour waiting periods; ban on second-trimester abortions in clinics; and protection to public hospitals that refused to provide abortions. Other objectives were to reduce multiple abortions for the same woman (the anti-recidivist measure) and, more positively, to disseminate information through family-planning services and physicians' offices to foster early, safe abortion.

Thus many bills were hostile to women's reproductive rights, and a few turned out to be unconstitutional. For instance, parental, guardian, and

spousal consent requirements were viewed as "chilling" the abortion decision, enabling a parent or husband to unilaterally veto the woman's
choice. Patient's informed consent, initially resisted by pro-abortion groups
on grounds that privacy protected public disclosure of personal information, was accepted as normal medical record keeping, providing that "confidentiality" could be preserved.

A variety of single-purpose bills were introduced by Congress or by the
states that totally negated or confounded choice. Legislatures in state after
state rushed to present bills that contained provisions relating to the right
of medical personnel to choose not to participate in abortion procedures,
counseling, or referral. Most bills did not indicate specific grounds for
refusal, such as moral or religious objectives. Nor did these measures
appear to provide comparable safeguards for persons who might endure
discrimination if they performed or assisted in providing abortion.

A crazy-quilt pattern was not uncommon. One bill in Texas would prohibit public employees and employees of publicly supported agencies from
participating in abortion except to save the woman's life. On the other
hand, two Wisconsin bills would authorize or require suspension of a physician's license for refusing to perform an abortion. By contrast, no legislation existed that reflected the rights of patients to obtain abortion,
although a Utah law prohibited the denial of public assistance or other
benefits to individuals who choose *not* to have an abortion.

Clearly, on a national level, the state was opting in favor of childbirth
and against choice and the newer life-styles. Voluntary sterilization, family
planning, artificial insemination, as well as abortion, were all morally suspect by conservative segments of the public, and a number of states moved
to prohibit the use of their facilities for such procedures, although Governor
of Georgia Jimmy Carter extolled the use of public funding for family
planning to offset the "debilitating effect of uncontrolled family size on
parents and their children" (Donovan 1973, 58–590). According to Carter,
public awareness about family-planning methods and expanded availability
of services would "minimize the demand for abortion services."

After 1973, hospitals acted to protect themselves from the abortion threat
by offering few or no services, claiming legal uncertainty, especially around
second-trimester abortion and the problem of staff resistance to abortion
service. But critics thought otherwise. Deborah Erb, a spokeswoman for
NOW, contended that the hospitals that refused to provide abortion services were in defiance of the Supreme Court decision and were acting "to
protect themselves from malpractice suits at the expense of those women
whose health care they have chosen to ignore" (*New York Times*, 16 March
1975, 34).

By 1977, pro-abortion forces confronted a medley of anti-abortion legislation proposed by the Ninety-fifth Congress, all calculated to protect
pregnancy and to limit or eliminate the abortion choice. Teenage pregnancy

bills designed to assist pregnant adolescents who opted for birth; prohibition on fetal research; restrictive abortion amendments on appropriations for foreign assistance, defense, and HEW; and the Hyde Amendment, which prohibited any use of Medicaid funds for abortion except for life-threatening situations, were among the anti-abortion measures proposed and eventually passed. With Medicaid funding cut off in large part after 1977, many low-income women have resorted to self-induced or illegal ("back-alley") abortions. According to the Center for Disease Control, there were an estimated 5,000 to 23,000 women in this category, involving a known seventeen abortion deaths between 1975 and 1979 (reported in Lader, 1984, 27). Nor was the anti-Medicaid decision achieved in a bureaucratic vacuum. Both President Carter and then-HEW head Joseph Califano were against federal funding for abortion. In 1978 Carter appointed Connie J. Downey to head his administration's study group on alternatives to abortion. Frustrated by the evidence, Downey disbanded the group, concluding that the only real alternatives are "suicide, motherhood, and some would add, madness." In a memo to HEW, Downey denounced the effort, saying that the panel lacked direction, scope, authority, or money necessary to attack the multiple problems underlying unwanted pregnancies (*New York Times*, 27 November 1978, 1:1).

In vain did pro-abortion and civil rights groups link the right to legal abortion with the responsibility of government to financially support that right. Carter's response suggests the extent to which elected officials legislated their personal morality into national abortion policy. Whereas Carter conceded that denial of federal aid for abortions could discriminate against poor women, he nevertheless added: "There are many things in life that are not fair... Government should not attempt to make opportunities precisely equal when morality is at issue" (transcript of news conference, *New York Times*, 13 July 1979).

Nor was the Burger Court showing any leadership regarding economic equalization for abortion rights. Testimony from the National Abortion Rights Action League (NARAL) before the Senate Labor and Public Welfare Committee asserted:

The Court proved no help. In refusing to expand the "fundamental interests" strand of the new equal protection to redress economic inequalities, it was negating the promising start by the Warren Court in 1966. In *Danridge v. Williams*, the Supreme Court declared that the intractable economic, social and even philosophical problems presented by public welfare assistance programs are not the business of this Court.

Medicaid for abortion went down in defeat, despite a court of appeals ruling in 1975.[6] This ruling stipulated that a "welfare payments statute which places special regulation on abortion, but not upon other medical procedures," cannot stand in light of the High Court's decision. However much abortion advocates argued the importance of federal support to pay for abortion, they were unsuccessful. The decision that had the most important implications was that of June 20, 1977, when the Supreme Court, by a six-to-three vote margin, held that the states are not required to pay for elective abortion and effectively returned to Congress and the states the decision as to whether or not to pay for abortion. In 1980 the Court went further by ruling that the federal government was not obliged to fund abortion for poor women even when such abortions were medically necessary.

Congress quickly followed up this ruling with the Hyde Amendment. This bill stipulated that the freedom to have an abortion, like the freedom to use contraceptives or attend private schools, is not accompanied by a grant of money in the Constitution (*Washington Post*, 1 July 1980, A-1, A-8). In a full-page ad run in major newspapers, Planned Parenthood quoted Justice Stevens, who said about the decision to prevent federal funding of abortion: "The harm inflicted upon women is grievous . . . tantamount to severe punishment . . . an unjustifiable and, indeed, blatant violation of the duty to govern impartially" (*New York Times*, 6 July 1980). According to Planned Parenthood, 300,000 poor women and teenagers would be at jeopardy on the assumption that the government has a greater legitimate interest in protecting the potential life of the fetus than it has in protecting the woman's life and health.

Whereas the Hyde Amendment took an indirect, if short, step toward ending abortion (and many critics add contraception, sex education, and efforts to help infertile couples have children), the Human Life Amendment offered at once a total ban on all abortion and a major challenge to judicial supremacy. First proposed in 1973 by Senators William Buckley and Jesse Helms, the Human Life Amendment is the most serious effort to reverse state protection from the woman to the fetus. Calling for legislative action to overturn the 1973 Supreme Court decision, the Reagan administration, nearly a decade later, demanded that the time had come to call a halt "to the second guessing by courts of state laws regulating abortion" and to judicial creation of "increasingly intricate" rules limiting legislative powers over the abortion issue (*New York Times*, 30 July 1982). "Vesting the court with broad authority to second-guess legislative judgments is inherently anti-democratic," the Reagan-inspired Justice Department brief said. Noting that the Constitution contains no mention of the word "privacy" or "abortion," the brief asserted that constitutional abortion rights were based on "a combination of shadows," rather than on any explicit constitutional guarantees.

The Reagan administration's move against the *Roe* decision occurred in the context of strong resistance by legal scholars about the wisdom of entering uncharted constitutional waters. Even Professor John T. Noonan, an ardent advocate of an anti-abortion constitutional amendment, expressed doubt about the efficacy of the convention method: "I am reluctant ... because of the fears a constitutional convention engenders among lawyers ... it has never been tried. The lawyers and the liberals who distrust the people will be in opposition. It is a last resort."[7] Because there are few ground rules or precedents for it to follow, a constitutional convention raises controversial questions about Congressional authority, presidential role, organization of the courts, non-representativeness, and others.

Abortion may only be the wedge for forcibly restraining the federal judiciary. By May 1982 the more than thirty anti-abortion proposals pending in Congress to curb the Court's power to interpret constitutional right represent alternatives to a constitutional convention. Promoters view with alarm certain rulings in recent decades. Among the most controversial are busing as a means of desegregating public schools, declaring the right of women to have abortion, prohibiting state-sponsored prayer in public school, and expanding the rights of criminal defendants. What these measures have in common is their effort to assimilate marginal and stigmatized groups into society: blacks, women, nonbelievers, and criminal offenders.

Crippling the courts could be dangerous, though. Even conservatives (e.g., Senator Barry Goldwater of Arizona) have joined liberals and the legal establishment in warning that legislation to curb the courts could cripple their ability to check the excesses of popular rule, nullify the protections written into the constitution, and subject the liberties of all Americans to a "tyranny of the majority" (*New York Times*, 16 May 1982, 1, 36).

Let the people decide in public opinion polls, a final strategy for determining the legitimacy of the Burger Court abortion decision, was applauded by liberals and pro-abortion forces. What have public opinion polls shown?

1. There is a steadily growing public affirmation of abortion for many circumstances (rape, incest, medical or mental health conditions).

2. About three-fourths of Americans polled endorse the woman's choice the first three months, and most respondents do not wish to see the law repealed.

3. About half of the Catholics surveyed disagree with the idea that abortion "should not be allowed under any circumstances."

4. As early as 1976, 66 percent of 1,500 adults polled nationwide opposed a constitutional amendment to outlaw abortion, and, among more educated respondents, the percentage supporting the current abortion law rose considerably.[8]

Rather than presume that the community's morality is somehow contained in these facts, Dworkin (1967) suggests that public reactions must be passed through an analytical strainer to remove prejudice, emotional reaction, rationalizations, and parroting, after which they should be further tested for both sincerity and consistency. In the final analysis, contemporary morality has become the necessary function of the judge. Not the medical profession, which is ill-equipped to cope with moral dissension, but the courts have taken over the responsibility to facilitate "the emergence of an alternative consensus" when the environment is one of "widely perceived moral flux" (Tribe, 1973). That the judiciary system chooses to play out the legal fiction of constitutionality in the abortion issue probably benefits women. In the current medicalization of abortion, the Court remains the last political bulwark of woman's rights.

ABORTION AND MEDICALIZATION

The terms "medicine" and "medicalization" point to two distinct functions. Medicine involves a highly technical and professionally skilled group of practitioners who apply therapeutic expertise to the treatment of illness. "Medicalization," as a political activity, is a power instrument supported by the state in the service of social control. In the first case, the profession performs services in the patients' interests; the treatment is the objective. In the second case, the service is tangential to the primary goal of political dominance.

Medicalization assumed the central role after abortion was legal and was implicated in its transformation from "bad" to "sick" (Conrad and Schneider, 1980, 10–12). Medicine, rather than the family, church, or state, became the primary agent for regulating abortion.

At first glance, it was apparent that the medical system responded positively to the unmet demand for abortion, especially in altering service delivery, costs, and medical techniques. For example, before *Roe*, 52 percent of hospitals provided no abortion service, 39 percent provided therapeutic abortion only, and 9 percent provided elective abortion. After *Roe*, 44 percent provided no abortion, 7 percent provided therapeutic abortion only, and 49 percent provided elective abortion.[9]

Although there were few official figures on the number of legal abortions performed during the first year after the Supreme Court decision, interviews conducted by the *New York Times* in a dozen major cities disclosed that tens of thousands of abortions were being performed in cities where a year earlier it was impossible to obtain an operation (*New York Times*, 31 December 1973).

And while pro-abortion groups continued to wrestle with state-imposed residency rules, spousal and parent consent, and other restrictions, the medical system provided more safe, low-cost abortions than in any period of American history.

Citing Oregon, for example, we can see that the immediate impact of permissive abortion has been most evident in market and technological changes, a situation duplicated in all states which were in compliance with the new abortion law. Total costs for medical abortion in 1972 ranged from

$500 to $1,000 (Michigan data). A first-trimester clinic abortion in Portland, Oregon, cost approximately $150 in 1977 and about $200 in 1982, including physician, medication, and a month's supply of birth control pills. Technological changes, once hampered by illegality, had two effects: sophisticated techniques for early abortion encouraged medical referrals in early pregnancy, and more dangerous complicated surgical procedures (e.g., hysterotomy) nearly vanished.

Neither decriminalization nor legalization has seriously affected demographic trends. In general, fertility has been moving downward, in large part due to increased contraceptive use. Christopher Tietze (1973) has prepared estimates of the health and demographic impact of legalized abortion and concludes that about 70 percent of the legal abortions in the United States between 1970–1972 were drawn from the unreported illegal market. Table 10.1 summarizes abortion utilization trends in Oregon and the United States.[10]

In Oregon, the 1969 decriminalization policy encouraged official reporting of abortion but otherwise failed to effect substantial downward changes in fertility. The birth rate has actually increased slightly since 1973, when abortion was officially legalized, while the age of marriage for women has been rising. Once confined to married and older women (Westoff and Westoff, 1971), abortion is increasingly taking place among younger unmarried women with nearly 72 percent of all Oregon abortions involving women who are twenty-four years of age and under (1975). In Oregon, the nearly 10 percent drop in abortion among women having four children or more between 1969 and 1974 suggests that among older, married women with completed families, contraceptive access and utilization severely reduces abortion demand.

Although Oregon is largely representative of states during the decriminalization phase, it also differs from other similarly situated states in certain ways. Despite early decriminalization, Oregon never attracted a large out-of-state clientele, compared with New York, California, and Washington, D.C. Black utilization in Oregon is proportionate to the state's population, whereas blacks are overutilizers in heavily populated industrial states. This reflects Oregon's lower population base relative to other states but also its higher accessibility to contraception, especially for urban blacks (Portland data). And Oregon women appear to lead not only in the number of abortions per live births, but also for teenage abortion use, as compared with other states. Low-cost clinic abortion, available for major population centers and conducted within a favorable medical climate (features identified for Oregon), may be a crucial factor for encouraging the abortion choice. Contrariwise, the Oregon case shows that rural residency, access limited to relatively costly hospital service instead of low-cost clinic service, and a negative medical or community climate severely curtail or discourage abortion use.

Table 10.1

**Characteristics of Women Receiving Abortions
in United States and Oregon from 1969 to 1975**

Characteristic	Oregon							United States		
	1969	1970	1971	1972	1973	1974	1975	1972	1973	19
	%	%	%	%	%	%	%	%	%	%
Residence										
Abortion in-state	95.6	95.4	95.1	94.9	94.7	92.0	94.0	56.2	74.8	86
Abortion out-of-state	4.4	4.6	4.9	5.1	5.2	8.0	6.0	43.8	25.2	13
Age										
≤ 19	36.6	34.7	39.1	37.5	37.6	37.9	38.3	32.6	32.7	32
20-24	32.0	35.6	32.9	32.3	32.7	31.9	33.5	32.5	32.0	31
≥ 25	32.4	29.7	28.1	30.2	29.7	30.2	28.2	34.9	35.3	35
Race										
White	95.1	-	-	-	-	94.3	95.8	77.0	72.5	69
Black and other	4.9	-	-	-	-	5.6	4.2	23.0	27.5	30
Marital Status										
Married	-	27.7	29.3	29.9	31.5	29.0	27.3	29.7	27.4	27
Unmarried	-	72.3	71.7	71.1	68.5	71.0	72.7	70.3	72.6	72
Number of Living Children										
0	60.1	-	-	-	-	61.0	12.5*	49.4	48.6	47
1	11.6	-	-	-	-	15.7	38.3	18.2	18.8	19
2	9.6	-	-	-	-	12.7	29.2	13.3	14.2	14
3	7.1	-	-	-	-	6.2	11.7	8.7	8.7	8
≥ 4	14.5	-	-	-	-	4.4	8.3	10.4	9.7	9
Total Number of Abortions	1,407	7,196	6,997	7,143	7,447	8,794	10,064	586,760	615,831	763
Abortion Ratio (abortions per 1,000 live births)	41.6	199.5	207.3	222.4	234.6	263.0	311.1	180.1	196.3	24

* In 1975, 6,312 women receiving abortion failed to report the number of children.
  Since this was over 50% of the cases, these data remain questionable.

Table 10.2
Percentages of Abortion by Weeks of Gestation and Type of Procedure

Week of Gestation	Oregon						United States*			Death to Case Rate from 1970 to 1974 in U.S.
	1970	1971	1972	1973	1974	1975	1972	1973	1974	
Less than 12 weeks	65.5	74.3	81.1	87.7	89.2	91.3	82.2	83.4	86.7	1.7
More than 12 weeks	34.5	25.7	18.9	22.3	10.8	8.7	17.8	16.6	13.3	15.0
Type of Procedure										
Vacuum aspiration ("Suction")	51.5	61.9	73.1	80.0	88.2	89.3	65.2	74.9	77.5	1.8
Dilatation and Curretage	21.1	18.0	10.6	9.1	2.8	1.2	23.4	13.5	12.3	2.9
Intrauterine in- stillation (saline)	22.3	15.9	13.6	9.3	6.5	6.5	10.4	10.4	7.8	17.9
Hysterotomy/ Hysterectomy	5.1	4.2	2.6	1.6	1.2	0.9	0.6	0.7	0.6	38.1
Other	0.1	0.1	0.3	0.1	1.0	2.0	0.5	0.6	1.9	4.9

*Data from the Public Health Center for Disease Control, Atlanta, GA., 1974.
1
Deaths per 100,000 abortions.

Table 10.2 examines the changing pattern of abortion by the week of gestation and the type of procedure. This pattern provides a crude measure of access: Early, safe abortions (i.e., vacuum aspiration) signify relatively high access, whereas late, riskier surgery indicates low access and, conversely, higher barriers.

By 1970, one year after Oregon's decriminalization, more than one-third of women delayed abortion into the second trimester, a medically risky and costly abortion. More than 27 percent of these women required a saline injection or surgical intervention (D and C, hysterotomy), procedures that may involve costly hospital stays and high complication and death rates.

By 1975 the 90 percent of Oregon women who received abortion in the first trimester had a vacuum aspiration (suction), with only about 1 percent of the terminations completed by the now-outmoded D & C (or sharp curettage). In addition, surgical procedures involving high complication and death rates (hysterotomy and hysterectomy) dropped to half the number from 1970 to 1975. Clearly, the criminal abortion policy delayed abortion and retarded medical innovation. As long as abortion was legally restricted, the medical profession had no compelling reason and, in fact, a disincentive to update abortion procedures. Most physicians in the pre-legal period depended on the D & C, a suitable technique in cases of miscarriage or other conditions contributing to uterine bleeding. The persistence of this outmoded technique for more than twenty years after the availability of the low-risk suction method testifies to the technological lag induced by restrictive law. Overall, legalization had a salutory effect in raising the safety level of abortion (Tietze, 1979).

Permissive abortion also has had positive consequences for health occupations. There has been an expanded demand for gynecologists and related medical specialists in a declining fertility market. Medical abortion has led to the development of new organizations and professions (e.g., outpatient clinics, abortion counselors). And in states with high accessibility of abortion, especially for poor women, there has been a reduction in welfare rolls and a marked improvement in contraceptive practice for married, lower-income women (Jaffe, et al., 1981).

But medicalization also opposed the free flow of abortion services. The law expressly states that the physician's judgment was the single most significant criterion for legal abortion practice. This made doctors virtually immune from malpractice, while granting them maximum discretion (Babcock, et al., 1975, 943–958). Thus the Court led in undermining abortion rights by granting physicians prior protection over the pregnant woman's needs.

Certainly, constitutional reformers who argued for repeal asserted that the 1973 decision was motivated by institutional influences, specifically a response to medical pressure (Roy Lucas in conversation).[11] Once the furor of the anti-abortion movement and the New Right impacted on local medical systems, though, physicians were more likely to respond to immediate political and organizational pressures. According to Tatalovich and Daynes (1981), policymaking on "life-style" issues relates less to economic interests than to questions of traditional standards of behavior, sexual mores, and social status. The severe lack of social cohesion in abortion led to seething conflict over life-styles. This produced a zigzag pattern in legal policy in which permissive laws initiated to reduce inequalities in one time period shifted to more restrictive practices at a later time because of public outrage over what some citizens believed was state-imposed immorality (e.g., abortion as murder).

Current restrictions in abortion have their source in both legal and medical systems. That abortion law operates primarily for the convenience of professional or organizational ends and not the needs of women can be supported by the following items (see Greenwood and Young, 1976; Bond and Johnson, 1982).

1. The law specifically enables physicians and hospital groups to constitutionally deny service to abortion clients for personal reasons (i.e., conscience clause).

2. Patients are dependent on the physician's judgment and willingness to perform abortion service or refer them elsewhere. Patients have no legal recourse when denied professionally relevant information or medical services.

3. Health plans may or may not include abortion, depending on local health insurance or medical boards and employer groups.

4. Low-income patients, lacking either paid medical insurance or Medicaid, may be denied service, regardless of need. For example, abortion quota systems still operate in many public and private hospitals, primarily affecting the indigent (Jaffe, et al., 1981). Observers expect this number to increase dramatically as a result of the Supreme Court's one-vote majority in upholding the constitutionality of the Hyde Amendment. This amendment denies federal funding for abortion and places state protection for the potential life of the fetus before protection of the pregnant woman's own health. The Guttmacher Institute estimates that 295,000 abortions were funded in 1977 by the federal and state governments under Medicaid. The Institute estimates that 432,000 low-income women each year would have Medicaid abortions if they were available. Government sources put this figure at 470,000 (*Washington Post*, 1 July 1980).

5. Clinic abortion, accounting for approximately 80 percent of all abortions, is a segmental, low-skill service, enabling physicians to perform "piece work" at hourly fees without responsibility for organizational or client management. Many physicians admittedly perform abortion on a moonlighting basis, often in a city other than where their regular practice is located. The relatively higher complication rates for abortions performed under local anesthetic (typical of early-trimester clinic abortion) compared with general anesthetic (inpatient hospital abortion) suggest the hazards that occur for a fast-turnover service performed by servers with low professional commitment. Such medical "dis-service" may be analogous to health-care delivery for the welfare class. Unmarried pregnant women, regardless of social class, along with welfare beneficiaries, may share common attributes of dependency and stigma (see Kurtz and Diacopassi, 1975).

In addition, institutional groups are not only more successful in mobilizing the law and translating it into organizational advantages than are individuals, but they can also erect extra-legal barriers that effectively restrict access to less preferred or troublesome clientele (e.g., unconstitutional parent or husband consent requirements in abortion). Sharp variations in costs for similar services among different medical servers operate as a price discrimination mechanism, requiring lower-income clients to shop around for services. This often results in delaying abortion beyond the safe first trimester. For many practitioners, abortion is reported to be "dirty work," a boring, low-skilled, stigmatizing practice with few or no career advantages.

UNRESOLVED SOCIAL PROBLEMS

Medicalization is implicated in other related health problems for women: unmarried teen pregnancy, "late" abortion, and repeat abortion. Whereas the average age of marriage for women has risen along with their apparent option for fewer children, teenage women reveal strikingly distinct abortion and pregnancy patterns. To cite Oregon again, teenage abortion rates are nearly double those of other age-groups. The unmarried pregnancy ratio among teens is triple those of other age-groups. And 30 percent of teens carrying their pregnancy to term in that state are unmarried.

In 1977 the Population Institute summarized national trends on teenage pregnancy, which continues into the 1980s (Baldwin, 1976; Fox, 1982; Jaffe, et al., 1981).

- Nearly 1 million teenagers become pregnant each year.
- Teenagers accounted for just under one-fifth of all 1975 births; 52 percent of the out-of-wedlock births, and one-third of the abortions in the United States.
- Out of 595,000 births to teenage women in 1975, nearly 13,000 were to women aged fourteen or younger.
- The number of mothers under sixteen years of age has increased 80 percent since 1960.
- Of the approximately 10 million females aged fifteen through nineteen, as many as 20 percent will experience a premarital pregnancy before they are out of their teenage years.
- Three-fourths of all first pregnancies to teenage women are begun premaritally.
- Half of the brides in the United States who are younger than eighteen years old are pregnant.
- Almost one-fourth of women who have their first child in their teenage years have three more within a seven-year period.
- Young, poor, and black women are at highest risk of abortion complications and death because of delayed abortion, which is related to lower accessibility and information about facilities.
- Only one in five sexually active teenage women uses contraception consistently.
- Less than half the states explicitly permit teenagers to obtain contraception without parental consent.

With most young mothers having few or no job skills (pregnancy accounts for the largest single factor contributing to high school dropout among females), the implications for family life and social organization may be profound. Social service professionals observe that child abuse, welfare dependency, poor health, and deprived life-styles for mother and child are typical outcomes of early pregnancy (unpublished interview data from Portland, Oregon, 1976).

Repeat abortion and second-trimester abortion, which is now typically a saline injection, are related issues that pose a double problem. On the one hand, they reflect a distribution problem; the failure of institutional groups to disseminate contraceptive information and develop an effective, universally safe contraceptive. On the other hand, they represent a post- or non-contraceptive decision, which exposes the woman to unnecessary surgical risk and long-term medical complications (Tietze and Lewitt, 1977). In 1974 the Centers for Disease Control reported that 11.5 percent of women coming in for abortion had at least one previous abortion, despite the fact that abortion had been legalized for only one year.

Delayed abortion is particularly a serious problem. Second-trimester abortion patients, who experience postoperative disease and death rates far in excess of those who seek abortions early in their pregnancy, differ from first-trimester patients for the United States as a whole (Bracken and Kasl, 1975, 1008–1019; Bracken and Swigar, 1972, 301–309; Kerenyi, et al., 1973, 299–311). Delayed abortion, perhaps more than any other single indicator, shows the impact of differential access. For instance, in 1981 two-thirds of all the counties in the United States lacked an abortion provider (Jaffe, et al., 1981). The following trends highlight differences among women who seek late abortion:

Age	Increased percentage of young women
Race	Increased percentage of women of minority races
Marital status	Increased percentage of single women
Reproductive history	Increased percentage of women pregnant for the first time
Social class	Increased percentage of women from lower strata
Education	Increased percentage of women with lower levels of completed education
Employment	Increased percentage of women unemployed, without material support, or with lower incomes
Relationship to significant others	Relationship more likely to be distant, women more likely to keep news of pregnancy from partner and parents, women less likely to get financial help or more likely to refuse it when offered

Discovery of pregnancy   Increased incidence of late recognition
Decision to abort   Increased incidence of delayed decision

Although the medical system tends to define teen pregnancy, repeat abortion, and second-trimester abortion as "irresponsible" or as deviant acts, this may increasingly reflect a choice model among some women (Luker, 1975). Alternatively, increased abortion utilization, unwed pregnancy, and delayed abortion suggest the unresolved problems for women whose marginality and exclusion from legal and medical resources contribute to information distortion, limited control over life-styles, and frequent personal crises requiring professional mediation and control.

LANGUAGE AND LAW

In the Supreme Court's attempt to formulate general rules for laying out guidelines to the abortion choice, and in the concrete attacks and defenses that followed, the issues hinged on the nature of abortion as symbol, its language and meanings. Here, among other things, abortion law watchers asked if there could be a necessary connection between the legal symbol of abortion as free, a woman's right, and any particular object, event, or situation. It was not only the narrow legal rendering of what the Court said, but also the linguistic implications that endowed the legal structure with authority to originate certain freedoms as well as to constrain their expression. Hence the language of the abortion law became an important source of the law's legitimacy or, more properly, its failure to legitimate major doctrinal changes in women's reproductive rights.

Contrary to many legal scholars, legalizing abortion was primarily a sociological event, not a constitutional one. The "superprotected" right to abortion is not inferable from the language of the Constitution because women had no legal standing in the eighteenth century, and moreover, the technology of intervention during this time was crude or nil. In *Roe*, the privacy concept, hinged as it was to the intimacy of "motherhood," a traditional idea, was further linked to a vague enunciation of equal protection. This proved to be a more or less suitable peg on which the judicial policy choice was hung. Abortion has no necessary connection to motherhood, inasmuch as the exercise of abortion rights can avoid motherhood altogether.

The word "privacy" itself imposes an interpretation. From the *American Heritage Dictionary* (Morris, 1973), the English meanings of privacy denote:

1. seclusion from the sight, presence, or intrusion of others;

2. confined to one person; personal;

3. not available for public use, control, or participation;

4. belonging to a particular person or persons, as opposed to the public or government;
5. not holding an official position;
6. not public; intimate, secret;

And from the Latin derivatives:

7. *privatus*—not belonging to the state, not in public life;
8. *privare* (past participle)—release;
9. *privus*—single, individual.

What, then, does "privacy" mean? Social reconstruction of the privacy term yields the following meanings. Abortion releases women from the collective will in which the private functions of sexuality, conception, and childbirth were under patriarchal family and later state surveillance but does so in the context of a *laissez-faire* doctrine. Criminal abortion required official intervention, a denial of intimacy and personal control, a situation that ended once women could be legally treated as responsible individuals rather than subordinate to husbands, fathers, guardians, or their medical surrogates. After *Roe v. Wade*, physicians were empowered to play a crucial part in the personal decision; hence the relationship between the woman and her physician takes on a confessional role in an updated version of moral patriarchy. The secrets of sexuality and contraception, once limited to the priest, are now heard legally by the doctor. In other words, there are fairly severe constraints on privacy when it is activated at all.

At the same time, privacy implies that women remain excluded from policy decisions; *privatus*, they are largely absent in public life in sufficient numbers to influence public policy. As single individuals they must negotiate in a professional structure often with little public or government support. J. S. Mill (1947) speaks for the middle class in its single-minded thrust for individual liberty over mind and body and freedom from the constraints of father rule or the state. And while privacy undermines patriarchy and certain forms of state intervention, it merely substitutes another evil. Privacy is isolating and offers only an unidimensional concept of the human condition. It negates both the larger community and the thornier issues of social and economic inequality that are denied almost all women, but especially minority, teen, poor, and disabled women. The abortion decision did not solve women's gender role dilemmas. It merely opened the door to their complexity, as the final chapter on social policy explains.

NOTES

1. *Roe v. Wade*, 410 U.S. 113, 165–166 (1973). See also *Doe v. Bolton*, 410 U.S. 179, 197, 199 (1973).

2. An excellent overview of legal scholars' responses to the *Roe v. Wade* decision is found in Gunther, 1976, 248–254. See also Ely, 1973; Heymann and Barzelay, 1973; Tribe, 1973; Grey, 1975; and Dostro, 1975, 1250–1351.

3. The conflict role of law as an active social force in change and public policy is analyzed by Turk, 1972, 1976; Evan, 1980; and Chambliss and Seidman, 1982.

4. For an excellent review of the Edelin case as well as other major legal and medical issues following the Supreme Court abortion decision, see *Abortion Law Reporter*, Jane A. Cullen, ed., Women's Rights Clinic, Antioch School of Law.

5. *Abortion Law Reporter* 1 (January 1976): NARAL-1.0.

6. *Abortion Law Reporter* 1 (July 1976): Medicaid-16.1.

7. Quoted in *Abortion Law Reporter* 2 (May 1977):5.4.

8. Public opinion polls on abortion are summarized in the *Abortion Law Reporter*, vol. 2, May 1977, NARAL-8.1. Trends in attitudes toward abortion are further examined by Tedrow and Mahoney, 1979, 181–189.

9. *Abortion Law Reporter*.

10. Tables 10.2 and 10.3 were prepared by Davis and Farr (1982).

11. Roy Lucas headed the Rockefeller-financed legal committee that challenged the Texas and Georgia abortion statutes.

11

Women, Abortion, and Social Policy

SUMMING UP

The moral panic following the Supreme Court abortion decision had its origins in three sources: (1) the anti-feminist backlash, as women attempted to redefine their reproductive options; (2) public reaction to the state's effort to legitimate a new regulatory regime in reproduction; and (3) the supposed direct link of abortion with various catastrophic themes: breakdown of sexual morality, collapse of law and order, and emergence of various evils—for example, youth rebellion and minority uprisings—produced by the permissive society.

To dismiss the anti-abortion and anti-feminist outcry as merely the ravings of a Right Wing-obsessed Moral Majority is undoubtedly a mistake. The appeal from the Right would have little impact if most citizens felt thoroughly comfortable about reproductive choice. After all, the women's movement (and abortion specifically) initially represented efforts primarily by affluent groups to change deeply entrenched social patterns; these changes now affect every aspect of our institutional and personal lives. There inevitably remains a time lag, perhaps a generation or more, between a movement's success in the legal and political arenas and its wholesale acceptance by a majority of citizens. And there may be a considerable amount of backsliding (e.g., witness the ongoing battle over racial equality). Despite the furor of official debates at the federal level led by Senators Jesse Helms and Orrin Hatch and President Reagan's self-admitted pressure to tighten abortion regulations (without prohibiting them), anti-abortion forces probably reached their high-water mark by 1980. The margin of political gain has gradually dissipated since that time.

The action of pro-abortion lobbyists, as well as political funding by pro-abortion supporters of congressional and state candidates in the 1982 election, has seriously reduced the effectiveness of anti-abortion activists. Feminist organizations have realized a boom in membership. The National Abortion Rights Action League (NARAL) had barely 90,000 members in November 1980, but by November 1982 it boasted 140,000 paid members. Organized medicine continues to oppose curbs in the abortion law that would affect the delivery of medicine or the current counseling format. For instance, an Akron, Ohio, ordinance that would require physicians to emphasize the physical, mental, emotional, and moral pain after abortion was categorically rejected as "bad" medicine by professional leaders.

The notion of choice, however frayed the concept may be by its trivialized or sentimentalized treatment by the media and anti-feminist groups, resonates with the American doctrine of justice and fair play. Responsibility and freedom are deeply embedded in our ethos, and despite the efforts of certain sectors that resist the idea of choice for *some* groups such as women, the pluralistic ideal prompts a kind of reluctant reciprocity. In this sense, both anti-abortion and pro-abortion groups must listen to each other.

But the struggle for women's rights, of which reproductive control is a part, has not been won. The women's movement suffered a severe defeat with the loss of the Equal Rights Amendment (ERA).[1] Passage of pro-women legislation depends on signs of affirmation, such as the ERA, to maintain efforts to achieve the desired goal against powerful odds, perhaps most significantly, institutional and personal apathy. With the rise of exploitative and often vicious pornography, the setbacks to affirmative action and ERA, economic deprivation and cuts in financial and social aid for women and children, and the conservative temper of the times, it is apparent that we must continually address abortion as a justice issue that requires different abortion policies. These policies may differ by case: abortion for the teenager; for the divorced, single parent; for an older woman with a completed family; for the legislator and physician. These cases may present painful moral dilemmas.

For women to gain a free, rational, and just reproductive policy requires that we lay bare the structure of society's moral and political beliefs about reproduction. This book has attempted to show that a feminist morality of abortion must first confront the task of exposing the multiple realities of abortion, out of which a woman-centered abortion policy can be constructed and social needs and human costs determined.

As a social doctrine, abortion offers two contending, nonnegotiable positions: life for the woman or life for the fetus. Each argument is based on an elaborate rationale, which not only totally negates the opponent's position, but also represents a reversal form of reasoning. For example, both sides appeal to universal terms: good versus evil, clean versus dirty, freedom versus slavery, redemption versus annihilation. But what is good for one side (i.e., freedom for the woman, a pro-abortion image) evokes sym-
of the holocaust on the other (Powell, 1981). When these opposing
nes move into the political arena where they must be translated into

social policy, a profound stalemate occurs. There can be no moving back-ward. Once granted, the concept of reproductive choice infiltrates personal beliefs and institutional norms and becomes a way of life. But there is little moving forward either. Indeed, the various statutory restrictions on abor-tion have not altered women's behavior (approximately as many poor women received abortions after federal contributions to Medicaid were cut as before the 1980 act), but they do increase considerably the personal and financial costs of abortion for the individual woman. Endlessly stated and restated by anti- and pro-abortion partisans over the past decade, there has emerged no distinguishing core of objective or value-free recommen-dations for public policy concerning abortion.

But women may be losing the war over reproductive rights to an un-anticipated opponent. Technological breakthroughs may herald entirely new methods of reproductive control with the emergence of genetic en-gineering, recombinant DNA research, in vitro fertilization, artificial in-semination, cloning, nonsurgical methods of sterilization, and amniocentesis (which may promote late abortions resulting in the birth of a live fetus).[2]

The legal concept of "wrongful life" also links abortion to eugenics. As clarified by Robert Blank, a tort for "wrongful life" is a suit brought on behalf of an affected infant, most commonly against a physician or other health professional who, it is alleged, negligently failed to inform the par-ents of the possibility of their bearing a severely defective child. This failure to inform prevents "a parental choice in avoiding conception or birth of the child" (Blank, 1982, 3–4). Advances in prenatal diagnostic techniques, including amniocentesis, ultrasonics, and fiberoptics, combined with recent breakthroughs in fetal blood transfusions and fetal surgery, provide the information necessary to reduce substantially the number of children born with genetic and congenital defects. Because of the complexity of the issue and ambivalence of values on these sensitive life/death issues, the social-political ramifications could be profound. Blank says:

It is possible that unexpected consequences of wrongful life [court] decisions might in the long run lead to pressures on parents as well as the medical community to utilize all available technologies to eliminate those persons with severe genetic disorders. If this occurs, the courts might be condoning a very subtle form of eugenics, despite their intention to protect the rights of those born under conditions of wrongful life. (Blank, 1982, 5)

These technical and legal inventions signal the possible demise of woman as the creator of human life, or a view of women as the nurturer, the caretaker, the child-centered sex, whether or not the woman actually pro-duced offspring or not. What has throughout history been taken for granted is that the reverence for life begins with the feminine identification with mothering. Thus women's preeminent qualities of domestic giving and caring have contrasted sharply with the masculine characteristics of dominance in the public world. This dichotomy, for better or worse, appears to be ending. And what exists to take its place? Who will bear and care for the children? And who will offer the sacrifice for the next generation? For these fundamental questions of survival, the choice rhetoric simply will not do.

BEYOND CHOICE: THE SOCIAL CONTEXT OF REPRODUCTION

The entire choice discourse reflects an individualistic and libertarian social and political philosophy; it extols individual tastes and free decisions regarding reproduction in the same spirit as in purchasing a product or service in the marketplace. As a core cultural principle, reproductive choice assumes a group of independent and well-informed individuals whose personal resources allow for a pick-and-choose approach. But such liberal principles falter because they are grossly inadequate for dealing with those in situations of complete or partial dependency (e.g., the insane, children, the poor, and teenage, single, or pregnant women).

Despite the fact that pregnancy and childbearing may have exploited women, they have also provided significant social roles and meanings for women, as well as linking women to other women across generations and within kinship groups. Although there is only fragmentary evidence of the isolated survival of feral unsocialized children, it is evident that without nurturing such children remain severely limited—brain damaged and physically impaired. What such cases show us is that the human condition surrounding reproduction and childrearing demands high levels of social cooperation, trust, and interaction (Curtiss, 1977).

Until our own epoch, having a child has been a highly socialized, sociable event that identified the woman as fully adult and brought social privileges and emotional satisfaction to the woman, her husband, and both their kinship groups. Children have implied renewal, a new beginning, and hope. But in our post-modern society, pregnancy may be a traumatic event. For the educated woman, it may represent an unwelcomed intrusion into a tenuous, invariably highly competitive career. The interruption is not merely career-related, but may attack the fragile identity as well. For all women, but especially the economically disadvantaged woman, the costs of childbearing and childrearing are inestimable. Women continue to earn barely half of what men earn—fifty-nine cents for every dollar earned by a man; 80 percent of all women remain segregated in low-paying, clerical, retail sales, service, and factory jobs; women with a college degree earn an average of $3,000 a year less than a man with a high school diploma; and the feminization of poverty grows—two out of three women raising their children alone continue to live in poverty. After divorce, a woman stands to lose an average of 73 percent of her former income, while a man gains 40 percent. Among black women, the number who live at or below the poverty level is more than half. For the economically advantaged woman, society provides few or no incentives for taking on pregnancy or a child-bearing role. Among this group, the housewife/mother remains an object of futility or scorn. In the case of disadvantaged and poor women, abortion on demand absolves society, and men particularly, of the social and financial responsibility associated with pregnancy and child care.[3]

The choice concept offers other serious limitations. As part of the symbolism of the women's movement, this concept has been co-opted by advertisers, pharmaceutical interests, and other institutional groups to promote feminine or feminized products ("you've come a long way, baby"). This blunts the individual's awareness and clouds the issues that must be analyzed in order to examine real choice or to voice dissent. The legal rights argument, a corollary of abortion choice, provides us with a unique principle—that women are sole and exclusive determiners of reproduction. But these rights can be revoked, suppressed, ignored, or bypassed altogether, and thus an entire legal apparatus of lawyers, courts, and official hearings is required to assure that these rights may be effectively exercised (e.g., affirmative action efforts). Rights are also continuously subject to erosion and conflict and inevitably depend on the good will of powerful others (e.g., the good will of physicians to obtain abortion). In other words, rights are not a basic, universally accepted moral or social principle for constructing a woman-centered morality of abortion.

Finally, rights are contingent. A right can be maintained only so long as it is not overridden by other rights that have stronger claims. Being aware of our own past (including exploitation of women's bodies for men's purposes), can we imagine a situation in which a man's wish to parent his potential child in an ongoing reciprocal relationship is simply ignored, his request rejected as irrelevant or none of his business? Such situations may no longer be uncommon. Although abortion is incorrectly perceived by many observers as one-issue politics, it obviously is intricately tied into women's and men's expectations, our mutual roles, and our enduring capacity to live with each other.

In totalitarian states, abortion choice is nonexistent. When abortion becomes the preeminent solution to overpopulation, approximating or exceeding childbirth, as it has during various periods in Russia, the eastern European bloc nations, and China, the issue of rights becomes moot. The will of the state emerges as the dominant, overriding consideration.

For example, a *New York Times* reporter observed how vigilantes, in efforts to reduce the birth rate in Guangdong Province in China, abducted pregnant women on the streets and hauled them off, sometimes handcuffed or trussed, to abortion clinics. Other women were locked in detention cells or hauled before mass rallies and harassed into consenting to abortion.

The reporter referred to "aborted babies which were actually crying when they were born" (*New York Times*, 16 May 1982).

To make any sense, the structure of choice must be envisioned in a social-cultural framework. In China, women desire large families and strongly resist governmental interference in their reproductive lives. In Western liberal states that promote permissive abortion laws, women depend on state protection for the right to have small families through accessible, low-cost contraception and abortion. Cultural rules rarely promote total freedom, though. The most permissive abortion laws stipulate time and place limits. The idea of a mid-trimester fetus born "alive," kicking, crying, and recognizably human generates strong repugnance among most of us. We prefer to confine such relatively rare events to hospital settings, where medical intervention can shift categories quickly: from aborted fetus to live baby. Doctors who refuse such infants lifesaving equipment may increasingly jeopardize their medical careers.

On the whole, the ethics of abortion are rarely confronted by clinic or hospital managers. As an outpatient treatment, clinic abortion lacks certain of the medical rituals associated with other surgical procedures, but it remains firmly·entrenched in a medical, not ethical, regime. Abortion-on-convenience shapes the organization of services (e.g., rapid turnover, high patient volume, routinized services of physician as technician) and keeps costs low. This approach also produces the "mill-like" atmosphere found in many abortion clinics. Many women describe their clinic abortion experience as "terrible," impersonal, degrading, or traumatic. Because abortion services tend to be concentrated in urban-based facilities that operate for profit and that typically serve strangers on a one-time basis, the sense of anonymity and indifference is heightened. Add to that professionals and staff who may be hostile to women or to the abortion procedure, or at least who have not worked through their own ambivalence about gender roles and reproductive choice, and it is apparent that the costs of the procedure that fall almost exclusively on the woman extend far beyond the price of the abortion. And despite organized medicine's defense of legal abortion, there remains a serious disparity in the view of medical professionals between respectable medicine and abortion, thrusting abortion into a marginal place in the professional scheme of things.

The medical profession should not be "blamed" entirely for women's negative reactions. The retention of the abortion stigma is probably linked to the women's status and traditional values and goals. In my unpublished Portland, Oregon, sample of eighty-seven women who had clinic abortions (1976), most were white, young (fourteen to twenty-four), unmarried, and terminating a first pregnancy.[4] Uncertainty, confusion, uneasiness, guilt, fear, ambivalence, "changing my mind frequently," or "working through the decision carefully" characterized 83 percent, and among single women (seventy-one of the eighty-seven reporting), social, psychological, and economic issues were paramount considerations in their decisions to abort. Despite the internalized rejection of abortion as "killing," fear of trauma or inability to have future children, or, more commonly, regret, anger, and guilt among these single women, abortion was perceived as the "only" possible decision. Age, immaturity (not ready for children), lack of stable relationships, financial dependency, being a rape victim, or being overwhelmed with other living children made abortion necessary. Among single women, the stigma of being an unwed mother was pervasive.

Other studies support these Portland findings. In *The Ambivalence of Abortion*, Linda Bird Franke (1978) argues that, for the vast majority of single women who have had legal abortion, the decision to abort is relatively simple to reach. Particularly in middle-class communities, the attitude toward an unwed birth has not loosened in congruence with the loosening of social mores concerning sexuality.

Such women are neither independent and individualistic nor emotionally disturbed, another study shows (Burtchaell, 1980). Instead, abortion was perceived as a difficult situation to an "insurmountable problem" and, for most, an emotionally upsetting experience.

Abortion is not a universal trauma, though. Zimmerman's (1977) research involved interviewing women six to ten weeks after an abortion, examining the factors that contributed to the post-abortion adjustment. In the successful passage through abortion, social integration was the chief facilitator. Zimmerman says:

Emotional adjustment following abortion was more closely tied to social integration of the woman ("affiliated" or "disaffiliated") and her perception of abortion as a deviant act than to initial attitudes toward the pregnancy. These women believed abortion to be an immoral act, disapproved of by society and significant others. Coping with the consequences of their abortion decision took the form, not of changed attitudes toward abortion, which remained negative, but of disassociating the self from the deviant act by denial of responsibility—"no other choice." (Zimmerman, 1977)

These data on legal abortion after *Roe* suggest that law, moral attitudes, and culture do not change in symmetrical fashion. Instead, culture affects people's personal, moral, and political choices.

Cultural limits on the abortion choice impinge in two ways. They provide opportunities in keeping with changed cultural patterns and human needs. And they establish barriers through consensual rules. For example, reproduction based on the woman's decision opens up the possibility that women can make more meaningful commitments as they gain greater control over their lives; that population pressure can be abated; and that children will be both wanted and cared for by reasonably mature adults. At the same time, abortion exposes us to the tenuousness of our moral categories. The question of when life begins was not an issue when only a few women had legal abortions in protected medical enclaves, where the fetus was largely a nonissue. As for the hundreds of thousands of illegal abortions, "out of sight, out of mind." It was the woman who paid for her sin, while the man (sometimes) paid the bill.

But the current specter of 1.5 million abortions a year, almost one-third the total number of infants born annually, may create enormous disease for many persons. The issue of when life begins is now salient and must be faced, if not by feminists, then by physicians, nurses, lawyers, judges, or legislators. The common categories support the early (three months or less) period of pregnancy as appropriate for abortion, rejecting abortion in late pregnancy as inhumane. For the 10 percent of women who choose mid-trimester abortion and who are most likely to be teenage, older, or single, the late abortion remains fraught with difficulty. As political pressures on physicians increase for saving the lives of aborted viable fetuses, this will further compound the moral and emotional difficulties of women who finally seek abortion but come home with an unwanted child. As technology improves, the stage at which the fetus can survive outside the womb may occur much earlier than the twenty-six-week limit now established.

If, on the other hand, we use a different criterion, the concept of "person," as used in developmental psychology, the viability issue can be discarded.[5] Regardless of the stage of pregnancy during which the fetus can eventually be salvaged, it is the birth process that designates the beginning of "personning"; that is, the process of naming, giving a personal and family identity, creating living space for the new human being, and otherwise marking the event as a significant social and psychological reality versus the physical experience of being pregnant. For some women, this reality of "carrying a child" may occur much earlier than the actual birth, as some pregnant women begin planning their future lives around the birth early in their pregnancy. Thus we are left with the moral concept of intentionality, an issue we take up in the next section.

Physicians, nurses, and other medical attendants are also involved and must be considered in the dispute over when life begins if an effective woman-centered abortion policy is to be constructed. Because of professional socialization, many nurses remain highly resistant to the mid-trimester abortion. For the obstetric nurse, especially, who may work simultaneously in two worlds—disposing of dead fetuses through induced abortion and delivering live babies in the maternity ward—disorientation may occur. Specialized nursing staffs are probably required to reduce such dissonance.

Using the sociological criterion, biological life, then, is not the same as the social-psychological reality of life. We need not deny the human status of the embryo or fetus; rather, we would emphasize the qualitative and quantitative distinctions between the fetus as an emergent or potential human being and the socially designated status of the newborn child. To return to the eighteenth-century belief that the embryo existed completely preformed with the ovum as a microscopic homunculus or in the spermatozoa as an animalcule is to engage in fantasy, not rational policymaking.

In the final analysis, the definition of when life begins is an arbitrary one. It can be constructed in a lax or tight way, either to facilitate abortion or to reduce the number of legal terminations (and, by default, increase the number of criminal abortions and maternal mortality). Thus the issue of when life begins and how the woman should proceed in the event of an unwanted pregnancy revolves around who controls: the woman or society.

CONSCIENCE AND COMMITMENT

If women are to genuinely control their reproductive lives and options, we cannot abandon ethical reasoning, but rather must examine ourselves as moral actors evaluating, choosing, judging, and acting responsibly in the world.[6] Women have a duty to submit what they do to moral judgment, to examine the meanings of reproduction in terms of their own lives and the consequences of their actions for themselves and significant others. In this view, there is a kind of moral negligence that consists not merely in failing to do what one believes one ought to do, but also in evading or refusing to raise questions about the morality of what one does. Inadequate or confused moral concepts play a key part in the erosion of responsibility, exhibited by *not* raising certain questions. It makes no sense to shift from the pro-natalist role of "mindless motherhood" to merely another version of mindlessness, that of uninformed sexuality and abortion. But what are the moral considerations in reproduction?

First, moral decisions involve both intention and consequences, which often operate independently of each other. This means that because it is impossible to predict all the consequences of our acts, decisions made in good faith may produce unanticipated consequences. In a not untypical situation, parents may promote abortion as the only solution to their teen-age daughter's pregnancy, ignoring the girl's view of the situation. When a repeat pregnancy occurs a few months later, which the girl carries through to term, the parents suffer a strong sense of rejection and failure, interpreting this as an unconscionable youthful rebellion. Subsequent parent-child alienation implies that the meanings of both pregnancies remain hidden, while the negative consequences amplify throughout three generations.

Second, moral beliefs—conceptions of right and wrong—are never justified by appealing to nonmoral considerations. In a pluralistic moral universe, though, moral values and commitments are highly personal and often situational. For example, the woman with a career commitment who decides on late abortion after amniocentesis and the discovery of a deformed fetus makes a moral choice that is commensurate with her life goals. For another woman, say a full-time homemaker who has organized her life around her children, no fetus should be sacrificed, however physically or mentally deformed it may be. Prior commitments may also induce women to choose abortion at one point in their lives (say, late teenage or early married years) and opt for childbirth at a later period, when they feel more capable of devoting themselves to parenting.

Third, conflict is endemic to the sexual reproduction decision, whatever the eventual outcome. To be sexual or not to be sexual, to get pregnant or not to get pregnant, to carry to term or to abort, to choose a life-style oriented around children and family or to seek a career—these decisions, once silenced by a universal ethic of motherhood, present open agendas for modern women. Conflicting moral claims cannot be decided by appeals to "natural" law, however persuasively the sociobiologists argue, nor to the sacrosanct state of motherhood, as the New Right proposes. Caught between the self- (or couple) gratification of the new social ethic versus traditional female socialization, women confront an updated version of the double standard: Whatever choice is made, it will be her responsibility and burden. Thus the one-time counseling experience in abortion and the informal ad hoc socialization into parenting both represent wholly inadequate regimens. Pregnancy counseling needs to be recast in a larger network of reproductive and social supports, which might begin in the elementary school, but which would at least be available to girls entering puberty and beyond.

Fourth, there is no absolute moral authority to which all persons can appeal as a final arbiter. Personal conscience may find needed solace in pastoral or therapeutic guidance, but such counsel should more properly be perceived as open-ended recommendations, not as absolutist dogma. Intellectual rationales (his life-style or mine, his career or mine, youthful looks, marriage plans, and so on) are sometimes proferred as excuses for specific reproductive choices. Or "common sense," which appeals to something other than evidence or argument (e.g., everyone is doing it), supposedly serves the moral function. On the surface, almost any reason can be invoked for a particular reproductive decision, reasons that can actually obscure the woman's real values and needs. At the deeper level of beliefs, where conscience operates, though, the reasoning can be very different. Not to consider one's own beliefs in making reproductive decisions is to engage in false consciousness and bad faith. Meaningless and often psychologically destructive sexuality, followed by reluctant delivery or repeated abortions, is hardly a sign of a woman's emancipation. As a new form of psychic exploitation, "free" sexuality may cost dearly.

Fifth, emotional experiences of suffering are relevant to the moral argument. Thus the sanctity of fetal life (protected because of its potential personhood) must be balanced with the pain of the woman, couple, or family in the likely event of an unwanted birth. In this case, abortion serves as a lesser evil in a choice between negative outcomes.

Sixth, as linguists have shown, we use language to deaden our emotional awareness of the consequences of our actions and beliefs.[7] Cow is renamed "beef" and sheep becomes "mutton" in order to put distance between the living animal and the food that we eat. To justify war we dehumanize those who are killed, inventing jargon to disguise the killing ("mopping up" operation). By contrast, we have largely retained the emotionally loaded term "abortion," which is translated as the expulsion of a human fetus. The term also connotes stopping or arresting development; it does not imply the killing of a baby, as pro-life activists emphasize. What it certainly means is the intentional failure of a human organism to develop, progress, or mature, at a more or less early stage. It also implies the wilful intervention in the reproductive process, violating traditional norms of "natural" motherhood.

Seventh, we lack an adequate language to communicate the problems associated with a viable fetus born alive that is allowed to die. That appears, to most of us, closer to killing than the sterile procedure of vacuum aspiration conducted within the first twelve weeks of pregnancy. Unlike the whole-fetal-body deliveries of the mid-trimester abortion, in the suction technique no recognizable body parts are visible. The evacuation of a "conceptus," or an "abortus," does not appear to be taking human life when we observe merely the remnants of placental or fetal tissue prematurely passed or curetted. In fact, women, long adapted to menstruation, may find such a vision of bloody residue neither extraordinary nor traumatizing. For those of tender conscience or limited experience, though, the sight and sound of an abortion procedure at any stage may be a dreadful event.

Eighth, only a moral agent, one who is capable and free to make a decision that affects her, can be held responsible. In the still unresolved issue of parent or guardian consent for abortion for girls seventeen and under, should the person be treated as a moral agent who is capable of the active apprehension of moral choice? Some young women undoubtedly are. Other teens, overly influenced by peers and the media, may have a great gap to cross from subjective hedonism or fear to a genuine ethical stance.

We cannot blame youth for a culture that fosters inward lack of wisdom coupled with an outward presentation of self that seeks to conceal this lack. The "cool" front often papers over a "hot" interior: the adolescent in turmoil. What abortion teaches teens and mature women alike is that women must make the final reproductive decision without familiar signposts to guide them. What we are also learning is that freedom is not an all-or-nothing matter, nor is self-awareness. By making moral choices we expand our arena of freedom. And by having an inward awareness of our actions we become capable of conscious commitments to ourselves and others. Letting others pull our strings—whether physicians, clergymen, lovers, or parents—narrows our moral beam and, if we remain overly dependent, can eventually snuff out the light of moral independence altogether.

Ninth, the quality-of-life criterion is morally significant and operates at the personal and societal levels. Why should one conception of the good life (for example, the traditional view of happiness as the nuclear family) be the exclusive model? We are apparently in the midst of a severe rupture in our normative and economic structures that mitigates the dominance of the nuclear family. Less than one household in four now contains the working husband, at-home wife, and school-age children. But other family and household forms are emerging that may be equally satisfying and require social and political support for their continuity. Even the multi-generational family may be experiencing a resurgence, even if some "family" members are actually unrelated by blood or marriage.

At the collective level, the quality-of-life argument has even larger implications. Nuclear war, worldwide overpopulation, severe famine in Third World nations, racism, environmental protection, and energy conservation are intricately linked to abortion. For instance, does abortion evoke images of worldwide catastrophe, tantamount to an unjust war, as some alarmists insist? Although an extreme viewpoint, it is worth considering to what extent our culture remains mired in the nineteenth-century vision of the two-sphere doctrine: men making war and women reproducing the next generation of warriors. Considering the severity of the world's problems, this is absurd. What does it benefit the human species to have elaborate philosophical discourses on the sanctity of fetal life when at the same time we are overproducing world-annihilating weaponry. Famine and polluted food and water take longer to kill people, but if decimation of the world's powerless populations is on the West's hidden agenda, we are phenomenally successful. A reproductive policy that operates in tandem with human-centered rules for personal conduct and caring interpersonal relations, along with the cessation of economic and political exploitation, would go far toward promoting a more meaningful global quality of life. But how can we transcend the individual life-style mentality that ignores human need? We can begin by considering how a population policy can be mounted that will sustain gender equality, social diversity, and human survival.

ALTERNATIVE MODES OF POLICYMAKING

We can conceptualize the making of abortion policy in three ways: (1) hierarchy, or rule by experts; (2) politics, or rule by expediency; and (3) reorganization of social priorities, including shared social responsibility for sexuality, pregnancy, and child care.[8]

Hierarchy, or rule by experts, relies on centralized authority and a body of scientific and administrative experts, who are expected to offer a superior breadth and competence of analysis, as well as a comprehensive approach uncontaminated by ideology and special pleading. High technology facilitates the complex monitoring of entire populations—death, birth, migrations, food production, medical organization, level of political stability, and other social data. On the basis of this information, mathematically precise outcomes can be predicted for various policy proposals. For example, experts can make fairly accurate calculations of the increased number of unwanted pregnancies that would result from a population policy that requires teenage women to secure parental approval for an abortion. Their advisory role, however, restricts experts from implementing their opinions about the feasibility of such a policy.

Thus hierarchy, in and of itself, does not establish essential principles, tends toward impersonality and dehumanization, and, by definition, rejects equality and social differences. Scientists, hospital committees, and government bureaucrats operate as part of a chain of command, putting them at the disposal of their political superiors, who, themselves, may have conflicting agendas and be indifferent to the suffering of powerless people. Hierarchy, then, does not operate in a social vacuum, but takes its organizational shape and direction from political norms and conflicts.

Much of this book has presented the legal, medical, moral, and social problems resulting from an abortion policy determined by so-called experts. Modern developed societies, whether they are capitalist or communist, operate under a regimen of power, submission, and surveillance. Outside forces control. Hierarchical arrangements merely facilitate this control. For women to depend on this policymaking approach (experts to the rescue) is to risk losing all control over our own reproduction.

Politics, or rule by expediency, aims for a political strategy to guide the technical analysis. Whereas scientists can predict within a fairly narrow range the number of illegitimate births in an age cohort, their placement in the organization renders them powerless. For instance, such experts cannot determine what educational system best serves the deprived family's needs or how to encourage minority participation in the labor market.

Politicians, by contrast, lack the necessary information, invariably working with imperfect data and incomplete analysis. Yet they alone have the collective power to make the decisions. Reasoning may be based on trial and error, rules of thumb, routinized and habitual responses to categories of problems, and, inevitably, biased evaluations. Problems are typically treated incrementally—as they arise—and sequentially—paying close attention to the interplay between means and ends. The problem is rarely solved "correctly," for there are conflicting value judgments and one interpretation may contradict another. The goal is not to eliminate the problem, but to make an advance or to remedy dissatisfaction with a past policy, often using socially crude and expedient measures.

Political decision making takes as its single constant that goals and policies are in constant flux. The essential technique runs counter to that of hierarchy, which builds parts into wholes. The political solution is fragmentation—break up the problem into its constituent units and then reintegrate. Following a series of trial and error steps and gauging the public reaction is the political policymaking process. Analysis is not excluded here; it is only more limited in its scope and plays a secondary role to political interests.

In this sense, abortion has been almost totally politicized over the past decade. Since the Supreme Court decision in 1973, abortion has been overly susceptible to local option, undermining the original intent of the Court. Dissident groups' protest about the moral and medical propriety of abortion challenges constitutional guarantees for women's right to an abortion, rationalizes violence against persons and property, denies individual privacy, and rejects accessible medical assistance for poor women. Political compromises and expedient solutions have been proposed, challenged, rejected, and reopened continuously. Scientists and bureaucrats provide powerful analytical tests, showing the severe negative outcomes of overpopulation or of failure of poor women's rights to secure abortion. But in the day-to-day political struggles, such information is lost in the political melee.

Bear in mind that politicians are, above all, practical, not ideological; individualistic, not humanistic; male-oriented, not woman-centered. If fighting for abortion rights will help them survive in office, they will move with the times. If their jobs are threatened by dissenters who rage against abortion "murder," many will undoubtedly vote against abortion rights. The politics of disorder that has characterized women's struggle for equality requires that we reject an abortion policy constructed by impersonal experts or traditional politicians. Instead, a woman-centered policy offers a third way.

Reorganization of social priorities requires a critique of the existing system, including a blueprint for fundamental transformations in gender values and roles. Because the current social organization of reproduction disallows reproductive choice for many women—a point this book makes abundantly clear—existing policy based on expertise, bureaucracy, and politics must be examined for inherent limitations. These approaches merely reproduce class and gender inequalities. Is there any value to expert and political policy approaches? I would argue that even within the current policymaking mode there is the possibility of reform and the redistribution of essential benefits for women and children.

Certainly, as a first step, we can imagine an accretion of reforms—pregnancy disability benefits, child-care centers, maternity-leave provisions, and other reproductive-related reforms that support childbearing.

Such reformist efforts, however, will not alter the status of women and children unless we move beyond the individualistic framework of a woman's "right to choose" or the welfare state concept of women as clients.

The kind of humanistic transformation that is needed requires more than material or technological reforms or a pro-natalist reproduction policy. Fundamental institutional changes call for the creation of new values and altered social relations in the social, sexual, familial, economic, and political spheres. (See Rich, 1976; Chodorow, 1975; Dinnerstein, 1976; Merchant, 1980.)

Such value creations are essential for human survival and must be unleashed from their traditional family and sexual forms to a new set of social relations. Foremost among these revitalized relations is the care of children.

If new social priorities are to emerge, declares Adrienne Rich (1976), men must be "ready to share the responsibilities of full-time universal child care as a social priority." Responsibility for children dissociated from gender implies that it becomes dissociated from heterosexuality as well. Traditional child-rearing arrangements based on mother-right entails the inevitable subordination of women, involving deeply rooted cultural and psychic biases that divide the sexes and the generations.

We need to envision the conditions under which such a collective, shared, gender-free responsibility for sexuality, birth control, and child care can emerge. In a thoughtful paper on reproductive freedom, Rosalind Petchesky (1980, 661–685) outlines what these conditions would be. First, we would have to have the material resources for having and raising children, or for lessening these activities, in order to have a real alternative for *all* people. Currently, many women are without adequate material resources or social supports to transform nonadaptive sex roles or to change the traditional division of labor. An essential step, then, is to focus on the individual rather than on the family as the basic economic unit. This move will deliberately eradicate the sexual division of labor in the family and work force and establish equal participation and benefits in the labor force.

A second condition is the development and universal distribution of convenient, safe, and reliable methods of birth control. In order to secure good-quality contraception, a publicly funded health-care system must emerge in which maternal, prenatal, and child care are recognized as human rights, not privileges of wealth. As part of the reinstitutionalization of health and safety norms, we would eliminate reproductively hazardous environments where we work and live (e.g., nuclear waste, polluted water).

The provision of adequate jobs, incomes, housing, education, and social supports for all citizens is a final condition for a human-centered reproductive policy. The current maldistribution of wealth and unequal access to basic living necessities work to rigidify the divisions between classes and groups. An emancipatory ethic requires equalizing material conditions. As long as the political system remains part of an authoritarian and unequal economic order, democratic participation becomes a mockery, a convenient myth to quiet rebellion and political unrest.

The Reproductive Question, then, is ultimately the Human Question: How are we to organize a society that has as its core the positive qualities of trust, cooperation, and caring, rather than the negative qualities of resentment, competition, and indifference? In the framing of a moral outlook that proceeds from women's needs and experiences, the human values that women have historically been assigned to preserve expand out of the confines of private life and become the organizing principles of society. Such a gender-free society does not obliterate differences, but opens up to each person the fullest expression of both masculine and feminine attributes. Such human possibilities sound the death knoll for certain social types, such as professional warriors, sadistic heroes, and masochistic victims, but it can also signal the quiet triumph of a more humane world. Our human survival may depend on it.

NOTES

1. Analysis of the failure of the Equal Rights Amendment emphasizes the disjuncture between the people's views (as indicated in public opinion polls), which showed strong support for the measure, and politicians' inertia (see Boles, 1982; Daniels, et al., 1982; Elfin, 1982; and Palley, 1982).

2. Our ethics lag seriously behind our technology, as the literature on informed consent and pharmacologic treatment clearly shows (Gallant and Force, 1978; Katz, 1976; *Rutgers-Camden Law Journal*, 1975). In some instances, the market determines the ethics, regardless of scientific, professional, or feminist reactions. (For a popular view, see Hollister, 1982; for a feminist interpretation, see Petchesky, 1980, 661–685).

3. Issues of women's social condition and public policy are analyzed in detail in Boneparth, ed. (1982).

4. I am indebted to Gloria Riches, Portland State University student, for analyzing these data. Her analysis, which differentiated between single and married women, clearly shows the greater utilization and perceived need of abortion among single women.

5. An excellent analysis of the "person" concept is found in Lidz (1976).

6. Glover's (1970) thoughtful analysis of moral responsibility is particularly salient for considering the policy issues of abortion choice. See also Manier et al. (1977), for the fundamental (and perhaps nonresolvable) problems of individual versus system needs.

7. The relationships and antipathies between law, language, and ethics are nicely spelled out in a collection of essays edited by Bishin and Stone (1972).

8. Lindblom (1977) refers to these first two policy approaches as synoptic policymaking (rule by experts) versus strategic policymaking (political processes) and shows their inherent limitations for dealing with global problems.

Appendix A

Status of Abortion Laws-January 1971**

(Statutes provide that abortions are permitted for the reasons indicated and under the conditions specified.)

State	Year	Physi-cian	Hosp-ital	Life	Health	Physi-cal Health	Mental Health	Fetal Deform-ity	Forc-ible Rape	Statu-tory Rape (age)	Incest	Time Limit (Weeks)	M.D. Approv-al	Residency
Alabama	1951			X	X									
Alaska	1970	X	X[1]											X 30 dys.
Arizona	1865			X										
Arkansas	1969	X	X	X				X	X		X		3C	X 4 mos.
California	1967	X	X	X		X	X		X	X (15)	X	X (20)	2-3B[2]	
Colorado	1967	X	X	X		X	X	X	X	X (16)	X	X (16)[3]	3B	
Connecticut	1860			X										
Delaware	1969	X	X	X		X	X	X	X		X	X (20)[4]	1C-RA	X 4 mos.[5]
Dist.of Col.	1901			X	X									
Florida	1868			X										
Georgia	1968	X	X	X	X			X	X	X (14)			2C-3B	X
Hawaii	1970	X	X											X 90 dys.[6]
Idaho	1863			X										
Illinois	1874			X										
Indiana	1838			X										
Iowa	1843			X										
Kansas	1969	X	X[7]	X		X	X	X	X	X (16)	X		3C	

** Source: National Center for Family Planning Services, HSMHA, HEW.

254

State	Year	Physician	Hospital	Life	Health	Physical Health	Mental Health	Fetal Deformity	Forcible Rape	Statutory Rape (age)	Incest	Time Limit (Weeks)	M.D. Approval	Residency
Kentucky	1910			X										
Louisiana	1914			X									1C	
Maine	1840			X										
Maryland	1968	X	X	X		X	X	X	X			X (26)[8]	RA	
Massachusetts	1845		X[9]	X[9]	X[9]									
Michigan	1846			X										
Minnesota	1851			X										
Mississippi	1966	X		X					X[10]	x[10]			2C	
Missouri	1835			X										
Montana	1864			X										
Nebraska	1873			X										
Nevada	1861			X										
New Hampshire	1848			X										
New Jersey	1849			X[11]										
New Mexico	1969	X	X	X		X	X	X	X	X (16)	X		2B	
New York	1970	X										X (24)[12]		
N.Carolina	1967	X	X	X	X	X	X	X	X		X		3C	X 4 mos.
N.Dakota	1943			X										
Ohio	1841			X										

APPENDIX A (cont.)

State	Year	Physician	Hospital	Life	Health	Physical Health	Mental Health	Fetal Deformity	Forcible Rape	Statutory Rape (age)	Incest	Time Limit (Weeks)	M.D. Approval	Residency
Oklahoma	1910			X										
Oregon	1969	X	X	X		X[13]	X[13]	X	X	X (16)	X	X 150dys[14]	1C	X
Pennsylvania[15]	1860													
Puerto Rico	1913			X										
Rhode Island	1896			X										
S.Carolina	1970	X	X	X		X	X	X	X		X		3C	X 90 dys.
S.Dakota	1929			X										
Tennessee	1883			X										
Texas	1859			X										
Utah	1876			X										
Vermont	1867			X										
Virginia	1970	X	X	X		X	X	X	X		X		Board	X 120 dys.[5]
Washington	1970	X	X[17]									X (16)		X 90 dys.
West Virginia	1848			X										
Wisconsin	1858			X									2C	
Wyoming	1869			X										

C - Consultant; B - Therapeutic Abortion Board; RA - Hospital Review Authority   · Non-Visible Fetus

1 Abortion must be "performed in a hospital or other facility approved for the purpose by the Department of Health and Welfare or a hospital operated by the federal government or an agency of the federal government..." Abortion may not be performed unless "consent has been received from the parent or guardian of an unmarried woman less than 18 years of age..."

2 Two-member abortion board required through the 12th week of pregnancy, three-member board thereafter.

3 The 16-week time limit applies to rape and incest only.

4 After 20 weeks a pregnancy may be terminated to preserve the woman's life or where the fetus is dead.

5 Residency requirement does not apply if the woman or her husband works in Delaware or if she has previously been a patient of a Delaware physician or if her life is in danger.

6 "The affidavit (re: residency) of such a woman shall be prima facie evidence of compliance with this requirement."

7 Abortion must be done in a hospital "or other place as may be designated by law..."

8 After 26 weeks a pregnancy may be terminated to preserve maternal life or when the fetus is dead.

9 The statute prohibits "unlawful" abortion, or abortion which is "malicious" or performed "without lawful justification." Case law, however, sanctions abortion to preserve maternal life and protect maternal health COMMONWEALTH V. WHEELER (1944).

10 Statute does not specify whether forcible or statutory rape (for either) is meant.

11 The statute forbids abortions done "maliciously or without lawful justification." Case laws provide that abortions are permitted at least to preserve the life of the woman. GLEITMAN V. COSGROVE (1967).

12 After 24 weeks pregnancy may be terminated only to preserve woman's life.

13 "In determining whether or not there is substantial risk (to her physical or mental health) account may be taken of the mother's total environment, actual or reasonably foreseeable."

14 The 150-day time limit does not apply in cases of danger to life.

15 "Unlawful" abortion is proscribed but not defined.

16 Residency may be proved by affidavit.

17 Abortion must be performed in an accredited hospital or medical facility approved by the state Board of Health. Pregnancy can be lawfully terminated "with the prior consent and, if married and residing with her husband or unmarried and under the age of 18 years, with the prior consent of her husband or legal guardian, respectively."

Appendix B

MAJOR CATEGORIES OF STATE ABORTION LAWS	STATES HAVING SIMILAR ABORTION LAWS
I. Abortion allowed only when necessary to preserve the life of the pregnant woman	Arizona, Connecticut, Florida, Idaho, Illinois[1], Indiana, Iowa[2], Kentucky, Louisiana[3], Maine, Michigan, Minnesota, Missouri, Montana, Nebraska, Nevada, New Hampshire, North Dakoa, Ohio, Oklahoma, Rhode Island, South Dakota, Tennessee, Utah, Vermont, West Virginia, Wyoming.
II. Indications for legal abortion include threats to the pregnant woman's life and forcible rape.	Mississippi.
III. "Unlawful" or "unjustifiable" abortions are prohibited.	Massachusetts, New Jersey, Pennsylvania.
IV. Abortions allowed when continuation of the pregnency threatens the woman's life or health.	Alabama.
V. American Law Institute Model Abortion Law. "A licensed physician is justified in terminating a pregnancy if he believes that there is substantial risk that continuance of the pregnancy would gravely impair the physical or mental health of the mother or that the child would be born with grave physical or mental defect, or that the pregnancy resulted from rape, incest or other felonious intercourse".	Arkansas, California (does not include fetal deformity), Colorado, Delaware, Kansas, Maryland (does not include incest), New Mexico, North Carolina, South Carolina, Virginia.
VI. Abortion law based on the May 1968 recommendations of the American College of Obstetricians and Gynecologists allows abortion when the pregnancy resulted from felonious intercourse, and when there is risk that continuance of the pregnancy would impair the physical or mental health of the mother. "In determining whether or not there is substantial risk (to the woman's physical or mental health), account may be taken of the mother's total environment, actual or reasonably foreseeable".	Oregon.
VII. No legal restriction on reasons for which abortion may be obtained prior to viability of the fetus.	Alaska, Hawaii, New York, Washington
VIII. Legal restrictions on reasons for which an abortion may be obtained were invalidated by court decision.	District of Columbia, Georgia, Texas, Wisconsin[4].

I. A Federal District Court decision, Doe vs. Scott, 321 F.Upp. 1385 (N.D.III., Jan.29 1971), holding the Illinois abortion statute unconstitutional has been stayed pending appeal in the United States Supreme Court.

2.	In State vs. Dunklebarger, the Iowa statute which is couched in terms of saving the life of the woman, has been interpreted to suggest that preservation of health is sufficient. 221 N.W. 592 (Iowa, 1928).

3.	Although the Louisiana abortion statute does not contain an express exception to the "crime of abortion" the Louisiana Medical Practice Act authorizes the Medical Board to suspend or institute court proceedings to revoke a doctor's certificate to practice medicine in the state when the doctor has procured or aided or abetted in the procuring of an abortion "unless done for the relief of a woman whose life appears imperiled after due consultation with another licensed physician". La.Rev.Stat.Ann.37:1261.

4.	The abortion law of several other states have been ruled unconstitutional by lower state trial courts; however, these decisions are binding only in the jurisdiction in which the decision was rendered.

References

Adams, James Luther
  1965 *Paul Tillich's Philosophy of Culture, Science and Religion*. New York: Harper & Row.

Adler, Nancy E.
  1975 "Emotional Responses to Women Following Therapeutic Abortion." *American Journal of Orthopsychiatry* 45 (April): 446–454.

Alan Guttmacher Institute
  1977 *Teenage Pregnancy: The Problem That Won't Go Away*. New York: Alan Guttmacher Institute.

Arendt, Hannah
  1963 *Eichmann in Jerusalem*. New York: Viking Press.

Ash, Roberta
  1972 *Social Movements in America*. Chicago: Markham.

Babcock, Barbara Allen, et al.
  1975 *Sex Discrimination and the Law*. Boston: Little, Brown.

Baker, Tyler
  1974 "Roe and Paris: Does Privacy Have a Principle?" *Stanford Law Review* 26 (May): 1161–1189.

Baldwin, W. H.
  1976 "Adolescent Pregnancy and Childbearing: Growing Concerns for Americans." *Population Bulletin* 31. Washington, D.C.: Population Reference Bureau, Inc.

Banner, L.
  1984 *Women in Modern America: A Brief History*. 2d ed. New York: Harcourt Brace Jovanovich.

Barker-Bensfield, G. J.
  1976 *The Horrors of the Half-Known Life: Male Attitudes Toward Women and Sexuality in Nineteenth Century America*. New York: Harper & Row.

Bart, Pauline B.
1977   "Seizing the Means of Reproduction: An Illegal Feminist Abortion Collective: How and Why It Worked." Paper presented at the annual meetings of the American Sociological Association, Chicago, Illinois, September.

Barth, Fredrick
1963   *The Role of the Entrepreneur in Social Change in Northern Norway.* Bergen and Oslo: Norwegian Universities Press.

Bates, Jerome E., and Zawadski, Edward S.
1964   *Criminal Abortion.* Springfield, Ill.: Charles C. Thomas.

Berger, Peter
1967   "A Sociological View of the Secularization of Theology." *Journal for the Scientific Study of Religion* 11 (Spring): 1.

Berger, B., and Berger, P. L.
1983   *The War Over the Family.* Garden City, N.Y.: Anchor Press.

Berlant, J.
1975   *Profession and Monopoly: A Study of Medicine in the United States and Great Britain.* Berkeley: University of California Press.

Bernard, Jessie
1972   *The Future of Marriage.* New York: Bantam.
1981   *The Female World.* New York: The Free Press.

Bishin, William R., and Stone, Christopher D.
1972   *Law, Language and Ethics.* Mineola, N.Y.: The Foundation Press.

Blank, Robert H.
1982   "Legal Issues in Biomedical Research and Technology: A Policy of Wrongful Life?" Paper delivered at the American Political Science Association, Denver, Colorado, September.

Blumberg, A. S.
1967   *Criminal Justice.* Chicago: Quadrangle Books.

Blumer, Herbert
1951   "Collective Behavior." In *Principles of Sociology*, edited by A. M. Lee, 167–222. New York: Barnes & Noble.

Boles, Janet K.
1982   "Building Support for the ERA: A Case of 'Too Much, Too Late.' " *PS* 15 (Fall): 572–577.

Bolt, Merry; Wilson, Anne; and Larsen, Wendy
1979   "Women's Biology-Mankind's Destiny: The Population Explosion and Women's Changing Roles." In *Women: A Feminist Perspective*, edited by Jo Freeman, 3–18. 2d ed. Palo Alto, Calif.: Mayfield.

Bond, Jon R., and Johnson, Charles A.
1982   "Implementing a Permissive Policy: Hospital Abortion Services After *Roe v. Wade.*" *American Journal of Political Science* 26 (February): 1–24.

Boneparth, Ellen (ed.)
1982   *Women, Power and Policy.* New York: Pergamon Press.

Borders, J., and Cutright, P.
   1979 "Community Determinants of U.S. Legal Abortion Rates." *Family Planning Perspectives* 11 (4): 227–238.

Boston Women's Health Book Collective
   1979 *Our Bodies, Ourselves.* New York: Simon & Schuster.

Bracken, M. B., and Kasl, S. V.
   1975 "Delay in Seeking Induced Abortion: A Review and Theoretical Analysis." *American Journal of Obstetrics and Gynecology* 121: 1008–1019.

Bracken, M. B., and Swigar, M. E.
   1972 "Factors Associated with Delay in Seeking Induced Abortions." *American Journal of Obstetrics and Gynecology* 113: 301–309.

Bracken, M. B., et al.
   1973 "Abortion Counseling: An Experimental Study of Three Techniques." *American Journal of Obstetrics and Gynecology* 117 (September): 10–20.

Bumpass, L., and Presser, H.
   1973 "The Increasing Acceptance of Sterilization and Abortion." In *Toward the End of Growth*, edited by C. Westoff, 33–46. Englewood Cliffs, N.J.: Prentice-Hall.

Burtchaell, James T.
   1980 *Abortion Parley.* New York: Andrews and McMeel.

Caine, T. Allen, et al.
   1978 "A Survey of Research Relating to Abortion Issues." Paper presented to the Minnesota State Legislature. Abortion Counseling Services of Minnesota, 549 Turnpike Road, Golden Valley, Minnesota.

Calderone, M. S.
   1958 *Abortion in the United States.* New York: Hoeber-Harper Books.

Callahan, Daniel
   1970 *Abortion: Law, Choice and Morality.* New York: Macmillan.

Carey, H.C.
   1858 *Principles of Social Science.* Vols. 1 and 3. Philadelphia: J.B. Lippincott.

Chambliss, William, and Seidman, Robert
   1982 *Law, Order and Power.* 2d ed. Reading, Mass.: Addison-Wesley.

Chodorow, Nancy
   1975 *The Reproduction of Mothering.* Berkeley: University of California Press.

The Citation
   1971 "Special Issue—Medicolegal Aspects of Abortion." *American Medical Association*, December 15.

Congressional Record-Senate
   1964 88th Cong. 2d sess., Vol. 110. July 14: 16022–16023.

Connery, John, S.J.
   1977 *Abortion: The Development of the Roman Catholic Perspective.* Chicago: Loyola University Press.

Conrad, Peter, and Schneider, J. W.
   1980 *Deviance and Medicalization.* St. Louis: C. V. Mosby.

Cramton, Roger C.
  1976 "Judicial Law Making and Administration." *Public Administration Review* 5 (September-October): 551–555.

Cumming, E.
  1968 *Systems of Social Regulation*. New York: Atherton.

Curtiss, S.
  1977 *Genie: A Psycholinguistic Study of a Modern Day "Wild Child"*. New York: Academic Press.

Cutright, Phillips.
  1972 "The Teenage Sexual Revolution and the Myth of an Abstinent Past." *Family Planning Perspectives 4* (January): 24–31.

Daley, Mary
  1978 *Gyn/Ecology: The Metaethics of Radical Feminism*. Boston: Beacon Press.

Daniels, Mark R.; Darcy, Robert; and Westphal, Joseph
  1982 "The ERA Won—At Least in the Opinion Polls." *PS* 15 (Fall): 578–584.

Danridge v. Williams
  1970 397 U.S. 471.

Davis, Nanette J.
  1973 "The Abortion Market: Transactions in a Risk Commodity." Ph.D. diss., Department of Sociology, Michigan State University.
  1975 "Clergy Abortion Brokers: A Transactional Analysis of Social Movement Development." *Sociological Focus* 6 (Fall): 87–93.
  1982 "Researching an Abortion Market." In *Qualitative Methods: A Handbook of Social Science Research Methods*, edited by R. Smith and P. K. Manning. Vol. 2. New York: Ballinger.
  n.p.   "Gender, Deviance, and Social Control." In *Social Control of Deviance: A Critical Perspective*. New York: Random House. (forthcoming)

Davis, Nanette J., and Anderson, Bo
  1983 *Social Control: The Production of Deviance in the Modern State*. New York: Irvington.

Davis, Nanette J., and Farr, Grant M.
  1982 "Abortion and Legal Policy." Unpublished paper. Portland State University, Portland, Oregon.

Devereux, G.
  1967 "A Typological Study of Abortion in 350 Primitive, Ancient, and Pre-Industrial Societies." In *Abortion in America*, edited by H. Rose. Boston: Beacon Press.

Dinnerstein, Dorothy
  1976 *The Mermaid and the Minotaur*. New York: Harper & Row.

Doe v. Bolton
  1973 410 U.S. 179.

Donovan, Patricia
  1973 "Profile: Governor Jimmy Carter." *Family Planning Population Reporter* 2 (3): 58–59.

Dostro, Robert
1975   *California Law Review* 63 (Spring): 1250–1351.

Douglas, Ann
1977   *The Feminization of American Culture.* New York: Avon Books.

Downs, L.A., and Clayson, D.
1972   "Unwanted Pregnancy: A Clinical Syndrome Defined by the Similarities of Preceding Stressful Events in the Lives of Women with Particular Personality Characteristics." Paper presented at the Twentieth Annual Meeting of the American College of Obstetricians and Gynecologists, Chicago, Illinois.

Dunbar, F.
1945   "Motherhood." In *Psychology of Women*, edited by H. Deutsch, 179–201. Vol. 2. New York: Grune & Stratton.

Dupreel, E.
1922   *Les Variations Demographiques et le Progres.* Brussels: Imprimerie Scientifique et Litteraire.

Dworkin, L.
1967   "The Model of Rules." *University of Chicago Law Review* 35: 14.

Edelstein, Ludwig
1967   *Ancient Medicine: Selected Papers.* Baltimore: Johns Hopkins Press.

Ehrlich, Paul R.
1954   *The Population Bomb.* New York: Ballantine Books (Revised in 1968).

Einsenstadt v. Baird
1972   405 U.S. 438.

Ekblad, M.
1955   "Induced Abortion on Psychiatric Grounds: A Follow-up Study of 479 Women." *Acta Psychiatrica et Neurologica Scandinavia* 99 (suppl).

Elfin, Margery L.
1982   "Learning from Failures Present and Past." *PS* 15 (Fall): 585–587.

Ely, John Hart
1973   "The Wages of Crying Wolf: A Comment on *Roe v. Wade.*" *Yale Law Review* 82: 920.

Epstein, A. L.
1958   *Politics in an Urban African Community.* Manchester, England: Manchester University Press.

Evan, William P.
1980   "Law as an Instrument of Change." In *The Sociology of Law: A Social Structure Perspective*, edited by W. P. Evan, 554–562. New York: The Free Press.

Ewing, John A., and Rouse, Beatrice A.
1974   "Is Therapeutic Abortion on Psychiatric Grounds Therapeutic?" *Social Psychiatry* 1: 137–144.

Felsenthal, Carol
1981   *The Sweetheart of the Silent Majority: The Biography of Phyllis Schlafly.* New York: Doubleday.

Ferguson, Marilyn
  1980   *The Aquarian Conspiracy*. Los Angeles: J. P. Tarcher.

Firestone, Shulamith
  1970   *The Dialectic of Sex*. New York: William Morrow.

FitzGerald, Frances
  1981   "The Triumphs of the New Right." *The New York Review* 28: 19–26.

Folbre, N.
  1983   "Of Patriarchy Born: The Political Economy of Fertility Decisions." *Feminist Studies* 9: 2.

Foucault, Michel
  1976   *The Archaeology of Knowledge and the Discourse on Language*. New York: Pantheon Books.
  1977   *Discipline and Punish: The Birth of the Prison*. New York: Pantheon Books.
  1978   *The History of Sexuality*. Vol. 1. New York: Random House.
  1980   *Power/Knowledge*. New York: Pantheon Books.

Fox, Greer Litton
  1982   *The Childbearing Decision: Fertility Attitudes and Behavior*. Beverly Hills, Calif.: Sage Publications.

Francome, Colin
  1984   *Abortion Freedom: A Worldwide Movement*. London: George Allen & Unwin.

Franke, Linda Bird
  1978   *The Ambivalence of Abortion*. New York: Random House.

Freeman, Jo (ed.)
  1979   *Women: A Feminist Perspective*. 2d ed. Palo Alto, Calif.: Mayfield.

Freidson, Eliot
  1970   *Professional Dominance; The Social Structure of Medical Care*. New York: Atherton Press.

Freidson, Eliot, and Rhea, Burford
  1963   "Processes of Control in a Company of Equals." *Social Problems* 11: 119–130.

Gallant, Donald M., and Force, Robert (eds.)
  1978   *Legal and Ethical Issues in Human Research and Treatment*.New York: John Wiley & Sons.

Gebhard, P. H.; Pomeroy, W. B.; Martin, C. E.; and Christenson, C. V.
  1958   *Pregnancy, Birth and Abortion*. New York: Paul B. Hoeber.

Gerlach, L. P., and Hines, V. H.
  1968   "Five Factors Crucial to the Growth and Spread of a Modern Religious Movement." *Journal for the Scientific Study of Religion* 7 (Spring): 23–40.

Gilligan, C.
  1979   "Women's Place in Man's Life Cycle." *Harvard Educational Review* 49: 431–446.

Glen, Kristin Booth
1978 "Abortion in the Courts." *Feminist Studies* 1: 26.

Glover, Jonathan
1970 *Responsibility*. London: Routledge & Kegan Paul.

Goldstein, Leslie Friedman
1979 *The Constitutional Rights of Women: Cases in Law and Social Change*. New York and London: Longman.
1981 "The Constitutional Status of Women: The Burger Court and the Sexual Revolution in American Law." *Law and Policy Quarterly* 3 (January): 5–28.

Goldstein, M. S.
1984 "Creating and Controlling a Medical Market: Abortion in Los Angeles After Liberalization." *Social Problems* 31: 514–529.

Gordon, L.
1976 *Women's Body, Women's Right: A Social History of Birth Control in America*. New York: Grossman.

Greenwood, V., and Young, J.
1976 *Abortion on Demand*. London: Pluto Press.

Grey, A.
1975 "Do We Have an Unwritten Constitution?" *Stanford Law Review* 27: 703.

Grisez, Germain G.
1970 *Abortion Myths, the Realities and the Arguments*. New York: Corpus Books.

Griswold v. Connecticut
1965 381 U.S. 479, 85 Supreme Court, 1678.

Gunther, Gerald
1976 *Individual Rights in Constitutional Law*. Mineola, N.Y.: Foundation Press.

Gusfield, Joseph R.
1963 *Symbolic Crusade: Status Politics and the American Temperance Movement*. Urbana: University of Illinois Press.
1980 "Foreword." In *Deviance and Medicalization*. P. Conrad and J. Schneider. St. Louis: C. V. Mosby.

Hall, Robert E. (ed.)
1970 *Abortion in a Changing World*. Vols. 1 and 2. New York: Columbia University Press.

Hammond, Philip E.
1966 *The Campus Clergyman*. New York: Basic Books.

Handlin, Garrett
1968 *Exploring New Ethics for Survival*. New York: Viking Press.

Hardin, Garrett
1973 *Stalking the Wild Taboo*. Los Altos, Calif.: William Kaufmann.

Hart, H.L.A.
1963 *Law, Liberty and Morality*. Stanford, Calif.: Stanford University Press.

Harting, Donald, and Hunter, Helen J.
   1971   "Abortion Techniques and Services: A Review and Critique." *American Journal of Public Health* 61 (October).

Henshaw, S.; Forrest, J.; Sullivan, E.; and Tietze, C.
   1982   "Abortion Services in the United States: 1979 and 1980." *Family Planning Perspectives* 14(1): 5–15.

Henslin, J. M.
   1971   "Criminal Abortion: Making the Decision and Neutralizing the Act." In *Studies in the Sociology of Sex*, edited by J. M. Henslin, 131–135. New York: Appleton-Century-Crofts.

Hesburgh, Theodore
   1972   "A Concerned Catholic." In "Population: The U.S. Problem, the World Crisis." *New York Times Supplement* (April 30): 11.

Heymann, and Barzelay
   1973   "The Forest and the Trees: Roe v. Wade and Its Critics." *Boston University Law Review* 53: 765.

Hofstadter, Richard
   1965   *The Paranoid Style in American Politics*. New York: Knopf.

Hollister, Anne
   1982   "Small Miracles of Love and Science." *Life* 5 (November): 44–55.

Hughes, Everett
   1972   *The Sociological Eye: Selected Papers*. Chicago: Aldine, Atherton.

Humphries, D.
   1977   "The Movement to Legalize Abortion: A Historical Account." In *Corrections and Punishment*, edited by David F. Greenberg, 205–226. Beverly Hills, Calif.: Sage Publications.

Huxley, Julian
   1963   *The Human Crisis*. Seattle: University of Washington Press.

Hymowitz, Carol, and Weissman, Machaele
   1978   *A History of Women in America*. New York: Bantam Books.

Jackson, Jesse
   1972   "Population Control Is Subordinate to Wealth Control." In "Population: The U.S. Problem, the World Crisis." *New York Times Supplement*, April 30, p. 12.

Jaffe, F. S.; Lindheim, B. L.; and Lee, P. R.
   1981   *Abortion Politics: Private Morality and Public Policy*. New York: McGraw-Hill.

Jansson, B.
   1965   "Mental Disorders After Abortion." *Acta Psychologica Scandinavia* 41: 87–110.

Jewkes, J.
   1939   "The Population Scare." *The Manchester School* 10: 1–12.

Katz, J.
   1976   "Human Rights and Human Experimentation." In *Protection of Human Rights in the Light of Scientific and Technological Progress in Biology and*

Medicine. Proceedings of the Eighth Round Table of the Council for International Organizations of Medical Sciences, World Health Organization.

Kerenyi, Thomas D.; Glascock, E. L.; and Horowitz, M. L.
1973 "Reasons for Delayed Abortion: Results of Four Hundred Interviews." *American Journal of Obstetrics and Gynecology* 117: 299–311.

Kerenyi, Thomas D.; Mandelman, Nathan; and Sherman, David H.
1974 "Mid-Trimester Saline Inductions." In *Abortion Research: International Experience*, edited by Henry P. David, 87–97. Toronto: D. C. Heath.

Keynes, J. M.
1922 "An Economist's View of Population." *Manchester Guardian Commercial*, August, pp. 340–341.

King, John F.
1969 "Abortion and the New Maryland Law." *Journal of the American Medical Association* 207 (March 24).

Kurtz, R., and Diacopassi, D.
1975 "Medical and Social Work Students" Perceptions of Deviant Conditions and Sick Role Incumbency." *Social Science and Medicine 9: 249–255.*

Kurzweil, Edith
1980 *The Age of Structuralism: Lévi-Strauss to Foucault.* New York: Columbia University Press.

Lader, Lawrence
1967 *Abortion*. Boston: Beacon Press.
1971 *Breeding Ourselves to Death*. New York: Ballantine Books.
1973 *Abortion II: Making the Revolution*. Boston: Beacon Press.

Lasch, Christopher
1979 *The Culture of Narcissism*. New York: Warner Books.

Lee, N. H.
1969 *The Search for an Abortionist*. Chicago: University of Chicago Press.

Lemert, E. M.
1951 *Social Pathology*. New York: McGraw-Hill.

Leonard, Emile G.
1961 *A History of Protestantism*. Indianapolis: Bobbs-Merrill.

Lewis, Oscar
1963 *The Children of Sanchez*. New York: Vintage Books.

Lidz, Theodore
1976 *The Person: His and Her Development Throughout the Life Cycle*. Rev. ed. New York: Basic Books.

Lindblom, Charles E.
1977 *Politics and Markets: The World's Political Economic Systems*. New York: Basic Books.

Luker, Kristin
  1975 *Taking Chances: Abortion and the Decision Not to Contracept.* Berkeley: University of California Press.
  1984 *Abortion and the Politics of Motherhood.* Berkeley: University of California Press.

Malthus, T. R.
  1803 *An Essay on the Principle of Population.* 3d ed. London: Johnson, 1–16.

Manier, Edward; Liu, William; and Solomon, David
  1977 *Abortion: New Directions for Policy Studies.* Notre Dame, Ind.: University of Notre Dame Press.

Manning, P. K.
  1971 "Fixing What You Feared: Notes on the Campus Abortion Search." In *Studies in the Sociology of Sex*, edited by J. M. Henslin, 137–163. New York: Appleton-Century-Crofts.

Marcuse, Herbert
  1970 *The End of Utopia.* Rampart, April, pp. 30–34.

Martin, John B.
  1961 "Abortion." *Saturday Evening Post*, May 20: 237.

Marty, Martin E.
  1972 *Protestantism.* New York: Holt, Rinehart & Winston.

Marx, Karl
  1919 *Capital.* Vol. 1. Chicago: Kerr, 689–711.

Mayer, P.
  1962 "Migrancy and the Study of Africans in Towns." *American Anthropologist* 64: 576–592.

Means, Cyril
  1971 "Phoenix of Abortion Freedom: Is a Penumbra of Ninth Amendment Right About to Arise from the Nineteenth Century Legislative Ashes of a Fourteenth Century Common Law Liberty?" *New York Law Forum* 17: 335.

Merchant, Carolyn
  1983 *The Death of Nature: Women, Ecology and the Scientific Revolution.* San Francisco: Harper & Row.

Mill, John Stuart
  1947 In *On Liberty*, edited by Alburey Castell. Northbrook, Ill.: AHM Publishing Corp.

Miller, William Robert (ed.)
  1971 *Contemporary American Protestant Thought, 1900–1970.* New York: Bobbs-Merrill.

Mitchell, Juliet
  1966 "Women: The Longest Revolution," *New Left Review*, November/December, pp. 11–37.

Mitchell, J. C. (ed.)
  1969 *Social Networks in Urban Situations.* New York: Humanities Press.

Mitchell, Juliet
  1971 *Women's Estate*. New York: Random House.

Mitchell v. Lefkowitz
  1971 Laws of New York 1971, Ch. 1098, p. 1944. U.S. District Court, Southern District of New York, 71 Civ. 2990.

Mohr, J. C.
  1978 *Abortion in America: The Origins and Evolution of National Policy, 1800–1900*. New York: Oxford University Press.

Monroe, K.
  1968 "How California's Abortion Law Isn't Working." *New York Times Magazine*, December 29.

Morris, William (ed.)
  1973 *American Heritage Dictionary*. Boston: Houghton Mifflin.

Nathanson, B. N.
  1972 "Ambulatory Abortion: Experience with 26,000 cases (July 1, 1970 to August 1, 1972)." *New England Journal of Medicine* 286 (February 24): 404.

Noonan, J. J. (ed.)
  1970 *The Morality of Abortion: Legal and Historical Perspectives*. Cambridge, Mass.: Harvard University Press.
  1979 *A Private Choice: Abortion in the Seventies*. New York: The Free Press.

Oakley, A.
  1979 "A Case of Maternity: Paradigms of Women as Maternity Cases." *Signs* 4 (Summer): 607–631.

Osofsky, J. D., and Osofsky, H. J.
  1971 "The Psychological Reactions of Patients to Legalized Abortion." Paper presented to the American Orthopsychiatric Association Meeting, March.

Overbeek, J.
  1977 *The Evolution of Population Theory*. Westport, Conn.: Greenwood Press.

Packer, H. L.
  1968 *The Limits of the Criminal Sanction*. Stanford, Calif.: Stanford University Press.

Pakter, J., and Nelson, F.
  1971 "Abortion in New York City." *Family Planning Perspectives* 3 (July): 5–12.

Pakter, J.; O'Hare, D.; Nelson, F.; and Svigir, M.
  1973 "Two Years' Experience in New York City with the Liberalized Abortion Law—Progress and Problems." *American Journal of Public Health* 63 (June): 524–535.

Palley, M. L.
  1982 "Beyond the Deadline." *PS* 15 (Fall): 588–592.

Parsons, Talcott; Shils, Edward; Naegele, Kaspar D.; and Pitts, Jesse R.
  1965 *Theories of Society*. New York: The Free Press.

Partridge, J. R.; Spiegel, T. M.; Rouse, B. A.; and Ewing, J. A.
   1971   "Therapeutic Abortion: A Study of Psychiatric Applicants at North Car-
          olina Memorial Hospital." *North Carolina Medical Journal* 32 (April):
          131–136.

Petchesky, R. P.
   1980   "Reproductive Freedom: Beyond 'A Woman's Right to Choose.' " *Signs*
          5: 661–685.

Peterson, K. J.
   1976   "Creating Division of Labor: A Case Study of Nonprofessionals Professing
          Self-Help." Ph.D. diss., Northwestern University.

Pilpel, H.
   1969   "The Right to Abortion." *The Atlantic Monthly*, June.

Pivar, D., Jr.
   1973   *Purity Crusade: Sexual Morality and Social Control, 1868–1900*. Westport,
          Conn.: Greenwood Press.

Population Institute
   1977   *Facts About Teenage Pregnancies*. New York: 77 United Nations Plaza,
          New York, New York 10017.

Potts, M.
   1971   "Legal Abortion in the U.S.A.: A Preliminary Assessment." *Lancet* 2
          (September 18): 651–653.

Potts, M.; Diggory, P.; and Peel, J.
   1977   *Abortion*. Cambridge, London and New York: Cambridge University
          Press.

Powell, J.
   1981   *Abortion: The Silent Holocaust*. Allen, Tex.: Argus Communications.

Rains, P. M.
   1971   *Becoming an Unwed Mother*. Chicago: Aldine-Atherton.

Rich, A.
   1976   *Of Woman Born*. New York: W. W. Norton.

Roe v. Wade
   1973   Supreme Court of the United States. 410 U.S. 179.

Rokeach, M.
   1970   "Faith, Hope, Bigotry." *Psychology Today* 3 (April): 33–37.

Ross, H. Lawrence.
   1970   *Settled Out of Court: The Social Process of Insurance Claims Adjustment*.
          Chicago: Aldine.

Rutgers-Camden Law Journal
   1975   "Medical Treatment and Human Experimentation: Introducing Illegality,
          Fraud, Duress and Incapacity to the Doctrine of Informed Consent." Vol.
          6 (Winter): 538.

Ryan, M. P.
   1983   *Womanhood in America: From Colonial Times to the Present*. 3d ed. New
          York: Franklin Watts.

Ryder, N. B.
  1979 "The Future of American Fertility." *Social Problems* 26 (February): 359–370.

Sarvis, B., and Rodman, H.
  1974 *The Abortion Controversy.* New York: Columbia University Press.

Schur, E. M.
  1965 *Crimes Without Victims.* Englewood Cliffs, N.J.: Prentice-Hall.
  1968 *Law and Society.* New York: Random House.
  1984 *Labeling Women Deviant: Gender, Stigma, and Social Control.* New York: Random House.

Scully, D.
  1980 *Men Who Control Women's Health.* Boston: Houghton Mifflin.

Scully, D., and Bart, P.
  1973 "A Funny Thing Happened on the Way to the Orifice: Women in Gynecology Textbooks." In *Changing Women in a Changing Society*, edited by J. Huber, 283–288. Chicago: University of Chicago Press.

Seaman, B., and Seaman, G.
  1977 *Women and the Crisis in Sex Hormones.* New York: Rawson Associates.

Shils, E.
  1966 "Privacy: Its Constitution and Vicissitudes." *Law and Contemporary Problems* 28.

Shiner, L.
  1966 *The Secularization of History.* Nashville: Abingdon Press.

Shorter, E.
  1982 *A History of Women's Bodies.* New York: Basic Books.

Sims, J. M.
  1981 "Abortion: The Myth of the Golden Age." In *Controlling Women: The Normal and the Deviant*, edited by B. Hutter and G. Williams, 168–184. London: Croom Helm, in association with the Oxford University Women's Studies Committee.

Skolnick, Jerome H.
  1966 *Justice Without Trial.* New York: Wiley.
  1968 "Coercion to Virtue: The Enforcement of Morals." *Southern California Law Review* 41: 588–611.

Smelser, N. J.
  1963 *Theory of Collective Behavior.* New York: The Free Press.

S.P.S. Consultants, Inc. v. Lefkowitz
  1971 U.S. District Court, Southern District of New York. 71 Civ.2931.

Studies in Family Planning
  1972 "Population and the American Future: Excerpts" 3. (May): 77–96.

Stycos, Joseph M.
  1968 *Human Fertility in Latin America: Sociological Perspectives.* Ithaca, N.Y.: Cornell University Press.

Sutherland, Edwin H., and Cressey, Donald R.
  1969   *Principles of Criminology.* 6th ed. New York: J. B. Lippincott.

Tatalovich, Raymond, and Daynes, Bryon W.
  1981   *The Politics of Abortion: A Study of Community Conflict in Public Policy Making.* New York: Praeger.

Tedrow, Lucky M., and Mahoney, E. R.
  1979   "Trends in Attitudes Toward Abortion: 1972–1976." *The Public Opinion Quarterly* 43 (Summer): 181–189.

Tietze, C.
  1971   "Early Complications of Abortions Under Medical Auspices: A Preliminary Report." *Studies in Family Planning* 2 (July): 137–143.
  1979   *Induced Abortion.* New York: The Population Council.

Tietze, C., and Lewitt, S.
  1977   "Legal Abortion." *Scientific American* 236: 21–27.

Titmuss, Richard M.
  1971   *The Gift Relationship.* New York: Pantheon Books.

Tribe, Lawrence H.
  1973   "Foreword: Toward a Model of Roles in the Due Process of Life and Law." *Harvard Law Review* 87: 1–53.

Turk, Austin T.
  1972   *Legal Sanctioning and Social Control.* Washington, D.C., Superintendent of Documents, U.S. Government Printing Office, DHEW Pub. No. (HSM)72–9130.
  1976   "Law as a Weapon in Social Conflict." *Social Problems* 23 (February): 276–291.

Turner, Victor W.
  1957   *Schism and Continuity in an African Society.* Manchester: Manchester University Press for the Rhodes-Livingstone Institute.

Tyler, Stephen A. (ed.)
  1969   *Cognitive Anthropology.* New York: Holt, Rinehart & Winston.

Vincent, C. E.
  1961   *Unmarried Mothers.* New York: The Free Press.

Webb, Darryl L.
  1976   *Social Issues Before the Court: A Case Approach.* Dubuque, Iowa: Kendall/Hunt.

Westoff, Charles, and Ryder, Norman B.
  1977   *The Contraceptive Revolution.* Princeton, N.J.: Princeton University Press.

Westoff, L. and Westoff, C.
  1971   *From Now to Zero: Fertility, Contraception and Abortion in America.* Boston: Little, Brown.

Wiest, William M., and Squier, Leslie H.
  1974   "Incentives and Reinforcement: A Behavioral Approach to Fertility." *Journal of Social Issues* 30: 235–263.

Willer, David, and Anderson, Bo
  1981 *Networks, Exchange and Coercion.* New York: Elsevier.

Wolfson, Margaret
  1978 *Changing Approaches to Population Problems.* Paris: Development Centre of the Organization for Economic Cooperation and Development.

Worthington, B. S.; Vermeersch, J.; and William, S. R.
  1977 *Nutrition in Pregnancy and Lactation.* St. Louis: C. V. Mosby.

Wrong, Dennis H.
  1964 "Population Myths." *Commentary*, (November, pp. 61–64.
  1967 *Population and Society.* 3d ed. New York: Random House.

Zald, Mayer N.
  1970 *Organizational Change: The Political Economy of the Y.M.C.A.* Chicago: University of Chicago Press.

Zald, Mayer, and Ash, Roberta
  1966 "Social Movement Organizations: Growth, Decay and Change." *Social Forces* 44: 327–341.

Zimmerman, Mary H.
  1977 *Passage Through Abortion.* New York: Praeger.

Index

Abbot, Reverend David, 115
Abortifacients, 185
Abortion: back-alley, 5, 98, 117, 119, 122, 180, 184, 200, 223; Belgium, 60; birth control, as, 59; California, 11, 117, 139, 177, 227; catheter, 91, 184; chain, 165–168, 178; Chicago, 171, 181; choice, xiii, xiv, 129, 137–138, 148, 179, 209, 210, 221, 224, 225, 227, 234, 238, 241; church doctrine, 42; committee, 10, 65–72, 75–77, 79, 81, 85, 119, 122, 209, 216; complications, 77, 84, 90, 99, 102, 104, 117, 160, 163, 181, 192, 199–201, 205, 214, 229-233; consultation, 66–67, 83; consumer, xiv, 123, 179, 182, 207; contraindications, 168; costs, 71, 79, 84, 86, 94, 98, 102, 103, 105, 114, 119, 122, 132, 134, 136, 141, 160, 163, 170–172, 176, 180–183, 186, 188, 192, 197–199, 201–204, 209, 211, 213-215, 226–227, 229, 242; counseling, 49, 61, 77, 82–83, 121–122, 124, 131–143, 146–149, 151, 164–166, 173, 175, 177, 181, 183, 194–195, 199, 202–203, 246; counseling advocate, 158–159; criminal (illegal), xiv, 3, 4, 5, 10, 12, 17, 32, 43, 44–50, 54, 55, 57, 59, 61, 64, 68, 81, 89–107, 109–111, 114–117, 120, 123, 139–141, 150, 154, 157, 159, 164–167, 170, 174–176, 178, 180, 181, 184, 195, 200, 208, 209, 211, 213, 214, 217, 223, 227, 230, 235, 244–245; delivery system, 11, 12, 182; dirty work, 89, 232; doctors' offices, 198; in Eastern Europe, 196–197; in England, 100, 139; in Europe, 60; facilities, 91, 182–186, 192–193, 197–203, 232; first-trimester (also early), 8, 192, 210, 213, 215–217, 227, 230–233; free-standing clinic, xv, 8, 49, 85, 105, 136, 138, 158–159, 168, 178, 180, 186, 192, 194, 197–203; incomplete, 67, 91–92; Ireland, 60; Japan, 100; law enforcement, xiv, 41–64, 91–93, 140, 146, 148, 179, 214; law reform, 113–116, 121–124, 126, 128, 136, 142–143, 145–146, 148–149, 150–153, 175, 180, 214–215, 219–226; legal, 3, 5, 18, 30, 58, 59, 60–61, 70, 77, 99, 113, 114, 118–119, 125–126, 132, 141, 153, 155, 166, 175, 177, 178, 180, 184, 199–200, 206, 209, 210, 214, 223, 226–227, 233, 242, 243–244; legitimation, 85, 121, 139, 145–147, 151, 153–154, 177, 198, 234; legitimation crisis, 12, 109; medical, 58, 84–86, 95, 114, 116, 132, 159, 174, 175, 177, 180, 181, 203, 206, 225; Mexico, 94; Michigan, 61, 71–72, 95, 97, 119, 141, 171, 172, 174–177, 181, 195; Michigan laws, 44–49,

About the Author

NANETTE DAVIS, professor of Sociology at Portland State University, has contributed frequently to journals in sociology and social science. She is the author of *Sociological Constructions of Deviance* and co-author of *Social Control: The Production of Deviance in the Modern State* and *Women and Deviance: Issues in Social Conflict and Change.*